Crowd-Based Business Models

Rajagopal

Crowd-Based Business Models

Using Collective Intelligence for Market Competitiveness

palgrave
macmillan

Rajagopal
EGADE Business School
Tecnologico de Monterrey
Mexico City, Mexico

ISBN 978-3-030-77082-2 ISBN 978-3-030-77083-9 (eBook)
https://doi.org/10.1007/978-3-030-77083-9

This Palgrave Macmillan imprint is published by the registered company Springer Nature Switzerland AG
The registered company address is: Gewerbestrasse 11, 6330 Cham, Switzerland

...to my grandchildren
Akhilesh &
Niharika (Khushi)

Preface

Companies of the twentieth century have long used teams to solve problems, take decisions, and develop business models. Market research organizations heavily used to depend on the focus groups to explore customer needs, and conducted consumer surveys to understand the market, while managers attended annual meetings to listen to shareholders in the past. But the words that need more comprehension such as *solve*, *explore*, *understand*, and *listen* have now taken on a whole new meaning through the technology platforms to acquire and analyze collective (crowdsourced) opinions on a greater scale. Indeed, the increasing use of information markets, wikis, crowdsourcing, the *wisdom of crowd* concepts, social networks, collaborative software, and other web-based tools constitute a paradigm shift for companies in making customer-centric decisions.[1]

The manifold growth of interactive virtual communities has led the companies to explore possibilities of seeking new ideas from the stakeholders, and coevolve business models over time in the competitive marketplace. Advances in digital technologies have given an enormous boost to the outsourcing business activities on public domain comprising several independent contributors. Crowdsourcing has emerged as a creative tool for companies today to expand their outreach

[1] Bonabeau, E. (2008). Decisions 2.0: The Power of Collective Intelligence. *MIT Sloan Management Review*, 50(2), 45–52.

to customers, map their perceptions, and understand behavioral implications of customers in business. Thus, this tool has led to collective intelligence, which helps the companies build the ***businessdesign cube*** integrating design-to-market, design-to-society, and design-to-value dimensions in business modeling process.[2] The analysis of collective intelligence not only opens a new range of business opportunities for companies, but also helps in exploring reverse innovations that have the potential for commercialization. Commercializing reverse innovation is a disruptive leap to hit a product in the target market, and it demands to develop organizational insight into how a new product could drive an impact in emerging market.[3] In fact, crowdsourcing has led to emergence of some entirely new business models. Such crowd-based business models (CBBMs) can lead to an important competitive advantage, simultaneously presenting new challenges to entrepreneurs and executives. Co-creation allows companies to continually tap the skills and insights of stakeholders and develop new ways of building value chain. Crowdsourcing platforms (physical and digital forums) are largely interactive for exploring new experiences and connections. The collective intelligence process grows organically in the organization as a system.[4]

The Crowd Dynamics

Conceptually, collective intelligence encourages a pro-customer and pro-society business modeling that helps businesses grow within the social ecosystem. However, determining the collective value to the firm and capturing value effectively from the mass information pose major challenges in developing the CBBMs. Building corporate goals and strategies on the crowd capital perspective and developing tactics and practices on the crowdsourced ideas often turns chaotic. In designing innovative

[2] Rajagopal (2021). The Design Cube: Converging Markets, Society, and Customer Values to Grow Competitive in Business, New York: Business Expert Press (*in press*).

[3] Rajagopal (2016), *Innovative Business Projects: Breaking Complexities, Building Performance (Vol. 2)-Financials, New Insights, and Project Sustainability*, New York: Business Expert Press.

[4] Gouillart, F. and Billings, D. (2013). Community-Powered Problem Solving. *Harvard Business Review*, 91(4), 70–77.

CBBMs for their industries, decision-makers get inspired by the appropriately filtered collective ideas in the context of social innovation, competitive advantage, technological feasibility, and economic viability.[5] Contemporary marketing has evolved alongside the customer-centric perspectives as a cognitive science, and has spanned across advanced marketing mix comprising twenty-seven elements. Therefore, customer value has become central to business modeling. Most companies develop marketing strategies (a principal constituent of business model) on assumptions of customer values, which might misfit while implementing a business model. Collective intelligence provides the real perceptions of customers and the rationale for new products and services.[6]

Philosophically, the crowd dynamics can be explained as collective intelligence, which reveals that no one knows everything, everyone knows something.[7] Information on collective intelligence is often raw and unclassified, so it appears highly disordered. The major challenge for the companies that tend to operate on collective intelligence is to classify the collective database and develop genre. Startup enterprises that depend on crowdsourcing of ideas, production, logistics, and services models classify the collective information. It is processed in small sets of building blocks of business operations that are combined and re-combined in various ways. The different collective intelligence systems emerging out of these small sets tend to maximize the market share, profit, social equity of enterprise, and customer value.[8]

Advancement of information technology has enabled crowdsourcing practices among innovation-oriented companies. Crowdsourced information is obtained through a designated website or through text mining. The designated call centers today are also capable of collecting crowdsourced data through an open call to the masses via the internet. Crowdsourcing is an artifact supported by information technology that has

[5] Tauscher, K. (2017). Leveraging Collective Intelligence: How to Design and Manage Crowd-Based Business Models. *Business Horizons*, 60(2), 237–245

[6] Rajagopal (2019), *Contemporary Marketing Strategy: Analyzing Consumer Behavior to Drive Managerial Decision Making*, Chapter 5 (pp. 121–149), New York: Palgrave Macmillan.

[7] Lévy, P. (1997). Collective Intelligence: Mankind's Emerging World in Cyberspace. New York: Plenum Trade.

[8] Malone, T. W., Laubacher, R. J., and Dellarocas, C. (2010). The Collective Intelligence Genome, *MIT Sloan Management Review*, 51(3), 21–31.

enabled organizations to collect and manage temporal and spatial information. Over the past decade, research and practice on crowdsourcing have continued to grow, evolve, and revolutionize the development of collaborative business models. Although numerous studies have been conducted in this area, it appears that the main components involved in the crowdsourcing processes remains limited.[9] The integrated business models with stakeholders' commitment can be explained in terms of their value proposition, and value creation and delivery through effective corporate social responsibility. These perspectives need to be discussed in terms of public information, consumption, and managing constituents of collective business ecosystems through global-local interactive information exchange. Though the literature proposes several conceptual solutions, there is a need to rethink on modular designs and co-creation of business models within global-local business dynamics.[10]

The concept of open innovation emphasizes that knowledge on new ideas, products, use values, and innovation is widely spread in the world, and it is not possible for the companies to explore this wealth to their fullest capacity. However, business ideas, concepts, and innovation processes are licensed from other companies. In addition, internal inventions not being used in a firm's business are also taken outside the company to get them licensed and sell them to client organizations to earn royalty. Most companies that intend to use open-market innovation apply tools such as licensing, joint ventures, and strategic alliances to bring the benefits of free trade to the flow of new ideas.[11]

Crowdsourcing has emerged as an effective tool for open innovation, which aims to boost idea generation in innovation processes. The underlying rationale of crowdsourcing is that the collective intelligence of a large number of contributors outside the firm's boundaries increases the likelihood of achieving high-quality ideas with exceptional business potential. Collective intelligence generates a plethora of new ideas, which need

[9] Modaresnezhad, M., Iyer, L., Palvia, P., and Taras, V. (2020). Information Technology (IT) Enabled Crowdsourcing: A Conceptual Framework. *Information Processing & Management*, 57(2), 1–14.

[10] Bridgens, B., Hobson, K., Lilley, D., Lee, J., Scott, J. L., and Wilson, G. T. (2017). Closing the Loop on E-Waste: A Multidisciplinary Perspective. *Journal of Industrial Ecology*, 39(1), 1–13.

[11] Rajagopal (2014), *Architecting Enterprise: Managing Innovation, Technology, and Global Competitiveness*, Basingstoke, UK: Palgrave Macmillan.

to be classified and differentiated to match with planned or on-going research. Accordingly, companies develop action plan to carry out open innovations by adopting the crowdsourced ideas. Various social media channels contribute to the dissemination of new ideas and serve as a pool of collective intelligence. However, the review of previous literature suggests that the overall effect of crowdsourcing on business modeling has not been thoroughly investigated. This book fills this gap by integrating the customer ideation in developing business models to achieve performance with purpose. Drawing on the resource-based view, the book argues how crowdsourced information can become a valuable resource for the firm to extract value from it, build value chain, deliver to stakeholders, and stay competitive in the marketplace.[12]

The literature on crowdsourcing has underpinned the role of digital technology to reach far beyond organizational boundaries and derive information from individuals within the organization in its innovation process. Consequently, the crowdsourcing has been dissected as umbrella model crowdsourcing, which occurs with the industry group companies under single corporate ownership, and societal crowdsourcing that has an outreach far beyond an organization. The Japanese innovation philosophy ***kaizen*** endorses intra-organizational crowdsourcing practice for continuous innovation by engaging employees. It has been argued in previous studies that individuals contribute novel insights because they consider an organization's innovation challenge from different perspectives. Building on the literature on creativity and absorptive capacity, this book discusses the influx of liberal ideas on innovation and their implications to ideation process and business modeling from the perspective business performance under dynamic market competition.[13]

Some previous studies reveal that the global sustainability drive has been influenced by new ideas emerging out of crowdsourcing. Most consumer products companies monitor consumer behavior and purchase

[12] Cappa, F., Oriani, R., Pinelli, M., and Massis, A. D. (2019). When Does Crowdsourcing Benefit Firm Stock Market Performance? ***Research Policy***, 48(9) https://*doi.org/10.1016/j.respol.2019.103825*.

[13] Boons, M. and Stam, D. (2019). Crowdsourcing for Innovation: How Related and Unrelated Perspectives Interact to Increase Creative Performance. ***Research Policy***, 48(7), 1758–1770.

decisions through the collective intelligence and build green alternatives.[14] The green consumption behavior has been largely influenced by the social media and crowdsourced opinions. Consequently, renewable energy consumption practices has been contributed by the crowdsourced lifestyle and sustainability concepts over time in food consumption and transport sustainability. Public policies and social consciousness also contribute significantly through the collective intelligence. Consequently, these factors catalyze transforming the consumption behavior at macro level. Therefore, many consumers are interested in modifying their consumption behavior with less impact on natural resources, particularly fossil fuels,[15] as the social dynamics reported through collective intelligence analytics has contributed to the changes in social lifestyle and values.[16]

Thematic Discussions

This book distinctively presents nine thematic discussions with live examples of small and large companies across the geographic destinations. At the onset, the concept and practices of crowdsourcing, which is identified as collective intelligence, have been discussed in the context of ideation process supporting the open-innovation goals of companies in various industries. Open innovations have extensively appeared in social development sector within the areas of community health, gender entrepreneurship, education, housing, and socio-economic infrastructure. The crowdsourcing has wide implications in social innovation, which are

[14] Paco, A. and Rapose, M. (2009). Green segmentation: An application to the Portuguese consumer market. *Market. Intelligence and Planning*, 27(3), 364–379.

[15] Chen, M. F. (2016). Extending the Theory of Planned Behavior Model to Explain People's Energy Savings and Carbon Reduction Behavioral Intentions to Mitigate Climate Change in Taiwanemoral Obligation Matters. *Journal of Cleaner Production*, 112, 1746–1753.

[16] Strupeit, L. and Palm, A. (2016). Overcoming Barriers to Renewable Energy Diffusion: Business Models for Customer-Sited Solar Photovoltaics in Japan, Germany and the United States. *Journal of Cleaner Production*, 123, 124–136.

co-evolved with 4As perspectives[17] comprising awareness (need, knowledge, and value), attributes (constituents of innovations, applications, and lifecycle), affordability (end user price, perceived value, 'me-too' feeling), and adaptability (ease of use, repeatability, social endorsement). Collective intelligence contributes effectively to the manufacturing process (farmer-members of agribusiness and dairy cooperatives in India, Japan, Israel and other countries) and stimulates continuous innovation.

The book discusses crowdfunding concept and practice in the context of social business and social innovations. A thematic discussion on how crowdfunding concept has evolved from non-profit philanthropic propositions to for-profit business models has been addressed in the context of contemporary philosophies and practices. The challenges and dynamics of crowdfunding has been explained as a systems approach. Crowdfunding through digital platforms has been growing rapidly since the early twenty-first century. Firms have conceived this approach as a creativity support tool to raise public funds through web-based technology and online payment systems for simplified transactions. The crowdfunding projects are driven by various motivations such as frugal innovations, social benefit, and Fintech ventures.[18] Epistemologies and practices on public investments, social equities, and social capital are addressed under this theme. The psychosocial behavior of non-profit organization makes significant contribution in raising and managing funds through the crowdfunding projects. The social objectives of crowdfunding often embed emotions and storytelling, which works as a compelling and effective strategy for engaging stakeholders for funding behaviors.[19]

The stakeholder management, decision process, and business governance are the major concerns in a firm that largely depends on the collective intelligence and crowdfunding. Management of crowdsourced information is complex and chaotic unless appropriate information screening

[17] Rajagopal (2020). *Barriers and Benefits towards Sustainability Driven Business Models*. In Editor(s): Hashmi, S. and Choudhury, I. A., Encyclopedia of Renewable and Sustainable Materials, pp. 318–327, Amsterdam: Elsevier. https://*doi.org/10.1016/b978-0-12-803581-8.10920-8*.

[18] Buttice, V., Colombo, M. G., and Wright, M. (2017). Serial Crowdfunding, Social Capital, and Project Success. *Entrepreneurship Theory and Practice*, 41(2), 183–207.

[19] Woodside, A. G., Sood, S., and Miller, K. E. (2008). When Consumers and Brands Talk: Storytelling Theory and Research in Psychology and Marketing. *Psychology & Marketing*, 25(2), 97–145.

parameters are employed. Therefore, decision-making based on the collective intelligence is often a difficult process. In this context, the path-of-least-resistance theory as a new epistemological domain has been discussed in the book to examine the feasibility of ideation as a key heuristic cue to decision-making. The quality of collective intelligence information depends on the external stimuli.[20] The book also examines the business scaling for mass production, which gradually commences by introducing new ideas and replacing the conventional business processes with collective ideas to gear up production toward economies of scale. Refurbishing business with collective intelligence helps companies to increase their business performance by introducing long-term engagement of stakeholders with the manufacturing and operational processes.[21]

Business modeling is a combination of long-term strategies for a firm to evolve consistently in a marketplace and the short-term tactics to overcome the market competition with quick, precise, and effective outcomes. This book discusses the theme on strategy sophistication and tactics in the context of learning organizations (lead thinking), new business order (stakeholders on the top of the organization, leadership (transactional and transformative), and social branding and control. Collective intelligence helps business organizations to coevolve with customers and decision-making process. Organizational learning is a continuous process, and it involves employees at all levels of management in sharing knowledge and innovative insights that support the business growth of the firm. Companies such as google, Procter & Gamble, Cisco Systems, General Electric, and Intel have experienced the benefits of continuous learning in building organizational capabilities, competencies, and leadership in the global marketplace. Organizational philosophy of the above companies has motivated emerging companies to practice learning through crowdsourcing and reach people by adding value to the organizational performance.[22] New ventures and SMEs capturing value from collective intelligence, explore business opportunities with business model sophistication

[20] Chan, K. W., Li, S. Y., and Zhu, J.J. (2018). Good to Be Novel? Understanding How Idea Feasibility Affects Idea Adoption Decision Making in Crowdsourcing. *Journal of Interactive Marketing*, 43(1), 52–68.

[21] Hawkins, G. (2001). Plastic Bags: Living with Rubbish. *International Journal of Cultural Studies*, 4(1), 5–23.

[22] Whelan, E., Parise, S., de Valk, J., and Aalbers, R. (2011). Creating Employee Networks That Deliver Open Innovation.*MIT Sloan Management Review*, 53(1), 37–44.

and exhibit critical importance toward the firm's integrated development. Accordingly, this book argues the strategy sophistication concepts with a quadruple helix approach over the conventional business models. Business model sophistication uncovers stakeholder facets of business model, explains economies of scope, instills cross-ideation opportunities, and involves users and the crowd.[23]

Social media and the virtual society are growing together with technology and are supporting the *Generation Next* business today. This is another icebreaking theme, which has been discussed in this book in view of the sensory entrepreneurship and business space (C-suit) co-creation through wisdom of crowds (collective intelligence). The concept of ***business model design space*** describes the opportunities and constraints of creating and capturing value from niche and frugal technologies.[24] The *Internet of Everything* has taken the firms a step forward by enabling them to connect with people to develop smart operational models in a wide range of industry sectors. These concepts have been discussed categorically in the book.

Consumers develop attitude and behavior in due course of time. The theory of behavior can be analyzed in the context of global markets. Consumer behavior is a complex process, which is developed through a chain of cognitive stages including perception and attitude leading to formation of behavior at the end. Disruptive forces like e-commerce, low-cost technology products, and tactical marketing strategies have captivated behavioral uncertainties and rapid shifts in the consumer experiences in the twenty-first century. Consequently, this book delivers a thematic discussion on consumer behavior and psychodynamics supported with the support of behavioral epistemologies. The consumer networks and advocacy have also been discussed in context of crowd- based business modeling.[25]

[23] Kesting, P., and Günzel-Jensen, F. (2015). SMEs and new ventures need business model sophistication. *Business Horizons*, 58 (3), 285-293.

[24] Wesseling, J. H., Bidmon, C., and Bohnsack, R. (2020). Business Model Design-Spaces in Socio-Technical Transitions: The Case of Electric Driving in the Netherlands. *Technological Forecasting and Social Change*, 154. https://doi.org/10.1016/j.techfore.2020.119950.

[25] Rajagopal (2019), *Contemporary Marketing Strategy: Analyzing Consumer Behavior to Drive Managerial Decision Making*, Chapter 1 (pp 3–33), New York: Palgrave Macmillan.

Crowd-based information offers a powerful metaphor that inspires diverse strategic frameworks to develop services business modeling in co-creating customer experiences and values. Collective intelligence helps firms to extend the outreach of services within communities. Consumer journey frameworks offer a crowd-based approach to explore customer experience and provide structured services for managing experiences by emphasizing how to improve touchpoints strategically.[26] Technological advances have fostered the Internet of Things vision, in which systems are inherently cyber-physical, increasingly contextual, and opportunistic in nature. On the information infrastructure side, Cloud, Fog, and Edge Computing provide virtualized services to manage collective intelligence. In the above context, the thematic discussions on collective services design with a crowd-based concept of reverse pyramid, representing a thinking triangle comprising design thinking, systems thinking, and value thinking, are central to the services theme in the book. The mosaics of collective intelligence on services can be mapped over time and space to develop semantics of services management, which induces complex interdependencies between idea generation and collective management of services.[27]

New product or market strategies can also emerge by considering the changing social and political perspectives. Toyota Motor's success with the Prius can be attributed to a growing interest in environmentally friendly products. Unilever's innovative product offerings in developing countries such as its Wheel detergent brand in India has derived high response to the unmet needs of bottom of the pyramid consumer segments. Effectiveness of the social media depends on the extent of participation of consumers on the network platforms and the degree of corporate involvement. Most companies become aware of the risks of social media manipulations and political advantage in business; and ignoring such risks may damage the stakeholders' value and corporate image in the long term. An understanding of the influence of various groups, their agendas, and their level of activism should be vital to a company to choose the right

[26] Lemon, K. N., and Verhoef, P. C. (2016). Understanding Customer Experience throughout the Customer Journey. *Journal of Marketing*, 80(6), 69–96.

[27] Martel, G., Aviron, S., Joannon, A., Lalechère, E., Roche, B., and Boussard, H. (2017). Impact of Farming Systems on Agricultural Landscapes and Biodiversity: From Plot to Farm and Landscape Scales. *European Journal of Agronomy*, 107(1), 53–62.

partners for involving socio-political networks in developing the business strategy. Companies should aggregate this information to identify the high-risk plots and need action areas in the business administration of the firm. It is also necessary to develop potential future scenarios that can consider the reaction of competitors and shifts in consumer patterns. Increased success on corporate and customers sides has laid the foundation for the co-create business models in which companies and social networks become the key parts of each other's capacity to deliver value.[28] Convergence of technology and customer value provides higher competitive advantage to the business. It allows technology driven businesses to interact frequently with the complex market players and customers to resolve operational issues like manufacturing, distribution, and marketing. The convergence marketing is woven around the five Cs comprising customization, community, channels, competitive value, and choice that drive the "fusion" in the corporate marketing strategies.[29]

Further to the above discussion on various themes related to collective intelligence and crowd-based business modeling, this book also opens a window to the future perspectives, which may evolve by the mid-twenty-first century. The artificial intelligence and collective intelligence enhance and complement each other and together serve as a hybrid concept. Both require training for personal development and high performance. The hybrid collective intelligence process coordinates with Industry 4.0 management processes and encourage firms of various sizes and industries to learn together.[30] The final thematic discussion in the book presents further perspectives of crowd-based business models. The role of people-business-governance, corporate citizenship, and social marketing model is central to this thematic discussion.

[28] Burgmann, J., and Prahalad, C. K. (2007), Co-creating Business's New Social Compact, *Harvard Business Review*, 85(2), 80–90.

[29] Wind, Y., and Mahajan, V. (2001), *Convergence Marketing: Strategies for Reaching the New Hybrid Consumer*, New York: Free Press.

[30] Gavriushenko, M., Kaikova, O., and Terziyan, V. (2020). Bridging Human and Machine Learning for the Needs of Collective Intelligence Development. *Procedia Manufacturing*, 42, 302–306.

Structure of the Book

This book categorically reviews the theories on information dissemination, collective intelligence, decision-making, stakeholder values, social innovation, and crowd-based business modeling. It also examines previous researches and analyzes the strategic and tactical stewardship of firms in managing collective information and implementing crowd-based business models. The book discusses new strategies suitable to co-create business models in association with the market players and consumers for the companies in emerging markets. This book significantly contributes to the existing literature, and serves as a learning post and a think tank for students, researchers and business managers. Accordingly, this book is composed of nine chapters, each supported by applied examples.

The chapters in this book are divided into three broad parts comprising the crowd foundation, crowd dynamics in business, and times ahead. At the onset of the book, Chapter 1 discusses ideation to design and market, open-innovation practices as the growing competitive trend and new product development using crowd platforms and social networks. Discussions in this chapter reveal that crowdsourcing has emerged as an ideation process through sharing individual ideas, emotions, and experiences on business-related perspectives raging from market trends to corporate strategies and social marketing to customer value creation. Continuing the conversation, Chapter 2 focuses on ecosystem of crowdfunding and its role in exploring new social businesses and managing those existing. In addition, the dynamics of crowd-based social innovation in vital sectors like health, education, and sustainability constitute the core topic of deliberations. Mapping the attributes of public governance in social business is also central to this chapter. The crowd-based business modeling in the context of crowd engagement in business has been explained in Chapter 3. This chapter discusses attributes of crowd-based business models and debate on contemporary practices on developing value-chain alongside the customer-centric marketing strategies to achieve competitive leverage. Broadly, this chapter discusses the evolution of crowd-based business modeling and its prospects with firms operating in emerging markets.

Decision space and collective intelligence constitute the central theme of Chapter 4, where discussions are knitted around stakeholder management, business governance, and decision-making process under the crowd-based business environment. This chapter discusses the ways and means of collective information-driven decision process by involving the stakeholders and managers. The business governance, scaling, and performance management have also been discussed in this chapter in the context of transformative relationship between data and people. In addition, attributes of interactive planning and governance, and value-chain management practices have been discussed in the crowd environment in the context of market competition and business growth. Chapter 5 focuses on conversations toward crowd-based leadership and organizational strategies. Accordingly, discussions on co-creation practices and managing wisdom of crowd in the milieu of brainstorming within crowd ecosystem, mapping perceptual semantics, and design thinking form the core of discussions in this chapter. Additionally, the discussion on attributes and impact of crowd leadership on businesses also adds thematic value to this chapter. Technology and 'generation-next' business constitute the core discussions in Chapter 6, which focusses on managing crowd-based business projects through the social media channels. This chapter discusses at length the impact of crowd-based information path on corporate decisions in reference to emotions and personality-driven behavior of customers and crowd-focused innovations. In this context, the chapter addresses the attributes of innovations and social transferability, ambidexterity, and growth of frugal innovations. In addition, this chapter also discusses the aspects of organizational design and innovation performance and the effects of future digital transformations of customer-centric innovations in business.

Chapter 7 discusses consumer behavior in reference to the cognitive theories. Cognition and perception and behavior analysis comprising motivational and decision theories are discussed in this chapter. Learning through influence of external factors on consumer behavior and relationships with other people that influence decision-making process of consumers has also been discussed in this chapter. The following Chapter 8 discusses emerging approaches on crowd-based service design and reverse services pyramid with focus on putting the *customer-first* effects. In addition, conversations on the social domain for services and the role of systems thinking in services also contribute to the core theme of this chapter. Some thoughts on value management in services are also shared in this chapter. It is argued in this chapter that services firms using collective intelligence are able to develop value-driven services business model and provide cost-effective utilitarian services with embedded aesthetic and emotional values. The concluding Chapter 9 of this book addresses future perspective in crowd-based business modeling and harnessing collective intelligence, as the digital technology and use of social network platform advance. The crowdsourcing practices endorse personal interactions between external buyers and sellers in the co-creation process, which appears as the new facet of future business modeling. Accordingly, this chapter discusses the pro-change business behavior of firms as a growing challenge among small and large firms across the regions, in view of the collective intelligence, social marketing strategies, and corporate citizenship behavior.

Value Perspectives

In view of the above arguments, this book discusses crowdsourcing, crowdfunding decision processes, technology, leadership, consumer behavior, crowd-based services designing, and future perspectives in the context of crowd-based business modeling and collective intelligence. Accordingly, this book is composed of nine chapters, each supported by real company examples. This book argues that most firms look for gaining competitive advantage in the marketplace by driving strategic moves, inculcating consumer consciousness on crowd-linked marketing approaches. The trends in crowd-based business decisions over the conventional corporate practice are felt by a greater number of companies as a customer-centric and value-driven approach, which integrate stakeholders, customers, and society. Sometimes such profound changes are introduced in the niche markets, which creates chain effects in consumer awareness, consumption patterns, and yields macro effects in large markets. Often crowd-based choices of the companies lean toward developing competitive differentiations that enable consumers to realize the social values and loyalty shifts in the competitive marketplace.

The book argues the rationale of putting the customer first through crowdsourcing and interactions on crowd platforms. It focuses on the crowd as the pivot of marketing and argues that the commitments of customers and stakeholders on advocating the need-based innovation and business strategies lead to social impact, and emotionally helps companies in growing their image, brands, and socio-political reputations. The book discusses new strategies suitable for the companies to develop crowd-based business models in the emerging markets and to co-create strategies in association with the market players, society, stakeholders, and customers. This book significantly contributes to the existing literature, and serves as a learning post and a think tank for students, researchers and business managers.

Some of my research papers on business modeling and customer-centric marketing in the emerging markets have been published in the international refereed journals that had driven new insights on the subject. Accordingly, filtered and refined concepts and management practices have been presented in the book that are endorsed with applied illustrations and updated review of literature on managing business in the overseas destinations. The principal audience of this book are working managers, and students of undergraduate and graduate management studies, research scholars, and academics in different business-related disciplines. This book has been developed also to serve as principal text to the undergraduate and graduate students who are pursuing studies in managing people, brand socialization, corporate governance, and social marketing. Besides serving as principal reading in undergraduate and graduate programs, this book would also inspire working managers, market analysts, and business consultants to explore various solutions on international business management. This book fits into the courses of Business Management, International Marketing, Business in Emerging Markets, Managing people in Business, Social Business Modelling, and New Product Management in various universities and business schools.

I hope this book will contribute to the existing literature, and deliver new concepts to the students and researchers to pursue the subject further. By reading this book, working managers may also realize how to converge best practices with corporate strategies in managing business at the destination markets while students would learn the new dimensions of marketing strategies.

Mexico City, Mexico
March 2021

Rajagopal

Acknowledgments

The pandemic and business shutdown in 2020 have reinforced many new approaches to maintain the business continuum and survive the social, economic, and business challenges. As institutional resources were confined during these critical times, the crowd dynamics was found remotely active. I have been teaching collective intelligence in M.B.A. program as a practice course at EGADE Business School in the past couple of years. The emerging storyboards on the crowdsourcing, crowdfunding, and crowd-based business modelling practices at the niche and macro-economic levels during 2020, have given many insights to me, which constituted the central theme of this book. I have also benefitted from the discussions of my colleagues within and outside the EGADE Business School and Boston University. I am thankful to Dr. Lou Chitkushev, Associate Dean, and Dr. John Sullivan, Chair of Administrative Sciences Department, Metropolitan College of Boston University for giving me teaching assignments, which enabled me to apply the research output on sustainability-based business modeling in the classes. I would like to acknowledge the support of Dr. Osmar Zavaleta, Interim Dean, EGADE Business School, and Dr Claudia Quintanilla, Director, Marketing and Business Intelligence Department of EGADE Business School, who have always encouraged me to take up new challenges in teaching graduate courses, develop new insights, and contribute to the existing literature prolifically. I also enjoyed discussions with the corporate managers on the subject, which helped in enriching the contents of this book.

I am thankful to various anonymous referees of our previous research works on globalization, consumer behavior, and marketing strategy that helped in looking deeper into the conceptual gaps, and improving the quality with their valuable comments. Finally, I express my deep gratitude to Arati Rajagopal who has been instrumental in completing this book. I acknowledge her help in copy editing the first draft of the manuscript and for staying in touch until the final proofs were crosschecked and the index was developed.

Contents

About the Author

Rajagopal is Professor of Marketing at EGADE Business School of Monterrey Institute of Technology and Higher Education (ITESM), Mexico City Campus and Life Fellow of the Royal Society for Encouragement of Arts, Manufacture and Commerce, London. He is also Fellow of the Chartered Management Institute, and Fellow of Institute of Operations Management, UK. Dr. Rajagopal is serving as a Visiting Professor at Boston University, Boston, Massachusetts since 2013 and is also engaged in teaching courses at the UFV India Global Education of the University of the Fraser Valley, Canada.

He has been listed with biography in various international directories. He offers courses on Competitor Analysis, Marketing Strategy, Advance Selling Systems, International Marketing, Services Marketing, New Product Development, and other subjects of contemporary interest to the students of undergraduate, graduate, and doctoral programs. He has imparted training to senior executives and has conducted over 65 management and faculty development programs. Dr. Rajagopal holds Post-graduate and doctoral degrees in Economics and Marketing respectively from Pandit Ravishankar Shukla University in India. His specialization is in the fields of Marketing Management, Rural Economic Linkages, and Development Economics.

He has to his credit 64 books on marketing management and rural development themes and over 400 research contributions that include published research papers in national and international refereed journals. He is Editor-in-Chief of *International Journal of Leisure and Tourism Marketing* and International *Journal of Business Competition.* Dr. Rajagopal served as Regional Editor of *Emerald Emerging Markets Case Studies* (2012–2019), published by Emerald Publishers, UK. He is on the editorial board of various journals of international repute. Currently Dr. Rajagopal holds the honor of the highest level of National Researcher-SNI Level-III. He has been awarded UK-Mexico Visiting Chair 2016–2017 for collaborative research on 'Global-Local Innovation Convergence' with University of Sheffield, UK, instituted by the Consortium of Higher Education Institutes of Mexico and UK.

List of Figures

PART I

The Crowd Foundation

CHAPTER 1

Crowdsourcing

Crowdsourcing has become a new normal for many customer-centric businesses, which narrows down the distance between companies and customers. Empowering the crowd comprising customers, stakeholders, and potential investors has shown encouraging results in improving business practices of companies and strengthened their competitive position. This chapter discusses the ideation process through crowdsourcing, which helps to serve open-innovation platforms and develop customer-centric innovations in a firm. In addition, this chapter comprehensively discusses the role of crowd-based ideation to design and marketing practices, open innovation, social networks, and new product development. This chapter argues that the crowdsourced information guides the manufacturing and business operations through the experiences of stakeholders, peers, gatekeepers, and customers.

Crowdsourcing is an ideation process of sharing individual ideas, emotions, and experiences on business perspectives raging from business diplomacy to corporate strategies, and social marketing to customer value creation. It is an informal pool of information, which circulates in the society, spread across the social media channels and conventional word-of-mouth forums. The open-innovation platforms and customer-centric innovations in a firm widely encourage crowdsourcing as a value-based tool to co-create community- and value-based business models. The crowdsourced information also guides manufacturing and business

Rajagopal, *Crowd-Based Business Models*,
https://doi.org/10.1007/978-3-030-77083-9_1

operations through the experiences of stakeholders, peers, gatekeepers, and consumers. Inspirational stimuli such as analogies are the prominent mechanism used to support designers (Goucher-Lambert & Cagan, 2019). Collective intelligence also helps the monitoring and evaluations of implementation and performance of crowd-based business models in companies. Collective intelligence also induces design-by-analogies and design-by-experience concepts, which helps in developing crowd-based business models (Moreno et al., 2014). Companies like Google, Amazon, AT&T, Walmart, and Pitney Bowes have found a way to delve into the collective intelligence of their stakeholders and workforce, and organize collective views categorically to improve the business performance of the firm.

1.1 Ideation to Design and Market

With increasing access to personal and digital information today, companies rely more on collective intelligence built through crowdsources than nurturing the inside-company ideas to advance their business. Consequently, innovations are not confined to a single path to reach out a market. Crowdsourcing has emerged as a dynamic people's approach over the isolated and individualistic ideation in exploring innovation, social values, and public–private business alliances. Previous research on innovation management suggests that the contribution of ideas drawn in isolation is often overvalued anticipating the customer preferences, which jeopardizes the commercialization of innovation. The crowdsourced ideas hold customer preferences at the grassroots and are contributed consciously. Such tendency is positively correlated with the attributes of consumer-centric and social innovations. With the advancement of human interface on social media, the trend of developing frugal innovations within the organization has been reverted to open platforms, which allows the voice of customers to be analyzed. The views of customers and stakeholders on developing new products have enhanced the scope of collective growth of firms in the niche market as compared to the conventional abilities of reaching the goals through in-company efforts. Teams confined to the corporate limits are also likely to overvalue the ideas they come up with, without exploring the market from the customers' perspectives. The social identity of business makes a significant contribution to the customer-centric growth of firms today. Consequently, crowdsourcing has emerged as a promising tool in developing business models (Sting et al., 2019).

Crowdsourcing has been practiced as relatively new tool to generate ideas and communications, and develop bottom-up business models by the regional and multinational companies. Most multinational companies such as McDonald's, LEGO, Samsung, and Starbucks have successfully founded their growth on the crowdsourced information. Such practice has evolved the ways to analyze needs, attitudes, and behavior of the consumer using the collective intelligence tools and techniques. McDonald's invited ideas from customers to know their preferences on burgers. Upon analyzing the collective contents, the company has been successful in marketing its products by ensuring customer value. The franchise exercised by the customers in suggested competitive and local value-based innovations in the existing product line and toward development of new products catering to the customer tastes had been a great contribution of the crowd. Starbucks, an American coffee brewing company, has a strong presence on multiple social networks, and it regularly encourages consumers to submit, view, and discuss submitted ideas along with employees from various Starbucks departments. The company has a dedicated website, which includes a leader board to track the user-generated contents. Similarly, LEGO, a creative toy company allows users to design new products, and simultaneously test the demand for the new product. According to the company practice, any user can submit a design, on which other users are able to vote for. The idea with popular votes is accepted and moved to production. The creator receives a 1% royalty on the net revenue on the shared design idea.

Chronologically, the practice of outsourcing has been observed as an organizational activity over a long time. In the twentieth century, such practice was commercialized by multinational companies as contests. By the beginning of the twenty-first century, exploitation of internet and social media to their fullest has driven the crowdsourcing approach more as a business tool than merely a social interaction platform. Toyota crowdsourced its logo in 1936, with the winner chosen from several submissions (Morozov, 2014). Crowdsourcing integrates the customer perceptions on the attributes of new products, associated problems, and possible solutions to reinforce them in the market. Consequently, crowdsourcing has been defined as an online-, mass-distributed designing-, problem-solving-, and production model to leverage the collective intelligence of consumer communities on digital platforms. Such peoples' action serves specific organizational goals and determines the mass action on products and services in the marketplace. Crowdsourcing has also emerged as an approach to customer engagement, and it inculcates value by providing freedom of speech with honor. Samsung, a global consumer electronics giant, has upheld customer freedom of speech to contribute bottom-up business concerns and realized the significance of crowdsourcing. Samsung has the largest crowdsourcing facility in Palo Alto, California, where the collective intelligence repository is maintained for periodical analysis of customer inputs. The company seeks innovative solutions from the crowd for the existing electronic products and technologies. Samsung, Amazon, Microsoft, Hewlett Packard, IBM, and many companies in the retailing and technology industry have encouraged community approach to share experiences, ideas, and resolve problems. Multinational companies also seek collaboration with other firms and interested individuals in text mining and monitoring blogging services. In 2013, Samsung partnered with product development platform Marbler to crowdsource ideas on how they could utilize newly discovered patents from NASA. The partner companies offered users the chance to help create Samsung's next product and earn a share of revenue along the way.

Crowd contribution serves as a significant resource for firms in finding new ideas and solutions to the problems of existing products and services. Collective intelligence drawn from user-generated contents offer potential payoffs to the contributions, which are valuable to the community and firm and have strategic effect on the market performance of the firms. However, a major challenge associated with the crowdsourcing ideas and solutions is that the crowd participation is an open concept and is not governed by employment or contractual laws that might stipulate code of ethical conduct, digital rights of intellectual property, and rights ownership of communication. Consequently, in managing crowdsourcing activities, firms use consumer opinion frequently in developing strategies and business models, and incorporate plans for obtaining permission from rights owners to use their crowdsourced content. Success of a crowdsourcing campaign depends on the organization's ability to attract, acquire, and analyze (3As process) the crowd information. Nonetheless, retaining the knowledgeable and skilled crowd, and indicating the need for a persistent and mutually beneficial arrangement between the crowd community and the organization appears to be a major challenge among both small and large firms (Franke et al., 2013). Crowdsourcing has been philosophically defined as a new trend using the wisdom of crowds on the Internet primarily for ideation initiatives and resolving problems of products and services within the consumer community. It converges cognitive and social factors comprising perceptions, semantics, social sharing, and interactive discussions. Managing crowdsourcing information needs huge information technology-based infrastructure and human resources. Since the mid-twentieth century, a number of crowdsourcing platforms emerged on various social media domains to facilitate the virtual interface of network members. However, the landscape of crowdsourcing platforms is widely dispersed but most tasks are controlled by the sponsors or domain owners. In the crowdsourcing process often finding a match between contributors' personal preferences and capabilities is difficult (Li et al., 2021). Figure 1.1 exhibits the attributes of crowdsourcing, which influence business modeling by creating social values.

With advancements in the information technology, crowdsourcing has emerged as a prominent community interface built around the 3S philosophy comprising share, simulate, and semblance as exhibited in Fig. 1.1. Sharing experiences of existing customers and needs of potential consumers along with the simulated utilization of products and services met enormous opportunity in the crowdsourcing process. Semblance is an attribute of crowdsourcing wherein information has a commonality in many aspects as it grows in a snowballing pattern. Consequently, despite the aggressive and heterogeneous perception among the crowd participants, homogeneity in information also prevails in crowdsourcing. However, large companies tend to control the information intricacy and density, crowd-behavior simulation (Narain et al., 2009), emotion contagion (Ta et al., 2017), and collision avoidance as predefined filters to refine the collective information. Emotional contagion is an observed behavioral change in one individual, which leads to reflexive production of the identical behavior by other individuals in close proximity, with the likely outcome of converging emotionally (Panksepp & Lahvis, 2011). Therefore, in crowdsourced information, there exists a significant, repetitive behavior and biasness.

The collective information repository serves as a source of open knowledge to the company, and at the same time, as a part of social movement to provide voice to customers to reach out to companies. This is an *outside-in* inflow of information, which helps companies in understanding the consumer perceptions, the trend of referrals, and styles of customer advocacy on products and services. Nonetheless, collective intelligence has

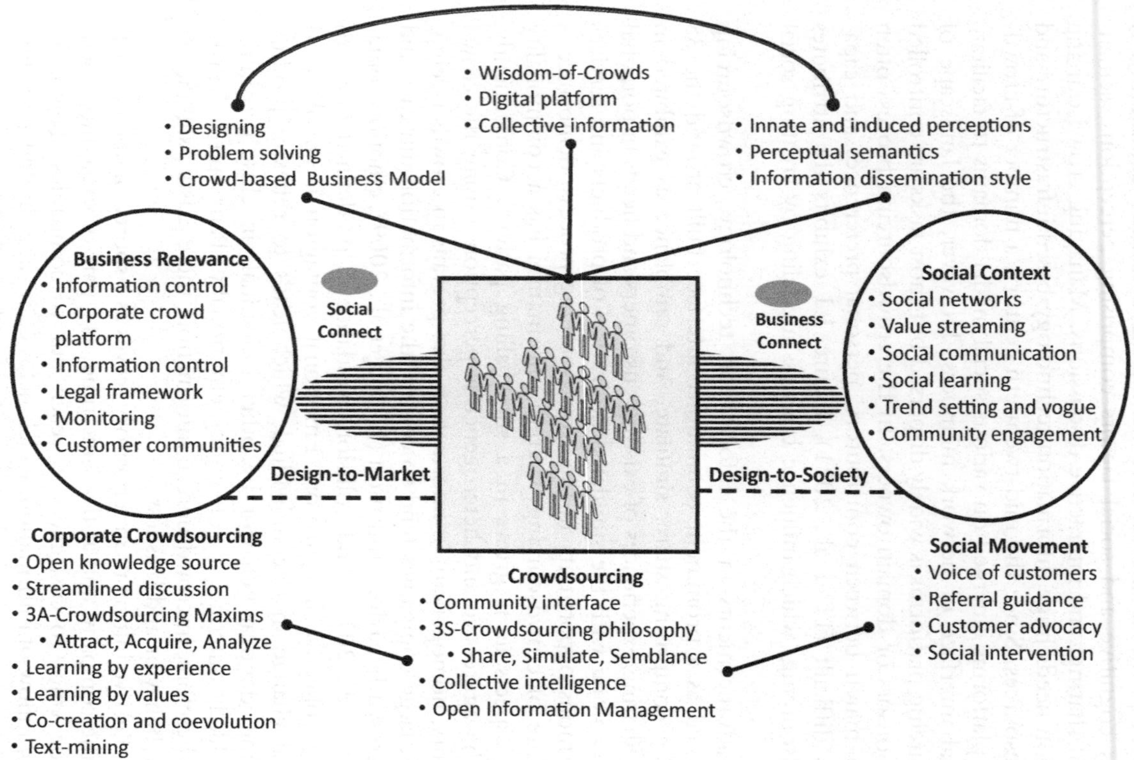

Fig. 1.1 Role of crowdsourcing in customer-centric business management (*Source* Author)

open information feeds that require companies to employ robust information filters for quality output. Most customer-centric companies have developed their social media page on Facebook to make customers stay abreast with the new products and share opinion on the existing products and services. Some companies like Microsoft, Apple, and Amazon have also promoted customer communities wherein the customers interact to share their experiences and resolve problems. Discussions on the companies' Facebook and customer communities are monitored periodically and streamlined by the designated employees and community leaders. Companies set the following crowdsourcing principles:

- Induct stimulant topics in business and society to attract crowd communication,
- Develop information screening processing and build information repositories to acquire and store information, and
- Analyze crowd communication systematically to use crowd inputs as the guide to business modeling and managing organizational performance.

Crowdsourced information enables companies to learn about customer perceptions and emotions through shared experience and values, co-create products and services, and coevolve with customers against competitors. In addition, text mining has also emerged as a tool to do research on user-generated contents across the web and derive necessary output on key terms. Text mining has become a popular qualitative research tool to extract meaningful data available in text form. Text mining sources range from academic literature to social networking sites, posts and comments about the news, voice of the customer, speech-to-text data, and more tangible, digitally published documents (Jung & Lee, 2020). Crowdsourcing practices are popular for co-creating product designs, problem-solving, and developing crowd-based business models as illustrated in Fig. 1.1. The *wisdom of crowds* refers to the phenomenon that the average view of a group of individuals on a given perspective can be similar or close to the acceptable response. It requires a large group diversity of opinions, but the collective error, the difference between the average opinion and the true value, remains small (Hertwig, 2012).

Crowdsourcing stimulates perceptual semantics among customers, stakeholders, and participants of social networks. Semantics exhibits connectivity of thoughts, perceptions, and values among customers on any given object or situation, or within an existing business ecosystem. Cognitive semantics is the continuity of the thought process that occurs in human mind. The cognitive semantics emerges as a process of thoughts and communication that connects to a core thought or mental state addressing the specific ecosystem (Brandt, 2005). Customers tend to develop compositions of contextual meaning and senses of given words, phrases, situations, concepts, or acquired information that affects the processing of complex thoughts, perceptions, and emotions. However, research on embodied cognition demonstrates that perceptual semantics is a synchronization of thoughts on lexical meanings and perceptual experience. The semantic thoughts are extensions of a principal thought leading to contextual interpretations and decisions. Therefore, perception-based information such as key terms in communication, advertisements, social media messages, and corporate announcements need to be meticulously drafted and posted (Rajagopal, 2021).

The strategic and tactical market approaches of companies, which include co-creation and coevolution (customer collaboration in innovation, strategy development, and managing communications), and competitive push (product attributes, pricing, delivery of products, promotions, packaging, and proliferation of products within the portfolios), play a significant role in driving the market thrust. In addition, social pull through community values also contributes to the customer values. The factors driving market thrust moderate the perceptual semantics and cognitive semantics. Accordingly, emotions keep changing, which affects the customer values. The value foundations are based on convergence of the corporate value-based goals and customer personality. Nonetheless, collective intelligence, derived from the social networks and market behavior, also affects the customer value in the short term (Rajagopal, 2021). Cognitive semantics plays a significant role in value creation among customers. Managers with large multifunctional teams in customer-centric companies monitor customer perceptions, and map variation in their perception to identify the origin of information contributing to the thought process, and modify the affecting words, phrases, or information accordingly (Govindarajan & Gupta, 2001). The ability to manifest self-generated thoughts in conscious and subconscious state of mind is central to cognition process. Collective intelligence exhibits plethora of perceptual semantics while sharing information, which is useful to companies in developing crowd-based business modeling.

Crowd creativity provides rich and applied manifestation of ideas, working strategies (draft), and user-generated contents to solve problems. However, such solutions largely remain untested, and stand on hypothetical grounds, which poses risks in developing and implementing prima *facie* public strategies due to social and legal risks associated with the 3I-elements comprising impulsive *ideation*, situation *interpretations*, and infringement of *intellectual property*. Consequently, companies relying on the crowd-based business modeling need to explore possibility of digital rights management to stand clear on the intellectual property issues while prospecting the crowdsourcing of solutions. The crowd-based information needs to be validated against the risks of using intellectual property and strategic fit on the business performance perspectives. Crowd commonly delivers raw information, which mitigates the risks associated with soliciting solutions on any uncommon or less occurring problem associated with the products and services. The unrefined crowd information is commonly proactive, premature, possessive, and persuasive, which needs to be judged within the social and business ecosystems (de Beer et al., 2017).

Many business ideas have benefitted creative companies like LEGO, Samsung, and Sony (gaming division products) by steering the crowd. The dynamic attributes of crowdsourcing of these companies have ranged from localization to globalization, and disruption to hybridization. As disruption in business has become a significant path to success, disruptive change requires firms to meet the challenges on the following key business indicators (O'Reilly & Binns, 2019):

- Applied Ideation with economic viability and technological feasibility to generate potential new business ideas,
- Incubation of crowd ideas and supported information to validate their applicability in the market, and
- Prospects of scaling them to reallocate the assets and capabilities required to grow the new business.

Amazon and IBM have developed approaches that address all the above indicators. Driving disruptive innovation in large companies requires firms to be ambidextrous to compete in mature markets where efficiency, control, and incremental improvement are essential to exploitation of the available market potential. Disruptive strategies help companies simultaneously compete with new technologies in emerging markets which need agile business strategies, salesforce autonomy, and understanding shifts in consumer behavior (O'Reilly & Tushman, 2013).

The process of ideation through crowdsourcing has been proved effective for developing new products, scaling production, or to drive an incremental innovation in the customer-centric companies. However, industrial products did not receive much impetus through the crowd-based ideation process as the business-to-business market segment widely operates on company specific, customized innovation and manufacturing processes. Such practice operates more on conventional wisdom than a generalized voice of customers to protect the competitive differentiation in products and services (Schilling & Hill, 1998). Customer-centric firms have learned to use the *wisdom of crowds* to generate product ideas, solve technical problems, and even develop advertising campaigns. Most firms, such as Xerox, IBM, Lucent, Intel, Merck, and Millennium rely on open innovation using the crowdsourcing practice. Such approach helps in establishing a customer-centric approach to gain advantage in the competitive markets. *Open innovation* is an outgrowth of collective intelligence, which helps in developing a crowd-based business model. It plays an enlightened role in research and development to manage and access intellectual property, advance its current business, and grow its future business (Chesbrough, 2003).

For example, Fiat Brazil developed a collaborative platform that combines crowdsourcing, open innovation, and creative commons in order to develop a model concept car called Fiat Mio. In the process of carrying out the innovative automobile project, the Fiat Mio team managed interactions over several months with a large number of participants from different nationalities. This led the project team to analyze more than 11,000 ideas for developing and testing appropriate innovation concept, and developing the prototype. The consumer belongingness to the innovation was evidenced by the company when Fiat Mio was launched in December 2010 at the Sao Paulo Auto Show as several people showed up to claim the prototype as their own. Submissions on the crowdsourcing platform allowed participants to communicate the idea of wheels that rotate 90 degrees to make easier parallel parking and use of cameras instead of rear-view mirrors and inter-vehicle communication to avoid collision. The Fiat Mio is a prime example of what can be accomplished by intelligent crowdsourcing of the new product development activities of a company. Such experiment has evidenced that instead of relying solely on internal abilities, connecting to a large community of engineers, startups, and other partners to circumvent the restrictions of limited resources and knowledge, and think outside the box could make the innovative business projects perform successfully (Saldanha & Pozzebon, 2015, Rajagopal, 2016a).

Crowdsourcing is a technology-driven, outside-in ideation approach. Companies often encourage collective ideation to initiate outside-the-box thinking, and analyze the perceptual semantics of consumers within the competencies and capabilities of the firm. The crowd-based ideation approach helps in generating public ideas at best; however, these ideas need to be validated from the operational perspectives. The problem with the crowd-based communication is that few people may be good at brainstorming with unstructured and abstract clues but may not be able to generate valid reasons for their perceptions. Many research studies raise also questions on the validity of crowd-based data due to lack of scope of fact-checking and storage of crowd information. Acquiring crowd-sourced information is a regular process for some firms like LEGO, Disney, and fashion apparel and accessory companies to generate ideas, and occasionally some great ones. Companies like the above approach to create new cognitive ergonomics for people to think outside of the organization, which offers ideas and post-buying perceptions, and deliver logical framework to validate their responses. Later, crowd-based ideas and perception are subjected to alignment with the corporate ideas, philosophies, action path, redesign processes, and removal of obstacles and intervening reviews; and the blueprint of new products and services are developed. For example, the Haagen-Dazs ice cream, and Marvel Comics have relied on crowd perceptions and ideas to design and deliver the products back to them. Such products and services are raised with consumer democracy, explaining the philosophy of *for the people and by the people* (Coyne et al., 2007).

Such crowd-based ideation has grown in a variety of ways, which has helped firms to converge with the creativity and value perspectives outside the firm. For example, companies like Apple, Google, Amazon, and Intuit managed the global digital rights allowing third-party products or services rights. LEGO and Procter and Gamble invited customers to suggest ideas for their new products and services while InnoCentive (open innovation and crowdsourcing company), and Alphabet Inc. Kaggle (A Google company of data management scientists) offered contests for participants to provide product solutions for business problems and market promotions. In addition, IBM, Wikipedia, and Facebook encouraged fostering networks or communities of interest to continue brainstorming for new business ideas with social interests (Huston & Sakkab, 2006).

Disruptive technologies have often gained impetus from the collective intelligence, and slowly tend to surpass the existing technologies in specific markets and geo-demographic segments. Conceptually, disruptive technologies suggest that the winning technologies have crowd contributions, and are not necessarily radical or superior technology. The disruptions in technology-led products may be more of utilitarian values than hedonic values with a dominant design generated through a process of social, economically disruptive ideation. Disruptive innovation is a process rather than a mere industrial output as it initially focuses on the niche markets to orient local consumerism. Crowd-based product designs are usually subjected to pilot testing in selected markets as they are viewed inferior to those in the mainstream market. Disruptive products focus on value and lean toward catering to the needs of consumers from the low-end niche markets (exceptionally high-end niche markets like crystal idols or precious metal crafts), and gradually enter the competitive mass market (Christensen et al., 2015). Initially, the disruptive innovations enter the niche markets, which are typically ignored by the upstream markets and local incumbents. Such innovations attract underserved consumers from these markets avoiding competition over time with incumbents while gaining market space (Huesig et al., 2014).

1.2 Open Innovation

Open innovation has emerged in the technology-led paradigm shift contributes by the crowd-based ideation process. IKEA, a creative home furnishing company, is an example of open innovation company which relies on both internal and external ideation process to advance their innovation process or to access new markets. Inbound, outbound, and coupled sources of information are associated with the open innovation domain. The inbound dimension includes practices that aim at internalizing external resources to innovate, whereas the outbound approaches toward information acquisition aim at outsourcing the company's internal resources to open new markets with new products developed through the collective intelligence (Radziwon & Bogers, 2019). The open innovation model is built around the external (crowd-based) and internal (in-company) ideas targeting both predetermined and alternate markets. Such innovations are congruent with the customer needs and preferred solutions at affordable prices. The concept of open innovation emphasizes that knowledge of new ideas, products, use values, and innovation are widespread in the world, and it is not possible for the companies to explore this wealth to their fullest capacity. However, business ideas, concepts, and innovation processes are licensed from other companies. In addition, internal inventions not being used in a firm's business are also taken outside the company to get them licensed and earn royalty by selling them to client organizations. Most companies that intend to use open-market innovation apply tools such as licensing, joint ventures, and strategic alliances to bring the benefits of free trade to the flow of new ideas (Rajagopal, 2014). The French multinational insurance firm, AXA, has relied on open innovations to develop customer-centric strategies and created 'AXA Labs,' as innovation outposts based in Shanghai and San Francisco. These outposts enabled the company to explore crowd-led ideation innovation and identify talented entrepreneurs, emerging trends, and new customer needs. The AXA Labs teams scout innovations in their respective regions to develop partnership alliances with the potential startups or adapt to the best-performing models tested in the industry by other companies. The Labs work closely with startup enterprises at every stage, to develop and accelerate disruptive business models.

The Internet and the open innovation have encouraged new ideas and solutions, which has made companies experience the longitudinal and latitudinal outreach in the consumer markets. Such ideas were based on developing products and services to provide consumer convenience, satisfaction, and enhance the business performance of firms. The main challenge faced in managing open innovation is measuring economic viability and technological feasibility accurately to enable the firms to take up innovation projects alongside the growing technology and develop convergence with the business model. Commonly, open innovations are low-priced and gain first-mover advantage in the market; however, these products operate in a predetermined niche to survive the competition. Most companies focus on employing new technologies to serve customers with value, which not only delivers competitive advantage over the existing products in the market, but is also able to create high-perceived value. For example, Nintendo with the Wii, and

Swatch with its fashionable and affordable watches provide the rationale of value-based innovation that is congruent with the customer expectation and the product design (Verganti, 2011). Customers evaluate the open innovation products in the context of 5 As comprising awareness (on product and market), attributes (competitive features), availability (routes to market and shopping options), affordability (price), and adaptability (perceived use value). To launch successful open innovation breakthroughs, most firms analyze the innovation-to-market ratio within a financial year to determine the market share and profit contribution of innovative products. Such analysis helps companies predict the rate of success of breakthrough innovations and expected perceived customer values. Accordingly, firms develop alliances and plan to grow in diverse markets by determining the degree of standardization and customization in the open-innovation products (Fleming, 2007).

Open innovations are getting popular among startup enterprises to develop customer-centric and value-oriented products. Nonetheless, the crowd-led ideation is criticized by some corporate management experts as an insecurely interconnected network of people and other entities, which generate substantial number of the supported activities (Longo & Giaccone, 2017). Such tasks are classified as open-innovation ecosystem initiatives. Most companies are leaning toward open innovation that balance in lowering the risk and generating quick returns on investment on innovations. The open innovations tend to lower the development costs of innovation by the greater use of external technology in carrying out the research and development activities. This saves time as well as money, and the firm no longer restricts itself to the markets it serves directly. Open Innovation is an emerging model in which companies invite innovation ideas from crowdsourcing and use external ideas, and screen them from the point of view of economic viability and technological feasibility of adopting the new ideas. Simultaneously, companies also encourage employees to share ideas within the company or industry group and determine the internal and external paths to market. Open innovation is based on co-created platforms of architectures and systems by various market players including consumers, distributors, retailers, and technology experts who set the innovation requirements and develop an appropriate business model (Rajagopal, 2016a). Creativity in innovation projects should be based on analyzing consumer preferences, scope of open innovation, and carrying out 'experience innovation' involving consumers and stakeholders of the company. Customer-centric companies develop innovative project designs that could generate high consumer use value, competitive differentiation, long and sustainable product lifecycle, and charter of serviceability of innovative products. Open Innovation is one of the central concepts for gaining competitive advantage in the marketplace. For example, large manufacturers from emerging markets such as Lenovo Group Ltd. (China) and Godrej Consumer Products (India), and Internet players such as Tencent Inc. (China) are pioneering new ways of industrializing innovation.

1.3 Social Networks

Social networks are growing rapidly and engage people in expressing their viewpoints on different genres of topics including business and innovation. Customers and stakeholders of customer-centric companies share their opinions or ideas on social media sites, such as Facebook, Twitter, or Instagram. The acquired information is subjected to analyzing contributors' preferences, backgrounds, task-related information, and social relationships to match corporate goals and contributors for crowdsourcing tasks (Li et al., 2015). As the competition is increasing in the global marketplace, most firms are reorienting their marketing communication strategies through customer-to-customer networking as the customer-driven communication is found more trustworthy and decisive. Consequently, consumers are adopting increasingly active roles in co-creating marketing communication with companies and their respective brands. Most of the emerging firms are working hard in developing online social marketing programs and brand campaigns to reach consumers where they 'live' virtually. However, the challenge faced by many companies is apparently the way to be active in social media, as most firms do not have clear understanding of how to manage the social networks effectively, and what performance indicators they should be measuring, and how. Further, as companies develop social media strategies, platforms such as YouTube, Facebook, and Twitter are too often treated as stand-alone elements rather than the part of an integrated system. Firms should invest in building strategies in a systematic way to understand and conceptualize online social media as an ecosystem of related elements involving both digital and traditional media (Hanna et al., 2011).

In the Internet age, firms are recognizing the power of the Internet as a platform for co-creating value with customers. Internet has impacted the process of collaborative innovation as a key process in value co-creation.

Distinctive capabilities of the Internet as a platform for customer engagement including interactivity, enhanced reach, persistence, speed, and flexibility suggest that firms can use these capabilities to engage customers in collaborative product innovation through a variety of Internet-based mechanisms (Rajagopal, 2016a). The network mechanisms can facilitate collaborative innovation at different stages of the new product development process (back end vs. front end stages), and for differing levels of customer involvement (high reach vs. high richness). Ducati, a manufacturer of motorbikes, and Eli Lilly, a multinational pharmaceutical company, are found actively engaged in encouraging customer involvement in developing new products (Sawhney et al., 2005). In pursuing growth through product innovation, companies should look at their customers as partners in creating and building value. Consumers today have near-instant access to all the information they need on virtually any product. Moreover, they are using this information to influence product development as individuals and, more importantly, through user communities and review groups (Johnson, 2006). Most companies ask their customers about their needs. Customers offer solutions in the form of products or services. Companies then deliver these tangibles, and customers just don't buy. Though customers are not experts and do not possess enough information to come up with solutions, the product research and development team of the company should work with the customers to find appropriate solutions. Customers should be asked only about the final product they want to use (Rajagopal, 2016b).

As re-communication in social networks like Facebook and Twitter is becoming common, many companies take advantage of such grapevine communication trend. A recent research identifies factors that increase the likelihood of re-tweeting communication, so that a firm's tweets will be shared with social networks among peers. Re-tweeting is desirable both because the original tweet reaches more people and a re-tweet is an endorsement from recipients to their followers. Opening a communication with an attention-grabbing headline is important to post the communications on social networks. Socializing the brand may drive enormous scope for re-tweeting as peers can use and act on the message, and save time and money on information search. The best practice of all communication strategies is when organizations combine several of these practices to get the most out of their marketing messages (Malhotra et al., 2012). Social networking and collaboration applications are extremely effective ways of converging forces of a business communication pyramid comprising the bidirectional flow of information among the firm, consumers, and market players (suppliers, service providers, retailers, etc.). The convergence of communication helps firms in managing crowdsourced information and sharing experiences on the innovations, improvements, and the temporary setbacks. People with common interests, or related role players can form communities to learn from and support one another on social media platforms. Social media can also help firms in cases where there is a need for creating more collaborative culture and drive the change initiatives (Rajagopal, 2013).

The collaboration and networking platforms empower employees, customers, and partners to be active participants in the global conversation. Social media tools and platforms provide an effective communications channel for the customer-centric business communication and as a transparent knowledge-sharing initiative across the organization. Firms must establish a process for delivering the voice of truth through the right communication in social media platforms by disseminating authentic, trusted, and believable information. This reinforces the idea that social media can be promoted by the firms as a tool not only to voice ideas and concerns, but also to get accurate and credible solutions on various issues of consumers. Social media and collective intelligence allow information to flow in multiple directions rather than just from the top down. For example, marketing firms crowdsource ideas and involve employees more directly in the innovative strategies. These firms also use social media channels and micro-blogs for sharing brief information. Firms can build greater internal loyalty by actively soliciting continuous feedback on issues related to the change. Social media is an important addition to a traditional change management program, one that can dramatically increase the acceptance of change and advance an organization more predictably toward its business goals. Collaboration and social media tools can reduce the time needed by an organization to navigate large-scale change programs and deliver a better solution for consumer-related marketing issues in the future. The prominent features of converging information acquired from social networks with business modeling is exhibited in Fig. 1.2.

Enormous growth in the information technology has shifted the social practice of face-to-face to digital discussion platforms. Such a shift has widened the outreach of customers and increased the inflow of participants' information. Consequently, social media has become a major

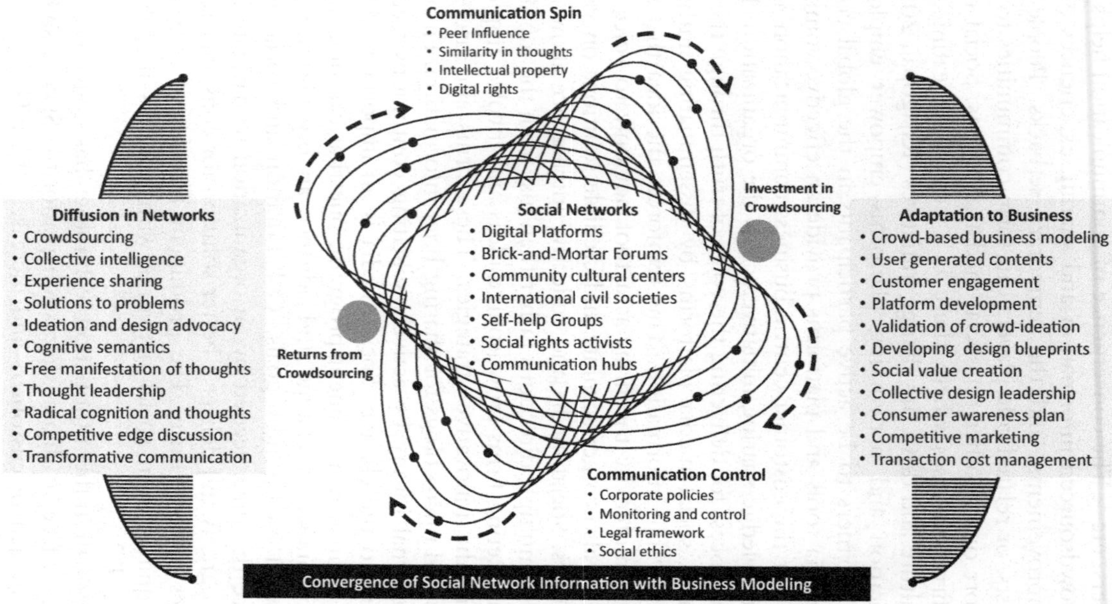

Fig. 1.2 Managing information of social networks for business modeling (*Source* Author)

tool for crowdsourcing and managing data related to collective intelligence. Figure 1.2 illustrates that the digital platforms for sharing personal opinions, new ideas, and experiences have transformed the conventional wisdom of people to stick to the brick-and-mortar forums, organize community meetings, and share experiences. Yet, community cultural centers serve in different sectors like social health, natural medicinal forums, handicrafts, and handloom cooperative centers as the places of human relations in developing countries. Social networks are also supported by the self-help groups working on specific social and economic themes like women empowerment, women entrepreneurship, sustainability, and many more. Similarly, social rights activists, business leaders, and political groups also promote communication hubs which attract participants to share their experience and new ideas related with the development of society and economy.

Crowdsourcing is one of the principal ways of acquiring information via social networks, which leads to generating a pool of ideation, experience sharing, and finding solutions to the existing problems. Such categorical information repositories build collective intelligence over time, which is harnessed by the companies for developing customer-centric and crowd-based business models. Participants also conduct design advocacy for the fashion products, consumer electronics, food and health, home décor, and other genres of public interest, which benefit customer-proactive companies to follow and fabricate. Intensive users on the social networks develop cognitive semantics by disseminating interconnected ideas and thoughts. Of which, thought leadership is built on the networks, and opinions gradually polarize to some flagship ideas. The business models of IKEA, LEGO, Google, and Sony Play Station are raised on such crowd-led central themes and ideas. Nonetheless, crowd communication needs to be filtered for radical thoughts and to extract the transformative communication that offers constructive measures in developing business models. Crowd-based business models are embedded with the following attributes:

- Integration of outside-in information of contributors on various genre of business needs,
- Use of network information technologies such as digital peer-to-peer platforms, and
- Transfer of customer value proposed or created by the predetermined crowd segment.

Building crowd-based business model requires firms to debrief the crowd with specific goals to stimulate information sharing by external contributors, which often emerge as a strong interaction of contributors and their resources on the social networks. The activities of these contributors can range from conducting microtasks to creating and delivering entire products and services to the firm's customers (Kohler, 2015). Customer-centric companies synchronize their marketing strategies with the user-generated contents and invest in engaging customer on effective and newer network platforms than those existing. Most firms co-create design blueprints by engaging the customers, and simultaneously enable creating social value. Consequently, customer-driven firms tend to develop collective design leadership over time. However, crowd communication spins around the peer influence and semblance of thoughts (similarity effect), which are monitored and controlled by the firms. The legal frameworks on social media and social ethics also govern the crowd-based information to some extent.

Social media has widened the opportunities for consumer-oriented firms to expand their market beyond the brick-and-mortar stores. Consumer networks are used by most firms to supplement the traditional sources of buyer insights with a wealth of information gathered by listening into community sites such as Facebook, LinkedIn, and Twitter, and customer forums and product review services. Monitoring the information flow on social media gives firms a unique access to unfiltered feedback from customers, which may not be possible to obtain through other means such as focus groups and surveys. Firms intending to experiment with monitoring the web can outsource the entire process to third parties, or build the capabilities internally. However, as the information technologies are evolving rapidly, firms need to carefully choose some of them to reach their consumers and avoid locking themselves into a solution that constrains their future capabilities. The grapevine effect triggered by the word of mouth is the primary factor among large segment of consumers in making their purchasing decisions. Its influence plays a pivotal role when consumers tend to buy a product or service for the first time or when products are relatively expensive. The social media-driven information factors tend to make people conduct more search, seek more opinions, and deliberate longer among the peers than they would otherwise do. The influence of word of mouth will probably grow along with the digital revolution and help consumers in making buying decisions. Thus, one-on-one communication architects the consumer opinion by analyzing personality of products or services, interventions in decision-making, responsiveness of brand or a company, and trust (PIRT). In the ambience of growing globalization, social media operates on a one-to-many respondents basis as product reviews are posted online and opinions disseminated through social networks. Some customers even create websites or blogs to praise or punish brands. Word of mouth is a potential way to acquire new customers as well as to retain the existing customers through building loyalty and trust in brand and company. On the contrary, this media may also lay negative effects among the peers by spewing dissatisfaction within the segment. Such developments in word-of-mouth platforms may even push firms to lose consumers (Yu, 2007).

Existing interpersonal communication theories describe word-of-mouth behavior in reference to focus on face-to-face interaction, which illustrates that the communicators are in close proximity and can significantly influence the buying behavior of consumers in a marketplace. The informal communication theories based on the principles of social cognition and interpersonal relationship development from social psychology suggest that, given enough time to develop peer interactions, individuals can create fully formed impressions of others based solely on the verbal content on Internet portals. It is imperative that marketers understand how these impressions affect the assessment and use of word-of-mouth information about products, brands, and firms, and consequential consumer behavior both spatially and temporally through the virtual platforms (Brown et al., 2007).

Social media has also turned customers into innovators by exchanging their ideas across the board with the companies. The new ideas on social networks are disseminated very fast and also filtered fast by the companies from the point of view of technological feasibility and economic viability. Recently, the consumers-as-innovators pattern has led to the framing of a new innovation paradigm, in which consumers play a central and very active role through their specific social network or company-based platforms. In this process, rather than seeing consumers simply as the market motivators, the new paradigm centers on consumers and other product users who get involved in the process. It explains why consumers are very important innovators who often develop products on their own (von Hippel et al., 2011). Content analysis of social media may also be helpful for the companies in launching a new product or mitigating negative word of mouth against the product, services, or the corporate image. The content analyses can focus on the current Internet performance of the company, hits on the website of the company, frequency of search, and traffic, and measuring the sales growth. This approach can give managers insights to make decision on investing further resources-financial and human resource, and time in social media. As social media activities achieve scale of returns over a period of time, the challenges of the company may be centered less around justifying funding and more on organizational issues such as developing the right processes and governance structure and identifying clear roles for all involved in social media strategy. Managers can identify the functions, touch points, and goals of social media activities, and approaches to measure their impact and manage their risks. However, companies may need to drive internal discussions on how to lead and to learn from social networks, competitors, and young consumers to stay competitive in the marketplace (Rajagopal, 2013).

Social media has increasingly drawn the attention of consumers and companies over the traditional media. Accordingly, most companies have redefined key factors of their marketing mix by reviewing the shifts in the consumer behavior and online word of mouth competing for innovations in the products, operations, and services strategies. Many companies consider staying active in social media as a viable alternative to traditional advertising and communication. However, managers should understand that both traditional and online social media should be complementary to each other rather than banking on either mode of media. A comparison of advertising and word of mouth shows that social media follow very different rules from traditional advertising. Social media can start conversations or build brand recognition, but the results are much more difficult to predict or measure (Armelini & Villanueva, 2011). While working with social media, some companies have realized that the problem-solving process begins with the identification of exchange content and goals such as what the customer needs, and how the company delivers solutions to meet those needs. The company's high degree of specialization may not often be ready to meet the shifts in consumer behavior as online interactive media drive the perceptions and attitudes of consumers faster than traditional communications (Tuli et al., 2007).

Consumers on social networks are largely driven by the speed of communication and volatility of the ideas, which often makes their need inconsistent and dependent on the supplier to diagnose a problem.

Consumer resources are, nevertheless, critical to the process in manufacturing and marketing contexts. They possess the knowledge needed for problem-solving concerning technological information, market insight, and project objectives in an unrefined form. The complexity and information asymmetry inherent in knowledge-intensive business challenge both supplier and consumer in value co-creation, it might be difficult for the company to communicate the value proposition in advance and to manage the service process to achieve the best service outcome. However, it has been observed that the common attitude of consumers interacting over the social networks is to place a heavy emphasis on the quality of interaction, product, and service process in reference to the company (Liu, 2006).

1.4 New Product Development

Innovation of new products is a complex process that needs to be carried out meticulously in the firms integrating the business and consumer use values in the marketplace. Firms engaged in innovating products should map consumers' needs, attributes of close substitutes, competitive threats, required product services, and estimated cost of marketing of the product in different markets. However, the rate of failure of innovative services is higher as compared to the consumer products. These products largely include credit cards, insurance schemes, hire purchase schemes, investment plans, and the like. The major factors that obstruct the process of innovative product development include:

- Limited creativity and paucity of customer-centric innovative ideas on products and services
- Fragmented markets and consumer segments
- Disruptive social networks for the diffusion of innovations
- Social and economic limitations of consumers
- Government policies and legal conditions
- Cost-effectiveness of the process of new product development
- Competitive marketing mix strategies to promote the innovative products and services
- Resource crisis at various levels in the process of innovative product development and inappropriate strategic decision toward launching innovative products in the market
- Innovation life cycle and sustainability of innovative products.

Most companies consider the process of innovative product development as colossal due to the cumbersome stage-gate process of manufacturing, organizational, and market-led intricacies in analyzing key indicators to launch and manage the products in the competitive marketplace. However, the process of developing an innovative product can be made easier by rationally dividing the chronology of process into two parts—an early stage, which focuses on evaluating prospects and eliminating bad bets; and a late stage that optimizes the market potential. Eli Lilly, following this approach, designed and piloted Chorus, an autonomous unit dedicated solely to the early stage. Chorus has significantly improved the efficiency of new product development and productivity at Lilly. Although the unit absorbs just one-tenth of Lilly's investment in early-stage development, it delivers a substantially greater fraction of the molecules slated for late second phase trials at almost twice the speed and less than a third of the cost of the standard process, sometimes shaving as much as two years off the usual development time (Bonabeau et al., 2008).

The new product has to be developed by the companies with great care. It is necessary to understand the need of the consumers, competitive threats, availability of post-sales services, and cost of marketing of the product. However, in the contemporary era of competition, continuous efforts in developing new products are essential for the companies though there exists risk of failure. The major factors that obstruct the process of new product development are:

- Limited creativity and paucity of new-product ideas
- Fragmented markets
- Social and economic limitations
- Government policies and restrictions
- Cost-effectiveness of the process of new product development
- Resource crisis at various levels in the process of product development to launching in the market
- Product development and launching time
- Short product life cycle.

Companies should strengthen their marketing network simultaneously while launching the new products. It has been observed that the failure of new products is often caused by the lack of organizational teamwork.

Thus, it is required to inculcate the team behavior in developing the new products and popularizing them in the test market segments. The results of the test markets may be further carried out in the larger segments. It is essential that the company should conduct brainstorming exercises to understand the basic and secondary needs for the product, list the product attributes, and identify the forced relationship of other goods and services with the new product.

Idea generation in the process of new product development is a major exercise. This technique calls for listing of all major attributes of the existing product and the needed attributes in order to improve the same product. The forced relationship of the new product with the existing accessories also needs to be studied *e.g.*, developing a new television set may be related to the consumer need for a clock, multichannel viewing on one screen, microphone attachment, and a built-in video game. Such forced relationship has to be identified by the company before launching the product. The morphological analysis calls for identifying the structural dimensions of a problem and examining the relationships among them. The need identification can be done by interacting with the potential and existing customers in a focus group meeting. The industrial marketers can identify new-product ideas working in association with the lead users of the product.

New product development and marketing cycle is also affected by the innovation diffusion cycle spread across the same stages as of product innovation cycle. In the introduction cycle often, the diffusion of information is low as firms do not put adequate resources in generating awareness on the innovation. Firms invite lead users in this stage to test the innovated product and influence early adopters on the usage of the product. Lead users form a small group but act as powerful referral and brand carriers. Firms spend adequate resources in the growth stage to diffuse product innovation attributes through direct communication on one-on-one basis to drive intensive effect on the innovation-led products among early adopters. Consumers in this group are strong followers of the lead users and stand as effective opinion leaders for influencing the early majority of consumers. Most companies deploy enormous resources in advertising, communication, and social media involvement during the late growth and maturity stage to drive customers who are less affluent, less educated, but ready to experiment the innovative products. The 'early majority' consumer segment constitutes a relatively larger segment than the previous consumer segments but is confined to the niche. However, the following stage is of late majority, which is a very large segment and often represents about half of the total number of consumers in a given market area. This consumer segment exhibits high adaptability with the innovative products and derives satisfactory value for money that makes the late majority consumers frequent buyers. Consumers in this segment are price sensitive, and there is the threat of defection when more attractive substitute products penetrate the market. However, a small number of consumers in each market segment are hard to drive for buying any innovative product as they are indecisive and difficult to convince. Such segment of consumers is found in all stages of growth of innovative products but is apparently huge in number during the decline stage of the product lifecycle (Rajagopal, 2016b).

Brainstorming has a major role in the idea generation process. Contemporary methods for ranking the relative merits of ideas generated by brainstorming sessions rely on comparing average scores across members of the group. The average is a measure of the overall merit assigned to an idea but it does not measure unanimity or the concentration of opinion across members of the group with respect to the idea under consideration. The standard deviation of responses is the accepted measure of group consensus but is rarely used in brainstorming possibly because the ranking of ideas is a more complex cognitive procedure when the two statistics, mean and standard deviation, are considered separately, or possibly because most voting schemes are very simple (Rajagopal, 2016b; Walsh & Wood, 1992). The ideation process in a more advanced way encompasses the following perspectives:

- 3Rs: Record, Recall, and Reconstruct
- Return on ideas to match with returns on investment in reference to time and organizational resources
- Brainstorming
- Define the problem as a question
- Select an idea link word or phrase from the list of people, place, or products
- Record a list of ideas associated with the selected idea link
- Choose the link connection and brainstorm the ideas about its potential relationship to the problem defined as question
- Repeat the above step till the time runs out
- Brain-writing
- Distribute blank paper to the participants

- Documenting the problem as a question
- Review the divergent thinking
- Record three ideas and then exchange them with other participants
- Draw the worksheet of ideas and list the best ideas in the lot
- Repeat these steps for 4–5 rounds until the time runs out.

Companies often begin their search for new ideas either by encouraging brainstorming, outside-the-box thinking, or by conducting quantitative analysis of existing market and financial data, and customer opinions. These approaches may produce acceptable ideas at best. The problem with the first method is that few people are very good at unstructured and abstract brainstorming while the second approach may cause fabricated databases usually compiled to offer biased information and customers can rarely reveal if they need or want a product they've never seen. The process of getting an organization to regularly generate lots of good ideas needs to be driven through the following steps:

- Create new boxes for people to think within to prevent their thinking process from going astray and to have a basis for offering ideas.
- Redesign ideation processes to remove obstacles that interfere with the flow of ideas, such as most people's aversion to speaking in groups larger than ten.

For example, how to improve an amusement park may need brainstorming. Response to these questions holds something that adults loved as children and that was reproduced in an expensive form for grown-ups. Further, asking brainstorming participants to ponder how their childhood passions could be recast as adult offerings might generate some fabulous ideas for new products or services (Coyne et al., 2007).

The pivotal role of creativity in organizations has been widely recognized by the academic community. Creativity is associated with the part of the innovation process which is labeled as idea generation. Ideation process for new product development can be stimulated through metaphors, pictures, and experience. It is rooted in the philosophy of rationalism and empiricism, implying 'the truth is out there' approaches. It is observed that defining cognitive idea generation is based on personal experiences and beliefs driven by individual and social information. However, these forms of cognitive-based idea generation process are individualistic and not amenable to team contexts (Bhatt, 2000). Managers engaged in documenting new-product ideas from users should communicate to them on the following lines:

- Use consumer language
- Keep idea simple, focused, and organized
- Keep clarity—from the consumers point of view
- Do not overpromise or oversell
- Focus on major consumer benefits
- Differentiate the brand from the competition
- Keep all concepts that will be tested in the same format
- Use experienced professionals to prepare the concepts
- Address the right target audience
- Understand the level of errors in information acquisition
- Include diagnostic questions.

The basic purpose of this exercise is to generate a large number of ideas. These ideas need to be carefully screened in the interest of consumer satisfaction as well as company's profit. In this process, the company should avoid the *Drop* and *Go* errors. The former attempts dismiss the good idea, while the latter attempts allow the poor ideas to move into the process of commercialization. Hence the purpose of screening the idea needs to be understood carefully. It is advised that the company should develop an idea-rating matrix on the basis of the emerging ideas and their usefulness. Product ideas have to be turned into concept and product concept can be turned later into the brand concept. Concept testing calls for testing of these competing concepts with an appropriate group of target consumers. Concepts can be presented physically or symbolically. The consumers' response may be summarized and the strength of the concept may be judged. The need gap and product gap levels may be checked and modified thereafter. The concept testing and product development methodology applies to any product or service. The business analysis includes the estimating sales as it would be of one-time purchase, frequently purchasing product or at regular interval purchase product. Estimates should also be made in relation to the tendency of first purchase, replacement purchase, or repeat sales. Besides, the company should also assess the marketing costs and the profits from the commercialization of this product (Rajagopal, 2016b).

Testing new products in markets is a scientific process. Successful test marketing leads to proper uses and also poses serious limitations. It provides a measure of sales performance, and the opportunity to identify and correct any weaknesses in the product or in the marketing plan. It is, however, expensive and arduous. Managers need to weigh the cost and risk of product failure against the profit and probability of success, the difference in scale of investment between a test and a national launch, the likelihood of being copied and pre-empted by the competition, and the costs in money and reputation of a product failure. Product development at this stage involves designing the prototypes on the lines of the derived concept that has passed through technical tests. The consumer testing of the product may be taken up in two forms—laboratory testing and home testing.

References

Armelini, G., & Villanueva, J. (2011). Adding social media to the marketing-mix. *IESE Magazine, 3*(4), 29–36.

Bhatt, G. (2000). Organising knowledge in the knowledge development cycle. *Journal of Knowledge Management, 4*(1), 15–26.

Bonabeau, E., Bodick, N., & Armstrong, R. W. (2008). A more rational approach to new-product development. *Harvard Business Review, 86*(3), 96–102.

Brandt, P. A. (2005). Mental spaces and cognitive semantics: A critical comment. *Journal of Pragmatics, 37*(10), 1578–1594.

Brown, J., Broderick, A. J., & Lee, N. (2007). Word of mouth communication within online communities: Conceptualizing the online social network. *Journal of Interactive Marketing, 21*(3), 2–20.

Chesbrough, H. (2003). *Open innovation: The new imperative for creating and profiting from technology*. Harvard Business School Press.

Christensen, C. M., Raynor, M., & Mcdonald, R. (2015). What is disruptive innovation? *Harvard Business Review, 93*(12), 44–53.

Coyne, K. P., Clifford, P. G., & Dye, R. (2007). Breakthrough thinking from inside the box. *Harvard Business Review, 85*(12), 70–83.

de Beer, J., McCarthy, I. P., Soliman, A., & Treen, E. (2017). Click here to agree: Managing intellectual property when crowdsourcing solutions. *Business Horizons, 60*(2), 207–217.

Fleming, L. (2007). Breakthroughs and the long tail of innovation. *MIT Sloan Management Review, 49*(1), 69–74.

Franke, N., Keinz, P., & Klausberger, K. (2013). "Does this sound like a fair deal?": Antecedents and consequences of fairness expectations in the individual's decision to participate in firm innovation. *Organization Science, 24*(5), 1495–1516.

Govindarajan, V., & Gupta, A. K. (2001). Building an effective global business team. *MIT Sloan Management Review, 42*(4), 63–71.

Goucher-Lambert, K., & Cagan, J. (2019). Crowdsourcing inspiration: Using crowd generated inspirational stimuli to support designer ideation. *Design Studies, 61*(1), 1–29.

Hanna, R. C., Rohm, A., & Crittenden, V. L. (2011). We're all connected: The power of the social media ecosystem. *Business Horizons, 54*(3), 265–273.

Hertwig, R. (2012). Tapping into the wisdom of the crowd-with confidence. *Science, 336*, 303–304.

Huesig, S., Timar, K., & Doblinger, C. (2014). The influence of regulation and disruptive potential on incumbents' submarket entry decision and success in the context of a network industry. *Journal of Production and Innovation Management, 31*(5), 1039–1056.

Huston, L., & Sakkab, N. (2006). Connect and develop: Inside procter & gamble's new model for innovation. *Harvard Business Review, 84*(3), 58–66.

Johnson, L. K. (2006). *Harnessing the power of the customer*. Harvard Business Publishing Newsletter, Cambridge, MA.

Jung, H., & Lee, B. G. (2020). Research trends in text mining: Semantic network and main path analysis of selected journals. *Expert Systems with Applications, 162*, 1–12.

Kohler, T. (2015). Crowdsourcing-based business models: How to create and capture value. *California Management Review, 57*(4), 63–84.

Li, Y., Qian, M., Jin, D., Hui, P., & Vasilakos, A. V. (2015). Revealing the efficiency of information diffusion in online social networks of microblog. *Information Science, 293*, 383–389.

Li, Y.M., Hsieh, C. Y., Lin, L. F., & Wei, C. H. (2021). A social mechanism for task-oriented crowdsourcing recommendations. *Decision Support Systems,141*, Art 113449. https://doi.org/10.1016/j.dss.2020.113449

Liu, C. (2006). Social changes and neighbourhood policy in Shanghai. *Policy and Society, 25*(1), 133–155.

Liu, A. H. (2011). Customer value and switching costs in business services: Developing exit barriers through strategic value management. *Journal of Business and Industrial Marketing, 21*(1), 30–37.

Longo, M. C., & Giaccone, S. C. (2017). Struggling with agency problems in open innovation ecosystem: Corporate policies in innovation hub. *The TQM Journal, 29*(6), 881–898.

Malhotra, A., Malhotra, C. K., & See, A. (2012). How to get your message re-twitted. *MIT Sloan Management Review, 53*(2), 61–66.

Moreno, D. P., Hernández, A. A., Yang, M. C., Otto, K. N., Hölttä-Otto, K., & Linsey, J. S. (2014). Fundamental studies in design-by-analogy: A focus on domain-knowledge experts and applications to transactional design problems. *Design Studies, 35*(3), 232–272.

Morozov, E. (2014). *To save everything, click here: The folly of technological solutionism*. New York: PublicAffairs.

Narain, R., Golas, A., Curtis, S., & Lin, M. C. (2009). Aggregate dynamics for dense crowd simulation. *ACM Transactions on Graphics, 28*(5), 1–8.

O'Reilly, C., & Binns, A. J. M. (2019). The three stages of disruptive innovation: Idea generation, incubation, and scaling. *California Management Review, 61*(3), 49–71.

O'Reilly, C., & Tushman, M. (2013). Organizational ambidexterity: Past, present and future. *Academy of Management Perspectives, 27*(4), 324–338.

Panksepp, J. B., & Lahvis, G. P. (2011). Rodent empathy and affective neuroscience. *Neuroscience and Biobehavioural Reviews, 35*, 1864–1875.

Radziwon, A., & Bogers, M. (2019). Open innovation in SMEs: Exploring inter-organizational relationships in an ecosystem. *Technological Forecasting and Social Change, 146*(C), 573–587.

Rajagopal. (2013). *Managing social media and consumerism: The grapevine effect in competitive markets*. Palgrave Macmillan.

Rajagopal. (2014). *Architecting enterprise: Managing innovation, technology, and global competitiveness*. Basingstoke, UK: Palgrave Macmillan.

Rajagopal. (2016a). *Innovative business projects: Breaking complexities, building performance (vol. 1)-fundamentals and project environment*. Business Expert Press.

Rajagopal. (2016b). *Sustainable growth in global markets: Strategic choices and managerial implications*. Palgrave Macmillan.

Rajagopal. (2021). *The design cube: Converging markets, society, and customer values to grow competitive in business*. Business Expert Press.

Saldanha, F. P., & Pozzebon, M. (2015). *Fiat Mio: The project that embraced open innovation, crowdsourcing and creative commons in the automotive industry*. Harvard Business School Press.

Sawhney, M., Verona, G., & Prandelli, E. (2005). Collaborating to create: The Internet as a platform for customer engagement in product innovation. *Journal of Interactive Marketing, 19*(4), 4–17.

Schilling, M., & Hill, C. (1998). Managing the new product development process: Strategic imperatives. *Academy of Management Executive, 12*(3), 67–81.

Sting, F. J., Fuchs, C., Schlickel, M., & Alexy, O. (2019). *How to overcome the bias we have toward our own ideas*. Harvard Business Review Digital Article. Harvard Business School Press.

Ta, X. H., Gaudou, B., Longin, D., & Ho, T.V. (2017). Emotional contagion model for group evacuation simulation. *Informatica* (Slovenia), *41*(2), 169–182.

Tuli, K. R., Kohli, A. K., & Bharadwaj, S. G. (2007). Rethinking customer solutions: From product bundles to relational processes. *Journal of Marketing, 71*(3), 1–17.

Verganti, R. (2011). Designing breakthrough products. *Harvard Business Review., 89*(10), 114–120.

von Hippel, E., Ogawa, S., & de Jong, P. J. (2011). The age of consumer innovator. *MIT Sloan Management Review, 53*(1), 27–35.

Walsh, P., & Wood, J. (1992). A new rule for assessing ideas from brainstorming. *Total Quality Management, 3*(1), 47–54.

Yu, L. (2007). The quality effect on word-of-mouth. *Sloan Management Review, 49*(1), 7–7.

CHAPTER 2

Crowdfunding

Crowdfunding has become a key approach in connecting people and equality distribution mechanisms. Digitalization enables various crowd-funding platforms. Discussions on concept and practices of crowdfunding for various social and startup enterprises are central to this chapter. The concept of crowdfunding is popular for designing and implementing the social business projects. Social and frugal innovations also attract crowd investors with the objectives of non-profit and for-profit business projects. This chapter critically examines the associated theories, practices, and criticisms on crowdfunding practices in developed and developing countries. The ecosystem of crowdfunding, social business practices, social innovations, and public governance constitute core discussions in this chapter. Factors that deter crowdfunding, and the effects of customer engagement in the crowdfunding process have also been discussed in this chapter. In addition, discussions on the key determinants of crowdfunding comprising social capital, structural perspectives, and customer relations also contribute to this chapter.

Crowdfunding has a chronological growth since the nineteenth century. In 1885, when the Statue of Liberty was shipped from France to the USA in parts, the fund raising to install the statue was a major challenge. However, a newspaper campaign and small donations had raised resources to build the working capital, which emerged as notably the first major 'crowdfunding' project. Modern crowdfunding, interestingly,

Rajagopal, *Crowd-Based Business Models*,
https://doi.org/10.1007/978-3-030-77083-9_2

is often traced to an internet campaign, which kicked off in the late twentieth century by British Rock band Marillion. Crowdfunding promoted by the sponsor could raise funds over fifty thousand dollars for the US tour of the musical band. Today, crowdfunding has become a major source of seed capital for the startup, and small and medium enterprises in developing economies.

Crowdfunding is steadily gaining momentum as an informal form of investment for investors globally. The World Bank has estimated that the current gap between the demand for finance by small- and medium-size enterprises and the existing matching supply of financial markets is approximately $5 trillion US Dollars worldwide. The Fintech solutions have tremendously expanded the outreach of startup, and small and medium enterprises to access formal financial resources. Though the Fintech solutions have provided increased financial inclusion, it has simultaneously increased competition driving the prices lower, and improving the quality of services offered. Nonetheless, driving access to transaction accounts and electronic payments has been a major challenge for these firms to ensure proper utilization and repay the credit. The emergence of peer-to-peer lending, equity crowdfunding, and initial coin offerings constitute a rapidly growing segment of fintech for meeting credit-, savings-, and investment needs (*e.g.* Gerber et al., 2012). Crowdfunding as an Internet-enabled network on a cause-specific platform for small businesses has proved to be a prolific way to raise money in the form of either donations or investments from multiple individuals. This new form of capital building has emerged in the wake of the 2008 financial crisis in North America and Europe to overcome the problems faced by artisans, entrepreneurs, and early-stage enterprises in raising funds. Crowdfunding takes advantage of collective intelligence, mass ideation, and crowd-based decision-making and innovation, and applies these to the funding of projects or businesses. The social networks, social profiles, and web-based communication tools are central to managing the crowdfunding campaigns. The social sources have raised billions of dollars in debt, equity, and donations for projects. Building a crowdfunding ecosystem depends on key enablers (individual sponsors) and fundraising companies to build trust among stakeholders linking the cause-related business model (World Bank, 2013). Crowdfunding has been successful in developing countries and the big emerging markets to support micro, small, and medium enterprises (MSME). Since 2017, *RupeeCircle*[1] crowdfunding financial management company has raised over nine million US dollars (INR 18.12 crore), giving an annual return of 15–25% to its investors through the investment in MSMEs.

Crowdfunding emerged as a new form of fundraising by stimulating informal public resources in the wake of the 2007–2011 financial crisis in North America and it revolutionized the fundraising process for social business, startups enterprises, and small and medium enterprises (SMEs) across the developing nations. The crowdfunding process is supported by most emerging firms through the social recognition and the increasing use of social media. The web-based Internet infrastructure reached the willing investors and supporters online to contribute funding for a social cause. Consequently, crowdfunding has become a principal tool in entrepreneurial resource planning and financial management, fostering economic empowerment and a democratic transformation of the financial sector in small enterprises. There are complexities in fundraising via social and voluntary approaches as compared to a formal institutional lending mechanism. Such funding complications are witnessed by the startup ventures mainly due to strict institutional lending requirements, which demands registrations of firms with the competent authorities. The crowd funded capital is also subjected to tax regulations in many developed and developing countries. However, due to the limited access to bank loans, entrepreneurs opt for alternative sources to fund their ventures. Crowdfunding serves as a conduit to entrepreneurs in raising funds, as fund-seekers overcome these limitations by transferring funds online through the platforms of web-based crowdfunding organizations. The applications of crowdfunding organizations facilitate inexpensive mass appeals allowing fund-seekers to reach millions of potential investors, with no costly intermediaries such as banks or underwriters (Agrawal et al., 2015).

Over time, irrespective of their organizational size and volume of business, enterprises have come forward to adapt to the new forms of collaboration, which make significant impact on consumers and stakeholder engagement. The collaborative decision-making outside the organization has been successfully experimented in the recent past, with crowdfunding

[1] *RupeeCircle* is a collaborating peer-to-peer fundraising company in partnership with the Mahindra Finance in India. The corporate details can be seen at https://www.rupeecircle.com/.

approaches managed categorically by crowdfunding companies. Crowdfunding is driven by community to contribute to collective resources, which leads to regional economic growth, community building, and general socio-political awareness. Crowdfunding is a community financial model in which investors contribute to funds raised in social- and sustainability-led business projects, in collaboration with government and local authorities under fund projects, to provide a community service. The development of social enterprises, fugal innovation startup enterprises, and sustainability-driven small and medium enterprises is an outgrowth of social engagement, empowerment, and public participation embodying crowdsourced and crowdfunded entrepreneurial activities. Consequently, crowdfunding plays a vital role in promoting innovation and entrepreneurship at low cost, and encourages operations in the niche market (*e.g.* Caré et al., 2018). The combination of social innovation and digitalization has encouraged crowdfunding to promote social and sustainable entrepreneurship, which drives new relationships between citizens, enterprises, and business organizations. The concept of urban entrepreneurship based on the attributes of sustainability and circular economy has gained increasing attention in the production and marketing segments. The concept of crowdfunding is contextual to urban entrepreneurship as investors feel that urban enterprises have better marketing conditions than semi-urban or rural demographics, though they also operate initially in the niche market segment. Crowdfunding in urban enterprises intends to create low-priced customer solutions, competitive product portfolios, and utilitarian gains to suit the urban ecosystem. The community entrepreneurial ecosystem is formed by entrepreneurs, neighborhood groups, and business promoters, whose three-way interactions form a triangle of community entrepreneurship within the urban ecosystem. It is driven by the factors such as urbanization, the democratization of innovation, technology, and collaboration (Johnston and Blenkinsopp (2017). A strong crowd-based business model is the key to the success of crowdfunding within the ecosystem constituted by the social and business-related factors as exhibited in Fig. 2.1.

The ecosystem of crowdfunding principally focuses on the concepts of design-to-society, design-to-market, and design-to-value. The crowdfunding business projects address the social causes such as education, health, housing, transportation, and sustainability to enhance the social values driving the quality of life standards, equality, and utilitarian values. Consequently, the crowd-based business models, which are aimed to stay

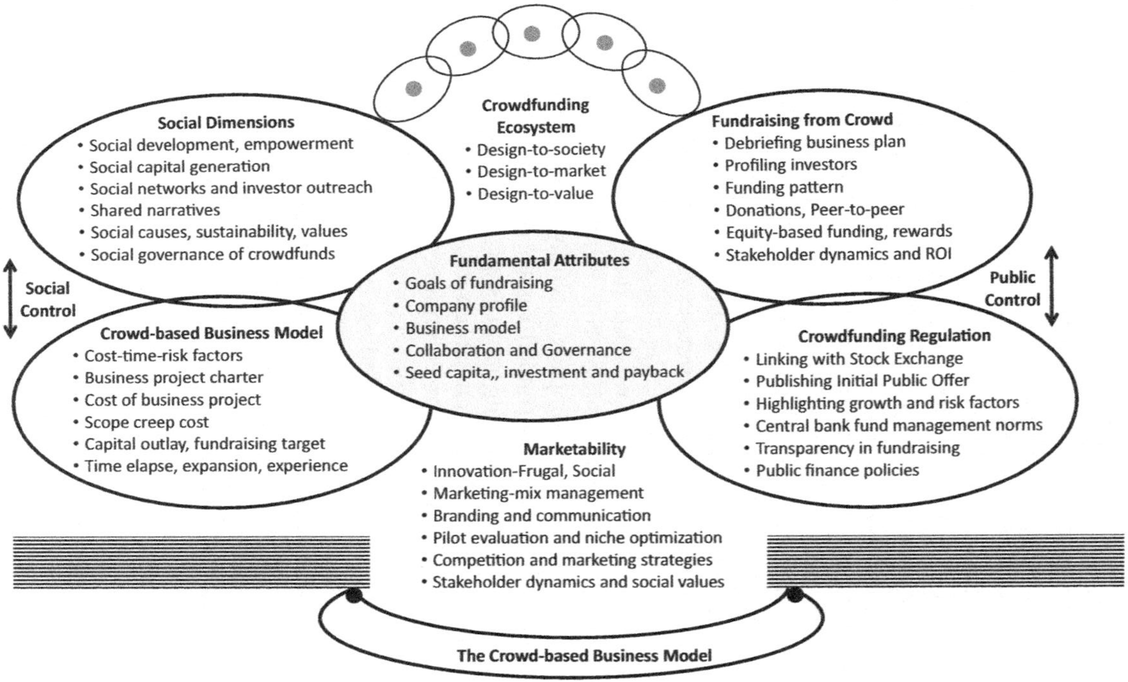

Fig. 2.1 Ecosystem of crowdfunding (*Source* Author)

competitive, earn profit, and serve with the predefined social norms, focus on design-to-market business strategies. The crowdfunding ecosystem is exhibited in Fig. 2.1, which illustrates that the ecosystem has five principal elements comprising social dimensions, crowd-based business model (CBBM) canvas, fundraising approaches, crowdfunding regulation, and marketability of products and services proposed under the CBBM. Crowdfunding has both social and public control, which ensures protection to investors and co-creation of social values.

The social dimensions of the crowdfunding business projects focus not only on achieving social development through empowerment of vulnerable segments like women and low-resource entrepreneurs, but also on generating value by improving the quality of life standards, and attaining the goals of social sustainability. The social capital generation is also aimed through social networks and enhancing the investor outreach while generating funds through crowd-based sources. Effective social governance of project communication, and shared narratives targeting social causes help in attracting crowd investors to raise the collective funds. Crowd-based business models face the challenge of cost, time, and risk overrun due to the project scope creep (deviation in project costs with addition tasks and time projections) unless the company carefully develops the business project charter within the predetermined capital outlay and cost structure of the project. However, unrealistic goals, performance tenures, and the scope of business expansion often cause setback to the crowdfunded business projects. The fund managers communicate the business plan to the investors and explain the fundraising options comprising donations, peer-to-peer funding, reward-based finding, and equity-based funding. The payback and returns on the investment process are also explained to the investors and stakeholders as illustrated in Fig. 2.1. Most developed countries have implemented the financial regulations on fundraising, which explain that the fundraising companies should be a registered business entity of a stock exchange that determines its legal jurisdiction. These companies should issue an initial public offer (IPO) by stating both the growth and risk factors to provide a transparent picture of the financial state of the company to the investors and follow the guidelines of the central bank in the fundraising process.

Crowdfunding is an attractive proposition as an alternative funding source for startups, which offers collective intelligence to frugal and disruptive innovations through the crowd advocacy organizational learning. Crowdfunding proposals are aimed at leveraging from open fundraising calls, requesting monetary contributions for small-scale commercial or social business. Nonetheless, many startups are hesitant to consider crowdfunding as there is no proper public policy or financial guidance on how the various types of crowdfunding projects can be managed to add value in different life cycle stages of the business (Paschen, 2016). Broadly, crowdfunding includes donations, peer-to-peer lending, public or private rewards, and equity-based funding. All categories of funding have the principal premise of raising financial resources from individual and corporate donors. Donation-based crowdfunding is arranged through the web-based social campaign for a social cause. The crowdfunding campaign is created for social innovation proposed by the not-for-profit social organizations.

Debt-based donations are peer-to-peer lending, which is a form of crowdfunding. In debt-based donations, the money pledged by investors is a loan, and must be repaid with interest by a certain deadline. Peer-to-peer lending is a form of organized social lending which typically seeks for guarantee form individual or institutions that opt for sponsoring the micro, small, and medium companies with pre-evaluated business model. The peer-to-peer lending is somewhat different than the pooled lending, which is followed by the chit-fund companies. The peer-to-peer lending companies invite individuals to invest in a portfolio of loans prequalified by evaluating the proposed business models by the clients (borrower). Investors may choose business projects, who applied for loans, with good credit history. Usually, the projects admitted for peer-to-peer funding include purposes of small business, home management, health requirement (surgery, hospitalization, and chronic disease treatment), or education. Investors can choose project by reviewing the general characteristics and expected outcomes. Due to the nature of such openness in business project, the crowd investment and lending face the risks of delayed payment, willful defaults, bankruptcy, or uncontrolled economic circumstances.

Reward-based crowdfunding offers incentives to the donors and investors on collective fundraising projects. Reward-based funding projects rely on the participating donors to assure their contributions to their project in return for a nonmonetary price like social recognition or souvenirs. This can be the product that the company aims to produce, a t-shirt, a thank you note, or even the backers' name on a website (Giudici et al., 2018). The value of the received reward normally increases according to the amount pledged. Such an approach serves as an effective strategy to promote the crowdfunding campaign and pre-sell new products and ideas to sponsors or donors. The rewards instituted for fundraising help the fundraising firms test the possible demand of the product, evaluate the trend, and seek social endorsement on the project. Rewards to fund contributors encourage the follow-up discussion and voluntary social roll-out of the campaign through focus groups. Usage of crowdfunding sites allows much bigger groups to participate on digital platforms and to carry out continuous improvements in the communication during the campaign so that the product can evolve strongly. The tensile fundraising projects for social causes, sustainability, development of women and children, and entrepreneurship are successfully tagged with the rewards (Young, 2013).

The equity-based crowdfunding allows small businesses and startups to part with a portion of their business profit or pay a dividend to the investors as stakeholders of the firm in exchange for funding. Contributors in equity-based fundraising campaigns receive shares of the business firms proportionately to their contribution. However, the majority of the developed and developing countries do not provide any legal support to equity assurances and distribution as crowdfunded companies are not registered in the respective stock exchanges and do not hold legal entities. In the USA, equity-based crowdfunding was restricted by the securities act of 1933, which required companies to constitute under the company's act and disclose their financial information to the Securities and Exchange Commission (SEC). After that the information was published to the public, the potential investors could make better decisions. Such practice is streamlined with the process of publishing Initial Public Offer (IPO) by stating the approved capital outlay, equity values, and risk indicators.

This law made the use of equity-based crowdfunding efforts difficult and expensive for smaller businesses (Young, 2013). Generating crowdfunding requires all transactions under Regulation Crowdfunding to take place online through a stock exchange-registered intermediary, either a broker-dealer or a funding portal. Companies seeking crowdfunding need to publish disclosure of information in filings with the regulatory authorities and to investors and the intermediary facilitating the offering. The key regulatory factors that have facilitated crowdfunding in developed countries include (World Bank, 2013):

- A regulatory framework, which ensures transparency in financial operations, speed of fund collection, and scale of business.

- Registration with the competent authority of fundraising companies, which serves as collection agents to ensure financial transparency.
- Monitoring of technology and Internet usage in the crowdfunding process to ensure transactional transparency.
- Publishing initial public offer (IPO) by the principal company soliciting crowdfunding, including the fund managers.
- Publishing investor protection policies, code of ethics, and categorical terms of reference.
- Monitoring social media market penetration and Internet usage, which is necessary to harness demographic and technology trends to drive collaboration and cultural shifts.
- A regulated online marketplace that facilitates capital formation ensuring prudent investor protections through education and training, and
- Developing collaboration with other entrepreneurial events and hubs to create opportunity and oversight for investors and entrepreneurs.

Developing economies have the potential to drive growth by employing crowdfunding to leapfrog the traditional capital market structures and financial regulatory regimes of the developed world. Crowdfunding events can be managed successfully by developing financial transparency, regulatory conditions in collecting and utilizing crowdfunds, and creating frameworks for early-stage finance that facilitate entrepreneurship. In addition, public policies fostering the local innovations using affordable technology could help the enterprises to gain market competitiveness within the industry.

2.1 Social Businesses

Social businesses have focused on the personality, background of social entrepreneur (knowledge and entrepreneurial background), and entrepreneurial performance (capabilities and competence). The social entrepreneurs have unique characteristics including knowledge, cognitive capacities, and altruistic values. Social innovation is an interactive bottom-up collective learning process implemented through social enterprises. As a boundary-spanning activity across the public and private sectors, the interactive learning process and the associated capability building for social innovation serve as the catalyst for wider social reform. Social innovations help value creation in emerging economies involving stakeholders and firms in the broader projects. The growing concerns of circular economy and circular business have reoriented companies toward developing sustainable business models with effective social value-chain management. Circular economy encourages sharing of ideas, processes, and outcomes that are widely connected with sustainability projects. Sharing the economy of consumers, stakeholders, and society related to the consumer products companies encourages them to develop a sustainable business model. Most companies are engaged in building and implementing sustainable business models in the social interest that helps in value chain creation and acquiring new customers. While sharing socio-cultural attributes of geo-demographic segments has been a long-standing practice in society, the sharing economy is used as an umbrella concept to exhibit the broad range of disparate consumption practices and organizational models (Habibi et al., 2017). The value proposition of both customers and social communities contributes significantly to the sustainable business modeling process. Value proposition describes the attributes of the product/service offering, the customer segments, and their relationship in the social deliveries, whereas value creation and delivery describe how value is provided to customers (the channel efficiency and value delivery process), including the structure and activities in the value chain (Osterwalder & Pigneur, 2010).

Social capital theory has been the strong theoretical motivation in crowdfunding research and explaining entrepreneurs' social capital as one of the main determinants of crowdfunding success. One of the several factors motivating people to fund a project through crowdfunding by following peer-to-peer or equity funding is primarily based on the quality of social interactions over spatial (across geo-demographic segments) and temporal (longitudinally over time) dimensions. The crowdfunding campaigns can be successfully realized through illustrative, information-rich, and exemplified (case studies) crowdfunding platforms. The quality of crowdfunding websites, trustworthiness of crowdfunding managers (agencies), and investor protection policies help investors in strengthening commitment to fundraising cause(s). Investors tend to review feedback and shared experiences to inculcate emotions and connectedness to a community and entrepreneurs. 'Interactions,' 'connectedness,' and 'similar interest' are the divergent variables of the concept of social capital, which affect the commitment to funding public projects (Gerber et al.,

2012). Nonetheless, fundraisers rely on their social capital (community strength, social sensitivity, and business trends) to support their campaigns. Some crowdfunding research only studies certain facets or dimensions of social capital, without covering all dimensions of social capital. Commonly, crowdfunding campaigns elaborate on the role of social capital at certain stages of the business project, by explaining the slow growth associated with the early stage of business making it difficult to capture the effect of social capital on crowdfunding. Contrary to this stage, the fundraising campaigns emphasize the gains at the stage of growth and maturity over time. Therefore, the relationship between social capital and crowdfunding performance has many psychosocial elements to be judged (Colombo et al., 2015). Unlike offline investment in which trust and reputation are built through interpersonal interactions, the greater distance between online investments makes it difficult for founders to build relationships with potential investors due to lack of the factors comprising transcendence, trust, and transparency (3Ts) among the investors, founders, and fundraising channels. Besides the 3Ts, lack of proximity, debriefing with founding companies, and visibility of business growth prospects also hinder the investment prospects in crowdfunding projects. Therefore, the crowdfunding domain still needs to gain a deeper understanding and investor dynamics about how public or social project creators can benefit from social capital and business projects (McKenny et al., 2017). Social capital affects crowdfunding performance, and develops relations within the virtual community in which community members interact with each other. The effectiveness of digital interactions on fundraising dynamics has different triggers such as tactical versus strategic benefits, trust versus social obligation (sustainability, climate change, and ecological conservation), and social versus political backing on the crowd-based projects. However, virtual communities have made significant progress in developed countries toward formation and evolution of social capital, thereby influencing crowdfunding campaign performance over time (Inkpen & Tsang, 2005).

Social businesses are the community-conscious organizations evolved within the social framework, which address co-creation of solutions to a predetermined social need or a problem. Among many social problems in the urban–rural environment, sustainable housing, green energy, natural resources management, transportation and logistics, and poverty alleviation are some primary areas for social enterprises to work with. Social businesses are evolved with stakeholders to serve the urban and rural demographics, which also serve the underprivileged consumers in a weak regulatory framework. In emerging markets, customers and members of social enterprises at the bottom of the pyramid are targeted for the basic benefits and services such as healthcare, education, and farm and non-farm activities. Social businesses use innovative business models to build solutions with the available resources and offer basic services to the stakeholders in a sustainable way. The principal objective of such social businesses is to create social impact and generate economic and social values in a sustainable manner (Mair et al., 2007).

The entrepreneurial marketing approach involves cost-effective activities by avoiding formal market research or involving mass promotion strategies to promote business. However, entrepreneurs of small and medium business segments significantly depend on their personal networks to collect information about consumers and the market. These entrepreneurs heavily use consumer psychodynamics and the interpersonal communication such as word of mouth to promote their products and services (Copley, 2013). The social facet of entrepreneurship education has closer proximity to innovation diffusion and business modeling than the formal teaching pedagogy or regulatory education to entrepreneurs. Though regulatory and social environmental resources are external to entrepreneurship education, they can be purposely integrated and aligned with the entrepreneurial touchpoints to expand and enhance customers' journeys, customer experience, and marketability of their products or services in the emerging markets (Homburg et al., 2017).

Traditional approaches to social enterprise strategy of both startup enterprises and large companies assume that the social behavior and values are relatively stable and predictable. However, new technologies and greater transparency have been combined to achieve the social business goals of sustainability. Such shift in the business environment has generated more risk and vulnerability among social enterprises in engaging with new innovative projects. Social enterprises that thrive to follow the integrated innovation strategies, as discussed above, can alter the consumer behavior quickly and manage the market demand. These enterprises experiment rapidly and frequently with products and services as well as business models, processes, and strategies, to achieve a sustainable market for innovative products. Innovation entrepreneurship is a convergence of startup enterprises and the sponsoring companies, which moves from the stage of initiation to the systematic project management to commercialization, and finally to developing sustainable innovation through incremental innovations. Companies need to invest substantial resources toward consumer education in order to create consumer demand. Besides, they also have to carry out product demonstrations such as 'do-it-yourself' and adaptive customization by allowing consumers to use the new products for a reasonable period and perceive value for money associated with the products. However, the opportunities for open innovation, incremental innovation, and enhancement of the use value of innovative products over the stages of product life cycle finally take the innovation business projects to the initiation stage of the next generation innovative products (Rajagopal, 2021).

The peer-to-peer fundraising has been successfully implemented in a legendary social enterprise, the Grameen Bank (rural financing institution) experiment of Bangladesh. This enterprise emerged initially as a self-help group for catering to the grassroot financial needs of the people. It aimed at serving the poor and needy members of the social institution who wanted credit (loan) for farm or non-farm production or service activities. Commonly, poverty spans into generations in developing countries due to the vicious cycle of low-income and disguised unemployment. Consequently, people fail to break the cycle of poverty in the short term. The credit system in Grameen Bank is based on a survey of the social background rather than on a pre-established banking technique, which provides the required information to develop a long-term process depending on the aspirations and commitment of the stakeholders and economic operators. In this social enterprise, the credit system serves the poor, and not vice versa. Therefore, credit officers visit the villages to get to know the borrowers. The focus of operations is on those poverty-stricken people, who need investment resources as they have no access to credit. The institution leans on solidarity groups that are small informal groups consisting of co-opted members coming from the same background and trusting each other. In addition, savings are associated with credit, without it being necessarily a prerequisite. In view of the above successful experiment of Bangladesh Grameen Bank, it can be stated that social enterprises tend to alleviate social problems with an objective to run sustainably, and any profits must be reinvested in the enterprise rather than funneled back to shareholders. Unlike a low-cost business, a social business determines up-front actions to those eligible and strives to maintain high quality of deliverables (Yunus et al., 2015).

Cultural diversity has multiple meanings. Diversity within a society refers to the richness of choice within that society. Globalization focuses on diversity across societies, that is, whether societies are becoming more similar. Cross-cultural exchange tends to favor diversity within a society but not across societies. Trade tends to increase the diversity over time by accelerating the pace of change and bringing new cultural goods with each era or generation. Cultural similarities tend to come together over time across regions. That is, although chain restaurants take an increasing percentage of restaurant sales, growth in dining out has led to an expansion of specialty food opportunities. While cross-cultural exchange alters and disrupts each society it touches, it also supports innovation and creative human energies. The *creative destruction* of the market creates a plethora of innovative and high-quality creations in many different genres and styles, and media cross-cultural exchange expands the menu of choice, at least provided that trade and markets are allowed to flourish (Cowen, 2002). Most companies tend to resolve the business situations within the company by conversing with the employees rather than simply issuing orders. Such interface strategy to resolve business situations promotes corporate image, products and services, operational flexibility, employee engagement, and strategic alignment. Organizational conversation reflects the essential attributes of interpersonal conversation structure with 4 Is comprising intimacy, interactivity, inclusion, and intentionality. Intimacy drives a bottom-up exchange of ideas through social media platforms in an organization, and shifts and develops behavioral involvement of the consumers in the discussion. Interactivity entails shunning the simplicity of monologue and embracing the unpredictable vitality of dialogue.

Marketing through social channels in the twenty-first century has succeeded in connecting consumers with companies, brands, and destinations by highlighting peer evaluations, consumer preferences, and motivations toward buying decisions. However, the contribution of marketing technology in establishing both product and customer interconnectedness across markets prompts companies to make the dynamic decision based on the market competition trends. The dynamic marketing decisions often develop inconsistencies in the consumer policies of the company, and the deliverables of brands are affected (Dass & Kumar, 2014). Public policies are focusing on macroeconomic disruption due to sustainability issues in developing economies (Béal, 2015). Therefore, large companies are developing alliances with local governments on public–private partnerships (PPP) in implementing sustainability norms and enhancing social value. The PPP initiatives in various geo-demographic sectors have generated social awareness among people and inculcated the environmentally conscious consumption in the society. Environmentally conscious consumption is one of the key concerns in the modern society, and it is increasingly affecting the urban consumers. However, consumers often overstate their willingness to purchase environmentally conscious products; the global purchasing of these products is relatively low. Most research studies on environmentally conscious consumption suggest that the purchase intention is driven by intrinsic factors such as demographics comprising income, education and social status, consumer cognition, and personality attributes (Tsarenko et al., 2013). In addition, external factors and social influences also affect an individual's environmental consumption behavior.

Companies with green business philosophies such as automobiles, energy, textile, and paper products have begun to transform the manufacturing process alongside the competitive landscape. These companies redesign products, technologies, processes, and business models through social enterprises to deliver the social value for their products and services (Nidumolu et al., 2009). Despite the success of some sustainable business models implemented by the manufacturing and operations companies, small, medium, and large-scale companies in regional settings are struggling with the challenge of integrating environmental plans into their core business strategies. Local companies develop low-cost sustainability projects with an objective to expand their outreach to customers and stakeholders. Sustainability has emerged as a megatrend for businesses in the twenty-first century. Companies plan transformative changes in the organization to create social values across the competitive marketplace (Lubin & Esty, 2010). The trend of sustainability has encouraged both high- and low- investment companies. The dominant belief about creating and developing sustainable business model in the customer-centric and industrial-marketing companies is driven by the idea of solving environmental and economic issues and providing high social values. The response of public policies helps in developing sustainable business models through social guidelines to move their businesses toward green and circular economy (Evans et al., 2017). Social and innovation subsystems include social values, entrepreneurship education, and utilitarian innovations. Management of resources, and factors of production, procurement and transactions of public goods constitute some significant factors of macroeconomic subsystem.

Most large and medium companies are committed to the sustainability practices, which have consistently been driven by the need to contribute to social value of business and reduce the negative impact of *for-profit* corporate philosophy. The *for-profit* philosophy focuses business growth and expansion with no philanthropic and social concerns. The sustainability commitment allows companies to invest in *not-for-profit* projects by advancing into the global sustainability agenda across the three bottom lines comprising economic sustainability, environmental sustainability, and social sustainability. Benefits of sustainability and green organizational practices in manufacturing, services, and facilities management are measured by substantial reduction in wastes (waste management), increased productivity and social values through efficient work practices, and optimization of consumption of natural resources (Ikediashi et al., 2020). Commitment to sustainability is a common responsibility that involves partnership of state, and public- and private sectors. Socially enlightened corporate sector tends to meet the sustainability commitments by involving stakeholders and raising crowdsourced funds in addition to that of the organization. Collective intelligence helps companies monitor social sustainability projects with the sense of public commitment and deliver social values. In addition, crowdsourcing, corporate funding, and social incentives appear to be more effective in promoting sustainability commitment (Sheu & Hu, 2009).

2.2 Social Innovation

Social innovation is an interactive bottom-up collective learning process implemented through social enterprises. As a boundary-spanning activity across the public and private sectors, the interactive learning process and associated capability building for social innovation serve as a catalyst for wider social reform. Social innovations help value creation in emerging economies involving stakeholders and firms in the broader projects (Rao-Nicholson et al., 2017). Innovating the sustainable business model is about creating superior customer- and firm value by involving stakeholders and market players such as supply chain and packaging partners. Sustainable business model of a company addresses societal and environmental needs through integrated business operations. Ecosystems of different business models are specific to the purpose and the corporate goals of the companies. Some companies that grow with social innovation objectives have a greater number of qualitative designs encompassing social needs, stakeholder education, user value generation, and bridging the corporate social responsibilities. Crowdsourcing or collective intelligence has emerged as dynamic tool in the business ecosystem today, which is supported by the stakeholders. They support companies in co-creation and coevolution process with stakeholders through social interaction, social innovations, and social governance. Business ecosystems linked with the sustainability goals drive public–private entrepreneurship (collaborations) to meet the sustainable development goals through social and frugal innovations.

Consumers also play a significant role in the innovation subsystem by co-creating products that add value to the social sustainability. End users share insights on low-cost innovations and the possible ways of their utility with the consumer communities. The consumer-led social innovations are supported by public policies and encouraged through the non-governmental organizations and public–private participation. End users contribute to the innovation processes by contributing to the design perspectives and stimulating demand for the innovative product. Thus, stakeholders, corporate managers, and policymakers remain apprehensive about the potential of end users driving sustainable innovation (Nielsen, 2020). Social innovations emerge as the product of social entrepreneurs driven by the knowledge-intensive social needs and contextual services. Social innovations are often addressed to the non-profit sector such as social health, natural resources management, farming activity, and domestic energy, which are sometimes referred to as the social policies and economy. Companies develop sustainable business models by critically examining the inputs of innovation subsystem and socio-economic resources. Innovation subsystem largely evolves within the geo-demographic niche and uses initially cost-effective local resources; and it later transforms to commercial propositions in alliance with large organizations (Dionisio & Raupp de Vargas, 2020). The intermediate level of social value creation is developed by establishing relationships with stakeholders that enables sharing of information, and co-creation and coevolution process of social innovation and business projects. The apex level of social value creation has been identified as the sense of belongingness among stakeholders of sustainable business projects. In addition, collaborative projects promoting stakeholder engagements in managing sustainable projects, innovations, and technologies contribute to the social value creation (*e.g.* Liu et al., 2020). The value-chain management, and deliveries of sustainable business projects show effective results when organizations follow collaborative work culture with autonomy and employee engagement. The corporate social responsibility projects of most multinational companies are implemented as a pilot to test the sustainability-based business model.

Broad macro-factors include ecology and environment, the needs that are contextual to principal social sector (health, housing, agriculture, energy, natural resources, and local industries), and relevant public policies. The macro-factors are affected by various micro elements in the implementation of sustainable business projects due to improper prioritization across the geo-demographic segment, which affect social values and lifestyle. In a broad context, the social entrepreneurship tends to co-create social innovations while implementing the sustainability projects in the region and coevolve with the collaborating organizations. Collective intelligence (crowdsourcing) helps to enhance the ideation process on socially sustainable business projects and leads to frugal or low-cost innovations. Frugal innovation is often associated with sustainability (ecological and social) as it is developed with an objective of minimizing the use of resources (raw material, production resources, energy, fuel, water, waste, financial resources) and maximizing the output within the given space, time, and application limitations. Frugal innovations are affordable and easily accessible as compared to conventional innovations (Weyrauch & Herstatt, 2016). The principal domains converging the social innovation process are exhibited in Fig. 2.2.

Social innovation is driven by three principal domains comprising social domain, entrepreneurial domain, and public domain, which determine the nature of social and business entrepreneurship and transformational leadership. The factors embedded in these domains influence the crowd-based business modeling for carrying out social innovation as illustrated in Fig. 2.2. The social services needed to support innovation in various sectors such as health, housing, education, and transportation call for social innovations through the support of the public domain. The social domain intends to promote sustainability-led businesses and drive bottom-up (local) economy. The public domain drives social innovation through the collective intelligence (crowdsourcing) for ideation and contextual information pooling, and crowdfunding to co-create and coevolve crowd-based business models. Regulatory policies of crowdfunding and other financial regulations are implemented by the government and central banks in developed and developing

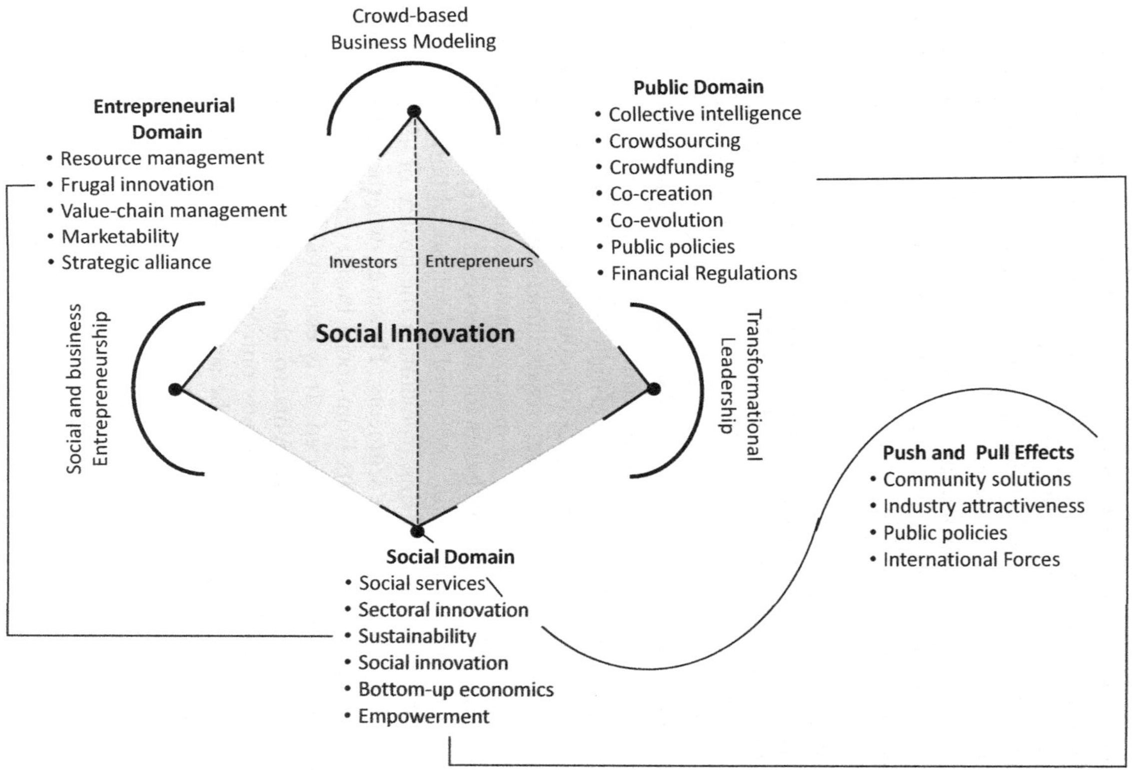

Fig. 2.2 Domains of social innovation (*Source* Author)

nations. Social entrepreneurship combines the resourcefulness of traditional entrepreneurship with a mission toward social development. The major concerns on resources management, frugal innovations, and their marketability approaches constitute the entrepreneurial domain, which contributes also to value-chain management among the key business partners including customers. Local enterprises managing social innovations also engage in building strategic alliances with large companies. In addition, exploring community solutions and industry attractiveness attributes create pull effects for social innovation through crowdfunding, while enforcement of public policies and international funding and business trends drive the push effect to encourage social innovation under the public domain.

The advancement of information technology has been radically adapted to the social and frugal innovations. The crowdfunding process has been leveraged by such technological advancement. Over time, companies evaluate the threats and opportunities of crowdfunding, and create new business options for the more-connected future of digital ecosystems. Consequently, many social innovation companies such as Uber, Airbnb, and Amazon are doing business successfully with the support of digitization, which offered opportunities for companies to leverage strong customer relationships and increase cross-selling. Simultaneously, many companies are deriving real value from social business using social media, social software, and technology-based social networks to enable relationships among people, information, and social capital. Social businesses play important role in decision-making to maintain the quality of life in most rural and suburban population segments. However, whether companies are able to derive positive benefits from social business is social business maturity need to be clearly explored. It is estimated in some research studies that incremental improvements to the existing social business practices contribute to positive business outcomes, and deliver benefits associated with the social business at the stage of maturity. The continuous improvement in social businesses requires a substantial change (Kane et al., 2014).

Some companies that grow with social innovation objectives have a greater impact on social needs, stakeholder education, user value generation, and in developing the corporate social responsibilities. Social values embedded in business models demonstrate corporate reputation and financial success besides the customer loyalty. The social business models include sustainability-led strategy and leadership, mission, communication and learning, social values and lifestyle, and loyalty and identification. Companies and stakeholders intending to proactively manage social sustainability need to undertake participatory projects with key partners and stakeholders on cultural change and development initiatives toward sustainability (Rajagopal, 2019; Schönborn et al., 2019). Large companies act pro-social as a part of their corporate social responsibility activities. In India and China, large companies prefer office furnishings, such as floor carpeting, which is manufactured by the community industries (hand-loom or power-loom enterprises). Thus, the social influence also plays a significant role in buying attitudes of industrial clients. Public policies in developing countries support sustainability projects through funding, accessibility, and adaptability to technology, and initial marketing. Public policies encourage co-creation of innovation, and public–private partnership in management of sustainability projects. These policies focus on improving the socio-cultural conditions and achieve higher economic gains while managing social innovation and sustainability projects. Social business models have emerged as the planning tools for entrepreneurs that help them think through all the core components of their ventures and rationally employ the investment decisions in the context of technology, attracting venture capitalists, and developing strategic alliances with large companies on commercializing social innovation projects (Colombo et al., 2013). Frugal innovation is the process of reducing the complexity and cost by taking cost-effective measures in manufacturing and following economies of scale. Usually, this refers to removing some conspicuous features from the product, such as an automobile, in order to market it in the bottom of the pyramid markets and emerging markets. Designing products for such markets may also call for an increase in sustainability of innovative products and selling through modern routes to market. However, profits earned on frugal innovations are much lower than high value-high technology innovative products targeted to the up-front or premier markets.

Social innovations also induce consumer behavior toward sustainable products and services, and generate social well-being. Social innovations are often seen as the products of social entrepreneurs, and are motivated by the knowledge-intensive social services. Social innovations are initiated with the crowd-based interactions and initiatives. Crowdsourcing has evolved along with the advancement of information technology on open-innovation platforms. The ideation process of social innovation has been enriched by the consumers, stakeholders, and corporate executives across geo-demographic segments. Sustainability-driven innovations are often skewed by social bias while evaluating the ideas within a narrow knowledge base. Social innovations today are generated through open innovation. Social organizations and companies engaged in corporate social responsibility projects rely on consumer preference and evaluative criteria to design innovations, which are supported by the crowdsourced ideas. In the crowd-based social innovation process, consumer engagement along with specialized expertise makes random ideas to be debated within the consumer communities. The crowdsourced and shared value on social innovation is driven by the predetermined or embedded social purpose like conservation of natural resources (land, energy, and water), sectoral production (farm and non-farm production), and organic consumption. Such social concepts involve reemphasizing the corporate social responsibility projects of a company and founding its social business objectives (Rajagopal, 2021).

Successful social innovations and sustainability-led corporate social responsibility projects periodically measure the shared value generated through crowdsourcing and social interactions. Coca-Cola spent months in monitoring and measuring the shared values on employability of youth in Brazil. This helped the company plan how to achieve business and social goals, and then establish intermediate measures to track progress. Entrepreneurs and firms develop social innovations by analyzing the social resources comprising social capital, capabilities, stakeholders, interactions, and outcomes. They identify strategies based on the existing or acquired competencies for activation, integration, co-designing, and co-creation appraising a qualitative way through shared values and the conditions to make each strategy feasible (Arena et al., 2020). Effective social innovators enlist external stakeholders in their efforts to understand social needs and to execute their strategies. The right market for a social innovation depends on whether the entrepreneur or the firm has a clear social purpose and understanding of the targeted problems. Creating social and sustainable innovation, therefore, should be aimed at delivering the frugal and long-term solutions and building a strong business case for social marketing. Innovation is critical to social and economic growth as most companies tend to develop local business models to explore marketing opportunities. Consequently, large companies have shown interest in sponsoring and acquiring technology-led startup enterprises, and making them more competitive in the regional marketplace. Social entrepreneurs use traditional techniques to go to market and scale-up quickly with limited resources against large companies that emulate market strategies not only to innovate quickly, but also to commercialize innovation rapidly across the market layers. Therefore, the behavior of large companies deters the local innovation and its growth initiatives (Rajagopal, 2021).

The convergence of business and society is driven through the transformational (change in social thinking) and transactional (value-based philosophy) thinking and co-creating solutions to the societal problems related to business sector. Social marketing strategies are the effective tools to align business goals with social development and value generation perspectives. Social innovations, sustainable development, green marketing, and implementing corporate social responsibility programs stimulate the enhancement of performance with social purpose. This linear path bridging the gap between society and business validates the design-to-society and design-to-market philosophies. Social validation of marketing programs by sharing customer experiences on digital platforms and generating user-driven contents creates the scope of co-creation of products and services effectively within the society and market. Sustainable customer products companies like IKEA, GE Energy, and Unilever focus on inducing corporate social leadership in managing the corporate social responsibility. However, while implementing society-linked business models, companies tend to develop community hubs for customer and stakeholder interactions on face-to-face, digital, or hybrid communication models. The interactions of customer on these platforms help companies document the voice of customers to support strategy designs. In addition, public policies, public–private partnerships, and social psychodynamics leverage companies in designing programs to evolve in vulnerable social sectors (health, education, housing, agriculture, and non-farm economic production) with meticulous business strategies. Social business is a value-led function involving customers, stakeholders, and entrepreneurs. The initiatives of involving the social entities in co-crating products and services help companies in driving quickly to social business due to wider acceptability among customers. Social businesses are more effective in outreaching bottom-of-the-pyramid customer segment and transforming demand for innovative products. Therefore, building social base for innovative products ensures reaping of higher gains as compared to the market-oriented competitive strategies. Co-creation is an upcoming phenomenon in business ecosystem, which involves society and business in sharing and adapting experiences of people respectively. It is a bidirectional dynamic of exchanging ideas, experiences, innovation concepts, developing prototypes, and commercializing generic thought into the business avenues. Experience co-creation is an art, which is portrayed by the business communities with the support of personal and digital interfaces to know the insights of all players, including customers, in the market operations. Co-creating business models with the underlying customer and stakeholder experiences has emerged as a new paradigm of strategy innovation. Customer-centric companies like Nestlé, Conagra, Amazon, Unilever, and Tata India are able to explore the public domain holistically today to innovate products and services with compelling value propositions through co-creating the strategy with effective employee engagement (*e.g.* Ramaswamy & Gouillart, 2008).

The growing concept of circular economy has given further boost to companies to adapt to the public–private policies of marketing sustainability-driven products. The potential activities within the circular economy movement include improving the performance and reducing the costs associated with recycled and sustainable products. These activities are largely focused on exploring and exploiting renewable energy, and solid and liquid waste, to regenerate products and services, and promote the sharing of products through maintenance and design. In addition, firms tend to improve product efficiency and removing operational waste from supply chains to optimize cost, benefits, and values with *closed loop* designs. The production loops have emerged as a tangible output with most manufacturing companies like automobiles, textiles, energy, organic food products, and companies delivering goods and services virtually. Replacing old materials with advanced renewable ones, or applying new technologies such as 3-D printing, have emerged as exchange solutions as a part of circular economy. Most industries already have profitable opportunities in each area (Bave & Swartz, 2016).

Successful co-creation of innovations has a major challenge of commercialization, which has driven the co-created products and services to evolve ambidextrously with society and corporations. Employee engagement and customer involvement are the pillars of coevolution process, besides resource pooling, distribution, and managing marketing mix (product, price, place, promotion, and psychodynamics) functions. Social business design is largely based on the psychosocial drivers that affect co-creation of innovations and strategies and the commercialization process. Customer and stakeholder participation in co-creating innovation and marketing strategies is effective in exploring the solutions to social problems and determining the needs. Participation in a social purpose is interactive and emotional as compared to the involvement of customers and stakeholders in an absolute commercial project. The social, cultural, and ethnic foundations nurture belief, trust, and loyalty perceptions during the collective efforts in innovation and developing marketing strategies. Companies carrying out co-creation process gain societal insights from the knowledge, attitude, and practices (conventional of intermediate) toward finding the social solutions. Most social entrepreneurs join co-creation projects and set mutual benefit goals with the business corporations. In addition, companies benefit from co-creation process in socializing their existing and upcoming brands by developing referrals and brand gatekeepers in the societal niche, which helps in enhancing the customer outreach. Societal engagement of business corporations opens avenues to enter the downstream markets alongside the mass and premium market segments, driving them to conquer the universe of market (comprising premium, upper mass, regular mass, lower mass, and bottom-of-the-pyramid market segment). In an interactive social and business environment, coevolution of businesses with the societal values provides competitive leverage to the companies and helps in achieving corporate social identity. The intrinsic factors within the social ecosystem that stimulate the co-creation process of social entrepreneurs, customers, and stakeholders include social responsibility-led self-esteem, voluntary behavior, social leadership, and active involvement in social media. The extrinsic factors of business ecosystem that attract co-creation and coevolution process with social stakeholders comprise social governance, public policies, public–private partnership, and the leverage of empowering social stakeholders toward promoting the social businesses (Rajagopal, 2021).

Developing co-created innovations and commercializing them have two distinct challenges. Marketing co-created brands have commonly slow organic growth within the organization and target markets. However, companies need to develop competence in marketing co-created and co-evolved innovation products by establishing social values consistently. There are many ways to categorize core competence. However, these may be broadly distinguished as market-access competence, integrity-related competence, and functionality-related competence. The market-access competence includes management of brand development, sales and marketing, distribution and logistics, technical support, etc. All these skills help to put a firm in close proximity to its customers. The attributes associated with competence like quality, cycle time management, just-in-time inventory management, and so on; which allow a company to do things more quickly, flexibly, or with a higher degree of reliability than competitors; constitute the integrity-related competence of a firm. Functionality-related competence leads toward improving the skills, which enable the company to invest in its services or products with unique functionality. Such competence drives companies toward capitalizing the products and services with distinctive customer benefits, rather than merely making it incrementally better. Functionality-related competence is becoming more important as a source of competitive differentiation, relative to the other two competence types.

2.3 Public Governance

The social business models are largely managed within the existing organizational design of the firm or through the public–private partnership design. However, crowdfunding for sustainable business models requires to route the funds through social or public organizational systems. All market players serve as key partners of the sustainable business projects and engage in ideation and innovation process. Among various types of resources, crowdfunding for sustainable projects has emerged as a promising approach. Governments, social organizations, and companies are actively encouraging the sustainable innovations. Public policies reinforce the accountability of companies for their eco-innovation initiatives and social consequences of their actions. Therefore, corporate social responsibility (CSR) has emerged as co-created and co-evolved projects to explore social priorities and implement CSR projects through the participation of business managers, social leaders, stakeholders, and government representatives. Political and social pressure is built on companies to design and deliver social responsibility contextual to social needs, development, and consumption patterns. Sustainable innovation is usually grown in generic ways instead of adapting to the tested corporate strategies. However, the mismatch of social needs and development goals corner the public approaches to CSR and remain disconnected from the companies. The Whole Foods Market, Toyota, and Volvo have invested enormously in the CSR projects to drive social innovations and gain competitive advantage. Some companies, which develop casual relations with the society to explore social needs and deliver social or eco-innovations, treat corporate growth and social welfare as a zero-sum game. CSR goals addressing social and eco-innovation projects are combined with the public relations campaign by most companies as they are increasingly important to competitive success (Porter & Kramer, 2006).

Broadly, public policies in both developed and developing countries support the sustainability- and circular economy-based business models anchored by the business companies. Public policies on innovation and sustainability are founded in the context of SDGs related development programs, state and international finding, and public–private partnership. The public policies also ensure that the sustainability and eco-innovation programs implemented by the government, non-governmental organizations, and by the companies as CSR, are properly monitored and continuously improved. The social drivers that influence innovation and sustainability in the context of social projects or CSR include social needs, sectoral development, social well-being and values, and economy. These attributes are spread across various innovation and sustainability projects across sectoral development and engage stakeholders in the designing and implementation of these projects. Business modeling is a structured process, which focuses on innovation and sustainability-led social and economic project, uses crowdsourcing (collective intelligence) for ideation process, and develops business models considering macro social attributes.

Sustainability and innovation are widely affected by the macro-factors comprising public policy, investment attractiveness, cooperation among stakeholders, consumers, state, and companies, market environment. Public policies in developing countries support sustainability projects through funding, accessibility, and adaptability to technology, and initial marketing. Public policies encourage co-creation of innovation, and public–private partnership in management of sustainability projects. These policies focus on improving the socio-cultural conditions of social and higher economic gains in managing social innovation and sustainability projects. Such public policies emphasize cooperation strategies and encourage social and business organizations to explore different types of alliances that combine productivity, spontaneity, and tangible outcomes in the context of managing sustainability projects, eco-innovations, management, and marketing. In this process, relationships among the society, entrepreneurs, and companies contribute significantly in promoting cooperation networks, which are characterized as an attractive strategy leading to better performance (Lin & Jin, 2016). Economic growth and proactive public policies tend to encourage the adaptation of greener and cleaner technologies in environmentally sustainable areas, which necessitates building proactive institutions and developing cooperation. The quality requirements in sustainable and eco-innovation projects encompass rigorous environmental standards, legal systems, property rights, eliminating socio-economic and political corruption, stakeholder education, removing cultural barriers, and improving the quality of financial information. In addition, the provision of incentives and subsidies to manufacturing firms undertaking technological innovations needs to be clearly drafted and implemented to help social and business organizations to comply with the environmental standards (Sethi et al., 2020).

As the global focus on sustainability and eco-innovations has increased and is supported by the public policies, the triadic market approaches comprising market-driven, sustainability-centered, and stakeholder-focused strategies have been categorically used by the companies in specific industries like fashion, consumer products, and social capital goods (health, energy and housing). The sustainability-based and stakeholder-based marketing strategies have been supported by the corporate social responsibility and societal ethics (Mena et al., 2019). Consumer-centric companies motivate consumers to use new products, perceive their use value, analyze value for money, develop consumption experience, and change their behavior. However, consumers often fail to develop sustainable consumption behavior as companies overpromise and under-deliver product values in the competitive marketplace. Value-based perception of consumers develops consumption attitude by evaluating value for money, competitive benefits, and utilitarian satisfaction. Often, a positive consumption experience guarantees satisfaction, and develops brand loyalty and sustainable behavior among consumers over time. Consumers who are active on social media also develop knowledge, perceptions, and motivations through the user-generated contents and experience sharing. As social media is dynamic, it attributes to the variable consumer behavior (Rajagopal, 2019).

References

Agrawal, A., Catalini, C., & Goldfarb, A. (2015). Crowdfunding: Geography, social networks, and the timing of investment decisions. *Journal of Economics and Management Strategy, 24*(2), 253–274.

Arena, M., Azzone, G., & Piantoni, G. (2020). Shared value creation during site decommissioning: A case study from the energy sector. *Journal of Cleaner Production, 251* (in press). https://doi.org/10.1016/j.jclepro.2019.119587

Béal, V. (2015). Selective public policies: Sustainability and neoliberal urban restructuring. *Environment and Urbanization, 27*(1), 303–316.

Beve, A. T., & Swartz, S. (2016, November). *Starting at the source: Sustainability in supply chains*. McKinsey & Co.

Carè, S., Trotta, A., Carè, R., & Rizzello, A. (2018). Crowdfunding for the development of smart cities. *Business Horizons, 61*(4), 501–509.

Colombo, M. G., Franzoni, C., & Rossi-Lamastra, C. (2015). Internal social capital and the attraction of early contributions in crowdfunding. *Entrepreneurship Theory and Practice, 39*(1), 75–100.

Colombo, M. G., Piva, E., & Rossi-Lamastra, C. (2013). Authorizing employees to collaborate with communities during working hours: When is it valuable for firms? *Long Range Planning*, 46(3), 236–257.

Copley, P. (2013). The need to deliver higher-order skills in the context of marketing in SMEs. *Industry and Higher Education, 27*(6), 465–476.

Cowen, T. (2002). *Creative destruction: How globalization is changing the world's cultures*. Princeton University Press.

Dass, M., & Kumar, S. (2014). Bringing product and consumer ecosystems to the strategic forefront. *Business Horizons, 57*(2), 225–234.

Dionisio, M., & Raupp de Vargas, E. (2020). Corporate social innovation: A systematic literature review. *International Business Review, 29*(2), 1–10.

Evans, S., Vladimirova, D., Holgado, M., Van Fossen, K., Yang, M. Y., Silva, E. A., & Barlow, C. Y. (2017). Business model innovation for sustainability: Towards a unified perspective for creation of sustainable business models. *Business Strategy and Environment, 26*(5), 597–608.

Gerber, E. M., Hui, J. S., & Kuo, P. Y. (2012). Crowdfunding: Why people are motivated to post and fund projects on crowdfunding platforms. In *Proceedings of the International Workshop on Design, Influence, and Social Technologies: Techniques, Impacts and Ethics* (Vol. 2, pp. 10–13). Northwestern University.

Giudici, G., Guerini, M., & Rossi-Lamastra, C. (2018). Reward-based crowdfunding of entrepreneurial projects: The effect of local altruism and localized social capital on proponents' success. *Small Business Economics, 50*(2), 307–324.

Habibi, M. R., Davidson, A., & Laroche, M. (2017). What managers should know about the sharing economy. *Business Horizon, 60*(1), 113–112.

Homburg, C., Jozić, D., & Kuehnl, C. (2017). Customer experience management: Toward implementing an evolving marketing concept. *Journal of the Academy of Marketing Science, 45*(3), 377–401.

Ikediashi, D. I., Ogunlana, S. O., Oladokun, M. G., & Adewuyi, T. (2020). Assessing the level of commitment and barriers to sustainable facilities management practice: A case of Nigeria. *International Journal of Sustainable Built Environment, 1*(2), 167–176.

Inkpen, A. C., & Tsang, E. W. (2005). Social capital, networks, and knowledge transfer. *Academy of Management Review, 30*(1), 146–165.

Johnston, L., & Blenkinsopp, J. (2017). Challenges for civil society involvement in civic entrepreneurship: A case study of local enterprise partnerships. *Public Money and Management, 37*(2), 89–96.

Kane, G. C., Palmer, D., Phillips, A. N., & Kiron, D. (2014). Finding the value in social business. *MIT Sloan Management Review, 55*(3), 81–88.

Lin, F. J., & Jin, Y. H. (2016). The effect of network relationship on the performance of SMEs.*Journal of Business Research, 69,* 1780–1784.

Liu, S., Xiao, W., Fang, C., Zhang, X., & Lin, J. (2020). Social support, belongingness, and value co-creation behaviors in online health communities. *Telematics and Informatics, 50* (in press). https://doi.org/10.1016/j.tele.2020.101398

Lubin, D. A., & Esty, D. C. (2010). The sustainability imperative. *Harvard Business Review, 88*(5), 42–50.

Mair, J., Martí, I., & Ganly, K. (2007). Institutional voids as spaces of opportunity. *European Business Forum, 31*(1), 34–39.

McKenny, A. F., Allison, T. H., Ketchen, D. J., Short, J. C., & Ireland, R. D. (2017). How should crowdfunding research evolve? A survey of the entrepreneurship theory and practice editorial board. *Entrepreneurship Theory and Practice, 41*(2), 291–304.

Mena, J. A., Hult, G. T. M., Ferrell, O. C., & Zhang, Y. (2019). Competing assessments of market-driven, sustainability-centered, and stakeholder-focused approaches to the customer-brand relationships and performance. *Journal of Business Research, 95*(4), 531–543.

Nidumolu, R., Prahalad, C. K., & Rangaswami, M. R. (2009). Why sustainability is now the key driver of innovation. *Harvard Business Review, 87*(9), 56–64.

Nielsen, K. R. (2020). Policymakers' views on sustainable end-user innovation: Implications for sustainable innovation. *Journal of Cleaner Production, 254.* https://doi.org/10.1016/j.jclepro.2020.120030

Osterwalder, A., & Pigneur, Y. (2010). *Business model generation: A handbook for visionaries, game changers, and challengers*. Wiley.

Paschen, J. (2016). Choose wisely: Crowdfunding through the stages of the startup life cycle. *Business Horizons, 60*(2), 179–188.

Porter, M. E., & Kramer, M. R. (2006). The link between competitive advantage and corporate social responsibility. *Harvard Business Review, 84*(12), 78–92.

Rajagopal. (2019). *Contemporary marketing strategy: Analyzing consumer behavior to drive managerial decision making*. Palgrave Macmillan.

Rajagopal. (2021). *Sustainable businesses in developing economies: Socio-economic and governance perspectives*. Palgrave Macmillan.

Ramaswamy, V., & Gouillart, F. J. (2008). *Co-creating strategy with experience co-creation*. Harvard Business School Press.

Rao-Nicholson, R., Vorley, T., & Khan, Z. (2017). Social innovation in emerging economies: A national systems of innovation-based approach. *Technological Forecasting and Social Change, 121*, 228–237.

Schönborn, G., Berlin, C., Pinzone, M., Hanisch, C., Georgoulias, K., & Lanz, M. (2019). Why social sustainability counts: The impact of corporate social sustainability culture on financial success. *Sustainable Production and Consumption, 17*, 1–10.

Sethi, P., Chakrabarti, D., & Bhattacharjee, S. (2020). Globalization, financial development and economic growth: Perils on the environmental sustainability of an emerging economy. *Journal of Policy Modeling* (in press). https://doi.org/10.1016/j.jpolmod.2020.01.007

Sheu, J. B., & Hu, T. L. (2009). Channel power, commitment and performance toward sustainable channel relationship. *Industrial Marketing Management, 38*(1), 17–31.

Tsarenko, Y., Ferraro, C., Sands, S., & McLeod, C. (2013). Environmentally conscious consumption: The role of retailers and peers as external influences. *Journal of Retailing and Consumer Services, 20*(3), 302–310.

Weyrauch, T., & Herstatt, C. (2016). What is frugal innovation? Three defining criteria. *Journal of Frugal Innovation, 2* (1), 1–17.

World Bank. (2013). *Crowdfunding's potential for the developing world*. World Bank.

Young, T. (2013). *The everything guide to crowdfunding*. Adams Media.

Yunus, M., Dalsace, F., Menasce, D., & Faivre-Tavignot, B. (2015). Reaching the rich world's poorest consumers. *Harvard Business Review, 93*(3), 46–53.

CHAPTER 3

Crowd-Based Business Modeling

Advances in the Internet-based technologies and a shift in the business philosophy of companies from market orientation to customer orientation have caused the emergence of crowd-based business models. The attributes of crowd-based business models include integration of contributors from outside the traditional boundaries of a firm, data mining through digital peer-to-peer platforms, and the transfer of value-creating activities to a crowd. This chapter discusses the evolution of crowd-based business modeling and its prospects with firms operating in emerging markets in the context of crowd engagement in businesses and deliberates on the role of various attributes of crowd-based business models. In addition, this chapter discusses marketing strategies, value chain management, and competitive leverage of firms using collective intelligence and customer-generated contents.

Crowd-based business models (CBBMs) are characterized by integrating investors from public, who are beyond the corporate boundaries. Companies relying on CBBM tend to bring the crowd interface by exploring new technologies and developing peer-to-peer platforms, and creating value to the customers and company through collective intelligence. This requires the firm to open certain resources and processes to external contributors, often resulting in strong interaction with these contributors and their resources. The activity of these contributors can

Rajagopal, *Crowd-Based Business Models*,
https://doi.org/10.1007/978-3-030-77083-9_3

range from conducting microtasks to creating and delivering entire products and services to the firm's customers. In this sense, CBBMs place even more importance on the crowd than traditional forms of crowdsourcing (Kohler, 2015). Over recent years, however, firms from different industries have started to develop new business models that fundamentally integrate crowds in value creation logic. The emergence of these crowd-based business models is both driven by advances in internet-based technologies and a shift in the role of consumers toward becoming so-called 'prosumers' (Ritzer, 2014). Crowd-based business models emerge out of the collective intelligence generated through crowdsourcing. As crowdsourcing evolves, new research finds a pitfall. Companies should be alert to: Consumer voting on the ideas submitted on open-innovation platforms is often skewed by social bias, or people's tendency to like and vote for ideas whose progenitors have liked and voted for their own. Collective intelligence (CI) led business models rely more on consumer preference and social criteria while evaluating the ideas that are generated through open innovation. Successful crowdsourcing ventures require more than an online platform and some kind of brand connection. Without an understanding of participant motivations and behaviors, casual attempts to leverage the wisdom of the crowd may backfire and lead to unintended results. Prominent examples of crowdsourcing failures are myriad. Consider General Motors, which provided users with web tools to make their own ads for the Chevrolet Tahoe, resulting in a number of viral videos that lampooned the company's products and the American automotive industry's gas guzzlers more generally. In the fast-moving consumer goods industry, Mountain Dew successfully crowdsourced part of its product development through the democracy contest series, but a similar project asking fans to name the brand's new apple-flavored drink brought on a slew of ironic suggestions, including Diabeetus (Fedorenko et al., 2017).

When Google bought Nest, a digital thermostat and smoke detector company, for $3.2 billion just a few months ago, it was a clear indication that digital transformation and connection are reaching critical mass, spreading across even the most traditional industrial segments and creating a staggering array of business opportunities and threats. The digitization of tasks and processes has become essential to competition. General Electric, for example, was at risk of losing many of its top customers to nontraditional competitors IBM and SAP, on one hand, big data startups on the other—offering data-intensive, analytics-based services that could connect to any industrial device. So, GE launched a multibillion-dollar initiative focused on what it calls the Industrial Internet. Adding digital sensors to its machines; connecting them to a common, cloud-based software platform; investing in software development capabilities; building advanced analytics capabilities; and embracing crowd-based product development. With all this, GE is evolving its business model. Now, for example, revenue from its jet engines is tied to reduced downtime and fewer miles flown over the course of a year. After just three years, GE is generating more than $1.5 billion in incremental income with digitally enabled, outcomes-based business models (Iansiti & Lakhani, 2014).

3.1 Crowd Engagement in Business

Crowd-based business models aim at value co-creation, which encourages customer engagement in business modeling and implementation process by serving as co-producers. In CBBM, customers employ their skills and competencies to create value in association with the business teams of the company. Customer engagement in business modeling process reinforces the transformational participation of creative customers as collaborators, co-developers, and competitors. Businesses have learned to draw on the competencies and resources of their business partners and suppliers to compete effectively; they must now include consumers as part of the extended enterprise. Harnessing these customer competencies won't be easy. Crowdsourcing demands high capability and competence of customers and stakeholders to participate in steering ideas, develop business models, and plan implementation. In this process the following attributes broadly affect the crowd-based business initiatives:

- Knowledge and experience in co-opting participants,
- Active customer engagement,
- Explicit, and ongoing dialogues on given theme,
- Mobility of customers communities,
- Evidence-based discussions,
- Customer diversity,
- Customers experience in co-creation, and
- Individual and group experiences.

Accordingly, firms need to revise some of the conventions processes in customer engagement, marketplace-pricing and billing systems, and value creation approaches, for instance—to account for their customers' new role (Prahalad & Ramaswamy, 2000).

There are many types of knowledge and skills that participants contribute to crowd-based business modeling in the crowdsourcing ventures such as crowdsourcing.com, and crowdworks.com. In the crowd-based business model canvas, information management is carried out through the following stages with embedded specific activities:

- Idea generation (generation of new ideas for products and services)
    - o Crowdsourcing
    - o Information screening
    - o In-house debate and idea adaptation
- Problem-solving (solutions to a customer or social problems or challenges)
    - o Need assessment
    - o Problem identification: micro, macro, discrete
    - o Solutions
        - 4As (awareness, attributes, affordability, and adaptability)
        - 4Cs (compatibility, competitive, competence, conflicts)
        - 4Rs (returns on investment, risk, recovery, responsiveness)
        - 4Ss (social orientation, strategic, services, satisfaction to users)
- Evaluation and selection (ideas/solutions)
    - o Discussion boards
    - o Customer communities
    - o In-company voting/consensus
- Forecasting (prediction markets for product success or market conditions)
    - o Marketability of crowdsourced ideas
    - o Competition forecast
    - o Profitability, continuity, and diversification

As the crowd information is filtered through the above stages, the business modeling processes move to the further stages including concept development, design thinking, analyzing industry attractiveness, cost structure, and revenue streams. These components are built around the functions of key partners spread across key activities to run the business through the crowdsources business model. Companies also map the key resources to support production and marketing activities, sales, and customer relationship management to create social and business values.

Among many consumer-centric companies, Procter and Gamble has been successfully consulting consumers into its research and development process. This company not only involves consumers and its employees in the co-creation of innovative products, but also works with its superannuated employees who have specific skills. Its co-creation platform, *Connect + Develop*, has helped in continuous innovation of a variety of consumer products, boosted product development process, and effectively enhanced the participation of consumers and employees in innovation process without adding additional costs (Bughin, 2014). Similarly, Heineken N. V., a Dutch brewery company, launched its co-creation platform in 2012, asking online gamers, beer drinkers, and environmentally conscious consumers to share ideas for improving its packaging to make it more sustainable. The winner, a German citizen, suggested a device (the Heineken-o-Mat) intended to turn recycling into a game. Starbucks had also called for the opinions and reviews of customers by providing a peer-interface platform for sharing views on sustainability. Interactions between companies and customers have helped in co-designing store ambiance, in-store music, and corporate social responsibility initiatives. However, using co-creation in business models and sustainability programs is often difficult for companies, as there remains a wide gap between the communication transparency and creativity in business modeling through various social and cultural approaches. Innovation in business models helps to align social and stakeholder benefits and revenue-stream management to leverage sustainable solutions (Rajagopal, 2019, 2020; Rashid et al., 2013).

The business model canvas has two facets: back end and front end, which have many elements from concept development to generation of revenue streams. The principal elements at the back end of the canvas consist of concept development, design thinking, industry attractiveness, market research, cost structure, and management of revenue streams. The front end of the canvas has elements contextual to the operations of the business model. These elements include organizational design, key partners, key activities, key resources, marketing channels, sales, customer relations management, and value propositions of the business model in the context of crowdsourced ideas and socially grown concepts as illustrated in Fig. 3.1.

The CBBM is associated with open innovation and encourages crowdsourcing in developing the business within the social and niche platforms. Crowd-based businesses are oriented toward transforming ideas into industrial economic and business frameworks. Consequently, companies develop agile business models by setting short-term goals, customer-centric objectives, and collective perceptions complementing the strategic profiteering goals. While screening crowdsourced information and developing proposals for crowdfunding firms also conduct extensive research to understand consumer behavior, competitive leverage, moderate values, and implementing CBBM in the niche markets and beyond (Bolton, 2004). Figure 3.1 illustrates the attributes of crowd-based business model developed in the context of collective intelligence.

Design thinking is a required exercise for developing appropriate business model based on crowdsourced ideation. Analysis of economic viability and technological feasibility of manufacturing and marketing processes defined in the CBBM is central to the innovations of targeted products within the social and market domains. The CBBM is expected to embed the identification of social needs and consumption patterns in the society. Accordingly, the design thinking process identifies the right innovation and technology to co-create the second-generation products from the industrial waste, maps product attractiveness, value spread, and determine its shelf-life and end of the cycle product state. The CBBM attributes broadly constitute the anticipated cost, time, and risk factors in a business operations matrix with the combination of various marketing mix elements. Industry attractiveness has always been a prerequisite for developing any type of business model. The industry attractiveness comprising new entrants, growth of substitutes, bargaining power of consumers and suppliers, and competition within the industry dominate the concerns of companies on developing appropriate marketing strategy and customer value. In an industry with fast-growing competition, consumers face complexities in developing sustainable perceptions and attitude to inculcate behavior. Rapidly emerging new brands (with crowd-based ideas) from unfamiliar companies attract consumers with low prices. Although most consumers tend to experiment with low-priced

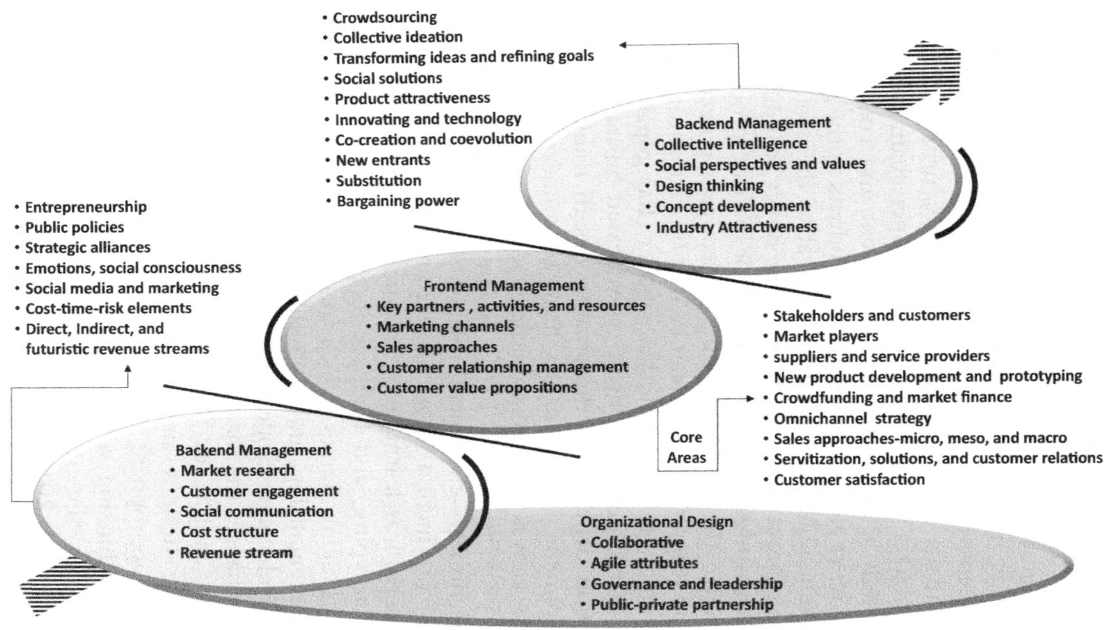

Fig. 3.1 Attributes of crowd-based business modeling (*Source* Author)

products and substitute the products that deliver satisfactory experience, they fail to develop sustainable perceptions and build attitudes toward repeat buying. However, industry attractiveness describes competition among traditional pipeline brands, which succeeds by optimizing the activities in their value chains. In addition, the crowdsourcing and collective intelligence have helped companies and their brand to streamline with the customer perceptions, brand value, and competitiveness. Uber (transport service), Alibaba (e-commerce), and Airbnb (urban housing); are growing in the market by improving the consumer chain and delivering satisfaction through active customer engagement and collective intelligence (Van Alstyne et al., 2016). Substitute products in the market affect the industry potential adversely, and pose threat to the customer preferences. Bargaining power of buyers refers to the direct or indirect pressure tactics to force the industry to reduce prices or increase product features in view to optimize the customer value. Buyers gain power when they have choices, and when their needs can be met by a substitute product or by the same product offered by another supplier (Rajagopal, 2019).

The success of the development of crowd-based business model and its implementation depends on the creative design thinking with high customer engagement, which enables firms to connect with all points on the business canvas. Accordingly, firms can launch manufacturing and marketing projects. Crowd-based design thinking is a continuous process, which connects customers, society, and businesses to manage the bricolage of production ideas. Most companies engaged in developing CBBM remain as learning organizations and invest in collective intelligence, prototyping, and feedback loops. The concept of CBBM has two design-thinking frames, which include opportunities for innovation and entrepreneurship, and marketing practices. The low-cost and high-use value products developed through collective intelligence attract consumers and enhances the marketability of innovative products, which are usually frugal, radical, or disruptive in nature. The crowd-based product or service designs aim at transforming the existing market and consumption appropriate the low cost, low risk, and short time span. Such design thinking will build a paradigm shift in the business ecosystem adapting to the crowdsourced and social involvement philosophy (Kirchherr et al., 2017). The success of CBBM depends on the extent of engagement of customers, stakeholders, and market players. Therefore, understanding customer needs and providing the desired solution through the crowd-based business model add value to business propositions. Such a business model helps end users, suppliers, manufacturers, and retailers, who would be interested in using the crowd-based innovative products.

Collective intelligence is also explorative as it is able to connect firms with isolated business ideas with success of such local experiments. The innovations developed in local markets are based on consumer needs and marketed within a niche at an affordable price to the consumers. These enterprises do not adapt to 'design-to-market' innovation approach. However, innovations with utilitarian values tend to drive high demand in local markets as they match with the sociocultural and ethnic values. For example, in 2016, an engineer entrepreneur of India designed a low-cost clay refrigerator, which requires no electricity and keeps the cooked food fresh and safe for five days uninterruptedly. This innovative product was branded as '***mittikool***' (clay-cool). It continued to function even in the event of irregular power supplies in the rural areas. The concept of this innovation has been later adapted to the 'design-to-market' strategy by a Chinese global giant Haier, which manufactured and commercialized non-compressor refrigerator. Instead of relying on a refrigerant, compressor, and evaporator to keep cool, it simply uses water and carbon dioxide (CO_2), plus a unique solid-state cooler. The product claims to save a significant amount of energy, provide more even cooling, eliminate all noise and vibration, and offer more usable space (Rajagopal, 2020).

Managing frugal innovations through CBBM is critical to the success of the competitive growth of the firm in the niche marketplace. The economic value of an innovation remains latent until it is commercialized in some way via a business model. Successful commercialization of an innovation leads to breakthrough in two different ways: in some instances, an innovation can employ a business model, which is already familiar to the firm; while in others a company has a business model that can make use of the innovation by licensing to third parties. To make CBBM competitively dynamic, firms need to consider the following actions (Chesbrough, 2010; Rajagopal, 2020):

- Articulating the value proposition based on collective intelligence by categorically analyzing the customer experiences,
- Creating customer value through new technology, process, or services, considering the 4As elements (awareness about crowd-based products and services, crowd-suggested attributes, affordability, and adaptability),

- Identifying appropriate market segments beyond niche and exploring new revenue streams,
- Defining required value chain structure to create market, diffuse innovation, and distribute the product through the determined supply chain,
- Estimating the cost structure and profit potential within the given value proposition and value chain,
- Building a crowd-based posture of the firm within the value network linking suppliers, customer, and democratize the business process, and
- Developing strategies to increase the market competitiveness in crowd-based business modeling.

Sustainable innovation is an outstanding way of achieving both competitive advantage and differentiation. Sustainable innovations are not limited to technology-led innovations. They are the innovations that generate higher perceived use value and social accountability. Sustainable innovations are strategic and grow slow in the market, but stay for long term in the market. The innovation is not necessarily a new product or product advancement, but also entails new ways to communicate products and operate in a new market or consumer segments.

The sources of innovation have become dispersed as the market is turning increasingly demanding and the users have formed their niche. Accordingly, innovation has shifted from technology to business models and is more focused on marketing than social needs. Many innovations are emerging in the market that is simplified or is scaling down on improving the existing products or services and positioning them as innovations. However, managers may align their business strategies with competitive advantages of markets and manage innovation in emerging economies to diffuse and commercialize (De Meyer, 2011). Traditional belief that positioning innovation of products and services makes a company competitive is a myth in the present state of global marketing. Thus, firms continually reinvent in large and small ways in reference to shifts in market demand and changes in the economy, and develop competitive marketing strategies in reference to shifts in the product and market behavior, knowledge of innovative products, and innovation positions. Though the firms may develop efficiency with regards to the above strategic positions of product/market, knowledge, and innovation independently, they are still risk-averse with the innovation (McDonough et al., 2008).

Innovations based on the existing needs of consumers are grown on a stronger commercial base than those developed with futuristic vision. Companies that engage in the latter type of innovation need to create demand among consumers and inculcate use value, which is a difficult proposition. Conventionally, innovations, which are co-created involving consumers and stakeholders, have strong foundation and easily taken ahead to the next generations. Innovations are improved to the design-to-market strategy by lowering the cost (frugal innovations) for gaining competitive advantage. Companies positioning innovations in the competitive marketplace also focus on continuous improvement on first-generation innovation and consider social perspectives to promote them in the market. Therefore, innovative products are extensively debated on social media and interpersonal forums. These innovations become market leaders generally in their third generation or ahead, as they focus on ambidextrous markets—premier and mass consumer segments. The design thinking emerges as an active strategy in advanced generations of innovations. Design thinking is a process of problem-solving through creative ideation. Design thinking in innovation is widely followed as co-creation for continuous improvement.

Crowdsourcing generates psychodynamics and helps in co-creating crowd-based business models aiming at doing business in consumer products in closed or open niche markets. Positive psychodynamics among consumers creates pull-effect for specific brands in the market. The pull-effect generates high consumer demand, which benefits companies in increasing market share and profit by reducing the marketing costs. Such costs for brands are spread across advertisements, in-store promotions, price discounts, and point-of-sales incentives to the consumers. The psychodynamics also generates referrals and brand advocacy behavior among consumers, which helps companies acquire new consumers at relatively low cost. Most firms involving social media as a marketing communication channel tap the knowledge and expertise of consumers for mutual benefit and for brand-building process rather than adopting a traditional knowledge-management approach where people dump their information in a giant database that nobody reads. Such firms can create an environment where they go through the peer-to-peer collaboration. Emerging firms may initially build very small collaborative tools that could enable their peer communication design to kick-off the consumer–company collaboration process and to get experience in understanding how it provides mutual benefits (Rajagopal, 2013).

3.2 Marketing Strategies

Guerrilla marketing is a competitive strategy concept of minor attacks on competitors continuously for a longer period. This strategy is generally followed by small businesses to promote their products or services in an unconventional way with little budget to spend. Guerilla marketing is also considered as an advertising tactic aimed at short-run myopic gains by the companies in the market. This involves high energy and imagination focusing on grasping the attention of the public in more a personal and memorable level. Some large companies use unconventional advertisement techniques, proclaiming them to be guerrilla marketing, but these companies have a larger budget, and the brand is already visible in the market.

Competition is found in all marketing functions including the prices at which products are exchanged, the attributes and qualities of products manufactured, the volume of products exchanged, and the methods of distribution and promotion. The school of thought, which has constructed the competition-related theories, may be categorized into two groups—economic theory and industrial organization perspective. The economists of the former group have discussed many different models of competition. The focus of their work is the model of perfect competition, which is based on the premise that, when a large number of buyers and sellers in the market are dealing in homogeneous products, there is complete freedom to enter or exit the market, and everyone has complete and accurate knowledge about everyone else. The latter group of the school of thought on competition in reference to industrial organizations postulates that a firm's position in the marketplace depends critically on the characteristics of the industry environment in which it competes. The industry environment comprises structure, conduct, and performance. Structure refers to the economic and technical perspectives of the industry in the context in which firms compete. It includes concentration in the industry such as the number and size distribution of firms, barriers to entry, and product differentiation. The competition theories have further laid emphasis on the market competition on functional dimensions, which include non-price competitions toward the product differentiation and quality competition. Products are differentiated when the products of different firms are not perfect substitutes, and companies may compete by changing the characteristics of the product they sell. Such strategies may not be necessarily appropriate to make a product better than the competitor, but may serve to differentiate it in order to create an appeal in a different ***market niche***.

Niche strategies provide a classic instance of such situations. No market is entirely homogeneous. There are always groups of customers that differ in terms of their needs. The possibility of the occurrence of niches, which individual competitors may occupy, always exists. Niches are unlikely to be complete, separate, and well-defined. There is always an overlap. However, if such niches are rather subtly defined, they may not always be obvious to all the players. Consequently, niche players may appear to compete, but in practice they do not do so or at least not fully. The competitive strategy of product differentiation helps the company in enhancing the product mix by introducing many varieties, which increase the range of consumer choice. However, it divides the market, leading to higher prices and costs for the firm. From an economist's point of view, this definition of competition appears closer to the category of monopolistic competition. In this case, it is assumed that a large number of buyers and sellers exist, with each seller producing a variety of the essentially differentiated product which characterizes the product group. This, in turn, accords the firms in question with some of the features of the monopoly described earlier, but at a more modest level. The precise level of power of monopoly enjoyed by each of the firms depends crucially upon the number of competing varieties in the market, and the distribution of consumers' preferences. In the contemporary analysis of competition and related strategies thereof, it is observed that the competitive firms intend to ascertain a continuous organizational learning process with respect to the value creation chain, and measure performance of the new products introduced in the market. In the growing competitive markets, the large and reputed firms are developing strategies to move into the provision of innovative combinations of products and services as 'high-value integrated solutions' tailored to each customer's needs than simply 'moving downstream' into services. Such firms are developing innovative combinations of service capabilities such as operations, business consultancy, and finance required to provide complete solutions to each customer's needs in order to augment the customer value toward the innovative or new products. The attributes of marketing mix that contribute to the developing competitive marketing strategies within the crowd-based business model are exhibited in Fig. 3.2.

Marketing strategies are derived by the firms in the context of business models co-created and coevolved with the customers and investors

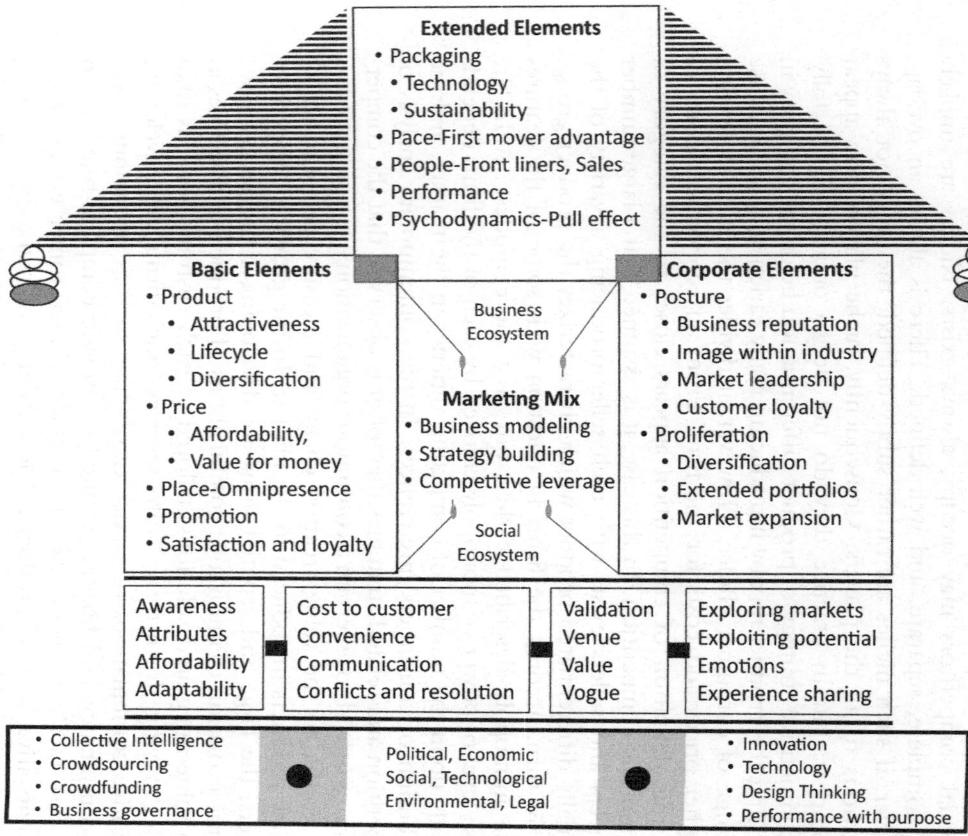

Fig. 3.2 Elements of marketing mix (*Source* Author)

in crowd-based business environment. Such collaborative business models provide competitive leverage to the micro, small, and medium firms built on collective intelligence. Figure 3.2 illustrates that marketing mix embeds 11Ps comprising basic elements (product, price, place, and promotion), extended elements (packaging, pace, people, promotion, and psychodynamics), and corporate elements (posture and performance). Products in the contemporary marketplace are consumer driven and developed as a solution to the consumer needs. The intangible factor of perceived use value and tangible preference of consumers determining the value for money of products governs the decision-making process for products, among consumers. Consumer-centric companies like Apple, IKEA, Procter and Gamble, and General Electric consider that design and marketing strategies, both are important tools in creating product preference, perceived use value, and deeper emotional value for the consumers. Product differentiation is another major challenge for consumer-centric companies to stay ahead of marketplace competition. Most companies believe that successful product differentiation allows the consumer brands to enter into mass market in the emerging markets. Product lifecycle determines the longevity of the product in the market, its perceived use value, and the associated value for money. Consumer thus prefers to measure the quality–price relationship in products considering the longevity and competitive advantages. Pricing is one of the most complex decisions facing any company. Along with a lack of academic interest (especially among marketing academics) in the field of pricing, this complexity has contributed to the dominance of simplified, cost-based formulas when levying prices. Price is considered the principal driver for determining profitability in a company. Price is also a cognitive determinant of consumer behavior that affects their buying behavior. Price is a sensitive tool for fixing profitability in consumer-centric companies. Every fluctuation in pricing leaves a significant impact on both the revenues and profitability of the company. Therefore, ineffective planning in pricing affects the profitability of products and services in a company. Accordingly, consumers assign different degrees of emphasis regarding price to determine their purchase decisions (Kohli & Suri, 2011). The increase in market competition has provided increasing choices of products and services altering the consumption patterns frequently. Such marketplace situation has developed a consumer philosophy of *touch, feel, and pick*, which makes consumers product loyal instead of brand loyal with instantaneous switching behavior. The emergence of e-commerce has prompted consumer-centric companies toward adapting to 'direct-to-customer' (DTC) distribution strategy. This strategy has been successful over the years as it helps companies in minimizing the cost, time, and risk (CTR) effects in managing distribution. The promotional strategies are evaluated by the companies in reference to its impact on the volume of sales, market share, and their contribution to the profit specific to the products and services. The promotional strategies of consumer-centric companies have turned into a large and growing part of marketing budgets of companies worldwide (Raghubir et al., 2004).

Packaging and marketing affect the business performance of production-led, sales-led, and marketing-led companies. Ergonomics of packaging today plays a significant role in establishing the product attractiveness, developing consumer preferences, defining the market, and determining price and the brand values. Etymologically, 'pace' indicates consistent and continuous speed in moving things. In the context of business, pace illustrates the marketing strategies for going ahead of competitors. Most companies in the competitive marketplace struggle to gain the first-mover advantage, increase the market share, and augment profit. People in the marketing mix constitute front-liners in markets, who manage sales of products and services. Selling is an art largely associated with the behavioral skills of the sales personnel of a sales organization. In a competitive marketplace, selling is performed using scientific methods of product presentation, advertising, and various approaches drawn to take the customer into confidence. Performance in the marketing mix is considered a hybrid element. This element is evolved through various factors comprising all basic elements of marketing mix, innovation and continuous improvement, organizational culture, employee engagement, and consumer involvement in co-creating products to enhance consumer value. Grapevine effect has emerged as an outgrowth of psychodynamics, which has evolved as collective intelligence, and is a critical element in creating tangible interactions among consumers in a competitive marketplace. The grapevine effect is contributed by the social media through word-of-mouth that stretches throughout the market irrespective of the various measures taken by the firms to build their brand and competitive posture. Grapevine develops psychodynamics among consumers by sharing various consumer experiences (Rajagopal, 2013). Figure 3.2 illustrates posture and proliferation as key corporate elements in the marketing mix. Posture of the company and its path of business proliferation by diversifying the business operations to new markets and expanding the product portfolios constitute the design elements in the marketing mix of a company. Corporate image develops the posture of a company within the industry and among the consumers in the marketplace. Among various facets of institutional growth, a social purpose, long-term focus, emotional engagement, partnering with the public, innovation, and team leadership would help in constructing building blocks of a more sustainable corporate reputation of a company (Kanter, 2011). Proliferation of business activities is commonly grown around product and market diversifications, and exploring new consumer segments for existing and future products developed using advanced technologies. Diversification strategies respond to the desire for growth when current products/markets have reached maturity and stability by spreading the risks of fluctuations in earnings. The diversification strategies would also be required for business security when the company may fear backward integration from one of its major customers.

Figure 3.2 also explains that there are many intangible elements that make major contribution to the marketing strategies. Most consumers show initial resistance because of low trust, relative risk, low value for money, and low knowledge on 4As elements consisting of awareness, availability, adaptability, and affordability prospects. The 4C's consist of consumer relations, convenience, cost to customers, and consumer conflicts in the marketing of products and services. Successful consumer products companies develop satisfactory relations with consumers during the process of prospecting consumers and providing post-sales services to build consumer confidence. As marketing technology is increasing rapidly, the expectation of consumers with a company is also growing up. The marketing performance of companies is also affected by the 4 V's comprising value perceptions of consumers, peer validity, venue and shopping experience, and vogue exhibited in the market. The sharing of consumer experiences on social media provides validation to the consumer perceptions and expectations on products and services. In addition, the 4E's elaborate in the marketing mix is associated with sharing consumer experiences on the social media and digital space, and developing perceptions led by emotions on brands. These elements allow the companies to develop strategies for exploring and expanding business in new geo-demographic segments and exploiting the markets by catering to the demand to the fullest possible.

The startup enterprises managing innovation need for the relatively smaller geo-demographic segments and at bottom of the pyramid may throw immense challenges for commercializing the innovations in the international markets. However, it requires a company to follow the institutionalized thinking that guides its actions in the global marketplace. The reverse innovations that are adopted by the sponsor companies need to make design adjustments, and fabricate for the mass consumers in the global markets in a radically simpler and cheaper way to serve the customer with high-perceived value. Companies can develop new products in emerging markets by using a radical change from below (generic innovation design) combined with smart leadership from top (upmarket strategy). The small startup enterprises may set audacious goals to match with the new organizational structure of sponsors, and adopt new design and commercialization methods. However, the startup enterprises may also nurture the reverse innovation provided they could arrange adequate resources to up-scale the innovation by shifting the gravity of business beyond emerging markets (Govindarajan, 2012; Rajagopal, 2016). Companies working with crowd-based business models usually develop products by following time-tested ideas of the crowd, which had overcome the constraints, and leveraged the benefits over the niche markets in developing economies. Such firms tend to develop and transform the crowd-based innovations by matching market segments to existing products, lowering the price by keeping essential features, redesigning technical specification of generic products, upholding stakeholders' value, and scaling up for penetrating into the low-income markets that could have mass appeal.

Buyers in emerging markets, who are price-sensitive, demand solutions on an entirely different price-performance curve and turn loyal to the brand if the innovative products satisfy the consumers, uphold the value for money, and offer competitive advantage. Consumers would demand new, high-tech solutions that deliver at low costs and match their personal standards of 'good enough' quality. In fact, the reverse innovation is not always a prolific solution for large companies to boost their revenue and business growth. However, reverse innovation is a bottom-up outcome of what consumers look for, and hence, embeds enormous potential for mass marketing. As the Darwinian effect in market evolution is seen in the global marketplace, the multinational companies are trying to uncover the remote niches of the mass market and bottom of the pyramid market segments. On the contrary, local companies are seeking expansion. The reverse innovations will power the future of large companies (international) to reach consumers in the lesser known markets. Hence, to stay noticed and sustain the market competition, multinational companies must just adopt reverse innovation beyond their home.[1] Successful and long-established multinational corporations, who are seeking explosive growth in emerging economies, must now learn new tricks in order to succeed. Reverse Innovation guides them about how to make innovation in emerging markets happen, and how such innovations can unlock opportunities throughout the world (Govindarajan & Trimble, 2012).

The main challenge faced in managing innovation projects is toward taking advantage of the growing technology and developing convergence with the innovation business project. Innovation-led products in the marketplace should gain the first-mover advantage to survive the competition. An innovation company being the first to launch a new product–technology convergence in the industry is relatively less important for an innovation-led product to survive than being first to envision its untapped market potential to enjoy the near-monopoly and build its brand. Most companies focus on employing new technologies to better serve customers' existing needs, while others strive to create products and services that will provide customers with a completely new reason to buy a product as innovative and unique. Online retailing and the digitization of merchandizing has changed the commercial landscape where virtual shelf space is infinite and consumers can search through innumerable options. Traditional marketing research methods such as test markets, focus groups, and controlled field experiments observe certain limitations. Some are vulnerable to observation and manipulation by competitors, while the virtual store not only addresses those limitations but also broadens the horizons of marketing research (Raymond, 1996). Realizing the power and the potential of social media for corporate life, customer-centric projects enable virtual collaboration in cross-functional projects through internal blogs, discussion boards, and YouTube channels. Such interactivity among the market players encourages global conversations and sharing of knowledge. Successful consumer companies engage in sophisticated virtual media campaigns to drive customers and create brand loyalty. Next-generation products are co-developed in open-innovation processes, and companies work on shaping their enterprise with Web 3.0 strategy (Marques et al., 2016).

[1] Extracted for the Vijaya Govindarajan's Blog (https://www.tuck.dartmouth.edu/people/vg/research Retrieved on February 11, 2016).

Most firms believe that competing through business models is critical for success, but developing appropriate business strategies to push technology and innovations through the business models is a difficult task. Technology firms focus on creating innovative models and evaluating their efficacy. However, the success or failure of a company's business model depends largely on how it interacts with the players within the industry and the competitive marketplace. Any business model will perform efficiently in pure monopolistic or temporary monopolistic market conditions. As firms build technology and innovation-based products in isolation of market competition, they routinely deploy conventional business models (Casadesus-Masanell & Ricart, 2011). Companies often design product lines by segmenting their markets on quality attributes that exhibit a 'more is better' or 'value for money' property for all consumers. Since products within a product line with marginal differentiation are close substitutes and consumers can self-select the products they want to purchase, they often threaten competition among the products within the product line. Multiproduct firms need to meticulously address the cannibalization problem in designing their product lines and avoid product overlaps. It has been observed that if lower quality products are attractive, consumers having concern for 'value for money' may find them beneficial to buy lower quality products rather than the higher quality products targeted to them.

The high-performing companies create cross-functional teams drawn from strategy, marketing, and finance to ensure the assumptions underlying your long-term plans, which reflect both the real economics of the company's markets and its actual performance relative to competitors. It has been observed that the high-performing companies use that rigorous analytic framework. Such companies ensure that the dialogue between the corporate office and the business units about market trends and assumptions is conducted within a rigorous framework, such as that of *profit pools*. These companies manage the resource deployments early to support the scheduled production and marketing activities. Proper resource management would in turn help the company create more realistic forecasts and more executable plans by discussing up-front the level and timing of critical deployments. Price wars are not the long-term solution to overcome the competition in oligopolistic. Therefore, in a modified pricing concept, most companies today believe in keeping the prices stable at higher end since the inception of introducing the products and attract customers through non-price stimulus such as quality, technology, services, and experience sharing. Slashing prices usually lowers profits for incumbents without driving the low-cost entrants out of business. Companies take various approaches to competing against cut-price players (Rajagopal, 2019).

Several barriers, however, make it difficult to enter an industry. Two cost-related entry barriers are the economies of scale, and the absolute cost advantage. In this process of competition, the new entrants face an uphill challenge of scaling at a high level of production or to accept a cost advantage. However, absolute cost advantage remains with the long-standing firms in the market, which possess technological and brand advantages for their products and services. The substitute products in the market affect the industry potential adversely and pose threat to the customer preferences. Bargaining power of buyers refers to the direct or indirect pressure tactics to force the industry to reduce prices or increase product features in view to optimize the customer value. Buyers gain power when they have choices, when their needs can be met by a substitute product or by the same product offered by another supplier. In addition, high buyer concentration, the threat of backward integration, and low switching costs add to buyer power. Similarly, the bargaining power of suppliers refers to their ability to force the industry to accept higher margins or reduced services, in the interest of augmenting or securing their profits. The factors influencing supplier power are the same as that of buyer power. In this case, however, industry members act as buyers (Rajagopal, 2012).

Testing the innovation-led products in markets is a scientific process. It provides a measure of sales performance and the opportunity to identify and correct any weaknesses in the product or in the marketing plan. Successful test marketing leads to their proper use, but at the same time poses serious limitations. It is expensive and arduous. Managers need to weigh the cost and risk of product failure against the profit and probability of success, the difference in scale of investment between a test and a national launch, the likelihood of being copied and preempted by the competition, and the costs in money and reputation of a product failure. Firms should conduct test marketing to rehearse the launching of a new product in a given market. Test marketing delivers results to improve marketing productivity and reduce the chance of product failures. It should be used in conjunction with the information on competing products and competitive strategies of the rival firms. Recent technological developments allow laboratory simulation of test marketing, which can significantly reduce the test-marketing costs (Cadbury, 1975; Klompmaker et al., 1976).

The best practices on innovating new products suggest holding the old ideas as raw materials for the new ideas. Developing innovative products moves around capturing good ideas from a wide variety of sources. In this process, firms should also keep the acquired and screened ideas by analyzing them with peers and applying them on pilot basis. Cross-pollinating ideas and innovation concepts would also make higher impact on innovation process by co-creating physical layouts and cognitive cosmos that allow people to interact on the core issues with one another and turn promising concepts into real services, products, processes, or business models. Most companies in the competitive marketplace desperately need to move ideas from one place to another to seed, synergize, and serve the market target. The most important lesson for entrepreneurs and leaders to learn in the innovation process is how to think about innovation and nurture it in the interest of the firm and market (Hargadon & Sutton, 2001). Creation of the processes required for efficient manufacturing and market delivery of a commercial product based upon the prototype characterizes innovation in the commercial stage. Innovative emphasis shifts from product function to process development and refinement. Process-focused innovations during this stage are likely to be radical rather than incremental.

Successful companies develop consumer-centric business models and focus on co-creation of values while working with the model. While co-creation with customers has brought widely publicized successes at some brand-name companies, the challenges in innovation business modeling exists in managing the risk of market competition and customer value. Consumer-centric companies, who fail to build and sustain consumer-centric business models, collaborate with larger companies on business-to-business prospects. Such shift in the focus does not always pay companies in a competitive marketplace. Co-creation skills are important for companies, essential to manage agile processes, quick test-and-learn cycles, and perceived values of customers. Co-creation focused companies gain value rapidly by delivering high-quality products and service innovation. Decision-making in marketing is influenced by various intrinsic and extrinsic elements. The intrinsic elements constitute organizational design, decision hierarchy within organization, decision cost-time-risk

(CTR) grid, and the marketing mix employed by the company in competitive marketplace. Supply chain players, market competition, business diplomacy, and innovation and technology are the extrinsic factors that significantly affect the decision-making process of a marketing organization. Organizational design in the multi-brand and multi-unit business models is decentralized, and it functions based on team leadership to reduce cost, time, and risk in decision-making. In the competitive marketplace, companies need to take decisions quickly and implement them cost-effectively to gain the desired benefit. The cost-effective decisions are largely tactical, while the strategic decisions are cost-oriented and spread over a long time. An effective marketing mix actively pushes the innovative and unfamiliar brands to serve the target markets by making clear passages through the competition. Marketers had been aggressive in launching innovation-led products as effective consumer solutions in linking the elements of marketing mix. Managers implementing the marketing mix often face the challenge of its best fit to the different market environments and consumer expectations. The marketing mix framework of a company moves in a pyramidal dimension, converging marketing policies of the company, people (intertwining salespeople and consumers), and process (presenting simple and transparent transaction processes to enhance organizational performance) within an organizational system (Comstock et al., 2010).

Companies often alter the marketing mix in tune with the market attributes at various destinations. However, strategies of selected elements of marketing mix are implemented in a minimum viable segment, determined as an effective niche to exploit less crowded territory, grow sales, develop customer value, and share consumer experience across the community. Companies have long used perceptual mapping techniques to understand how consumers feel about their brands relative to competitors', find gaps in the marketplace, and develop appropriate marketing strategies. However, consumer-centric companies need the coordination of strategies across several elements of marketing mix to develop an effective marketing mix canvas, and link the strategy implementation to business performance metrics such as product, price, place, promotion, and sales (Dawar & Bagga, 2015). Global concern for business development has led to a close competition of product standards to administer customer-oriented strategies for accrediting the product and the company with the welfare business theory. In the attempt to establish such theories, one of the important factors to be considered is evolving an efficient marketing mix system, which is a complex and important parameter that determines growth in business (Rajagopal, 2016). Companies, as first movers, also spend more resources to attract consumers and position their brands, which tends to lower the profit rate. However, efficient companies try to minimize the cost, time, and risk factors in launching and delivering products in the marketplace. Many companies believe that the first company in a new-product category gets significant breakthroughs in the markets and gets long-lasting benefits. However, it does not happen always. To ensure the advantages from the pace strategy, companies should monitor the gradual evolution in both the technology and the right opportunity to move in the market, which could provide them the first-mover advantage by influencing the consumers and creating demand in the neighboring markets (Verganti, 2011). A firm begins to sell its products in a competitive marketplace and thrives continuously on acquiring new customers. It launches new product lines or services in order to gain competitive advantages, retain the existing customers, enhance customer value, and gain competitive lead in the market. To compete in a dynamic and interactive marketplace environment, firms must transform their focus from just selling the products and services to value-added sales management to maximize customer lifetime value and encourage repeat sales.

In the competitive markets, products have categorically proliferated across consumer goods and services, attracting consumers toward their attributes and use value. To improve the product-line performance, managers should constantly monitor consumer behavior, coordinate marketing efforts, work with channel partners, and foster a climate and encourage transparency on the product-line performance. Managerial decisions are widely based on the relationships between different aspects organizational design, culture, and operations leading to performance. Investments in employees are often predicated well-rewarded and engage them in delivering improved service. Such performance results into customer loyalty, and enhances financial and market performance. However, in most corporate situations, managers fail to justify the assumptions underlying their competitive strategies. Consequently, they risk developing biased performance-boosting strategies for the company (Silvestro, 2016). However, as risk and market competition have increased simultaneously over time in urban markets, companies encourage consumers to experiment the new products, make improvements in products to converge the product-value with self-congruity of consumers, and reduce the impact of substitute products in the marketplace. Companies build their products compatible with substitutable goods by developing the brand loyalty, and generating effective psychodynamics among consumer communities (Gourville, 2006). In an aggressive marketplace, companies have realized that an appropriate fit of products into this strategy grid would help them leading the market as they can manage to streamline the consumer behavior, and reduce behavioral inconsistency among consumers.

Managing consumer conflicts is a major challenge for consumer products companies, as it is based more on cognitive platforms than the inefficiencies related to tangible products and services. Consumer conflicts commonly emerge due to incongruence with the needs and attributes of products, incompatibility of services and consumer relations, differences in perceptions, attitudes and values, and social influence on consumer behavior. Relating these conditions to the unique characteristics of services such as intangibility, heterogeneity, and co-production, suggests that many products and services are likely to generate conflict between manufacturing companies, service providers, and consumers. However, companies improve customer relations practices, and co-create peer-driven approaches to manage such consumer conflicts.

3.3 Value Chain and Competitive Advantage

A value chain is a network of activities for a firm operating in a specific industry. A business unit is considered as the appropriate level for construction of a value chain but not the divisional or corporate level of the firm. In the value chain, process, products, and services pass through all the activities with the predetermined chain in a proper order; and at each activity, the product gains some value. The chain of activities gives the products more benefit than the sum of the independent activities' values. It is important not to mix the concept of the value chain with the costs occurring throughout the activities. For example, dairy industry can be used to illustrate the difference between cost and the value chain. Milk processing activity may have a low cost, but the activity adds much of the value to the product, since fresh milk is significantly less valuable than the processed milk. Typically, the described value chain and the documentation of processes, assessment, and auditing of adherence to the process routines are at the core of the quality certification of the business. The requirement of an effective value chain process includes:

- Coordination and collaboration,
- Investment in information technology,
- Changes in organizational processes,
- Committed leadership,
- Flexible jobs and adaptable, capable employees, and
- A supportive organizational culture and attitudes

In the context of globalization, the value chain concept has been extended beyond individual firms to supply chains and distribution networks. Accordingly, it has been observed that the delivery of products and services to the end customer sets off different economic factors, each managing its own value chain. The industry-wide synchronized interactions of the local value chains can create an extended value chain and drive operational effectiveness in global business.

In the context of Thompson's (1967) typology of long-linked, intensive, and intervening technologies, it may be stated that the value chain and the value network develop distinct generic value configuration required to understand and analyze firm-level value creation logic across a broad range of industries and firms. The prolonged market interventions such as technology, prescribed and perceived use value of the products, deliver value by transforming inputs into products of the firm in order to gain competitive advantage. The intervening technology delivers value by resolving unique customer problems. Such market drivers may also deliver value by enabling direct and indirect exchanges of opinions among consumers. With the alternative value in the firm, value chain analysis is both sharpened and generalized into a value configuration approach that drives competitive advantage to the firms in the long run (Stabell & Fjeldstad, 1998). Analysis of the perceived values of customers toward new products is a complex issue. Despite considerable research in the field of measuring customer values in the recent past, it is still not clear how value interacts with marketing related constructs. However, there exists the need for evolving a comprehensive application model determining the interrelationship between customer satisfaction and customer value, which may help in reducing the ambiguities surrounding both concepts.

Improving customer value through faster response times for new products is a significant way to gain competitive advantage. In the globalization process, many approaches to new product development emerge which exhibit an internal focus and view the new product development process as terminating with product launch. However, it is the process output that really counts, such as customer availability. A study proposes that shortening the product life cycles should pay to get the product into the market as quickly as possible, and indicates that these markets should be defined on an international basis. The results of the study reveal that greater new product commercial success is significantly associated with a more ambitious and speedier launch into overseas markets as the process of innovation is only complete when potential customers on a world scale are introduced effectively to the new product (Oakley, 1996). The retail sales performance and the customer value approach are conceptually and methodically analogous. Both concepts calculate the value of a particular decision unit by analytical attributes forecast and the risk-adjusted value parameters. However, no scholarly attention has been devoted virtually to the question if any of these components of the shareholder value could be determined in a more market-oriented way using individual customer lifetime values. The value of a customer may be defined in reference to a firm as the expected performance measures are based on key assumptions concerning the retention rate and profit margin, and the customer value tracks market value of these firms over time. The value of all customers is determined by the acquisition rate and cost of acquiring new customers (Rajagopal & Sanchez, 2005). Nonetheless, building the customer value was an uphill challenge as most companies operating in developing countries failed to ensure the quality of delivery and protect the value for money perception of consumers. The lack of quality packaging and on-schedule delivery of consignments, and flaws in protecting the interest of consumers were the major concerns of an effective delivery system. Manufacturers have been concentrating on the quality of inputs (packaging, routing, cost, time, and risk) and outputs (quality of delivery, value creation, and competitive advantage) in distributions.

Customer lifetime value (CLV) is a key metric within customer relationship management. Although, most managers argue in favor of this metric, there are only a few studies that consider the predictive modeling of CLV. Customer lifetime value also represents the net present value of profits, coming from the individual customer, which creates a flow of transactions over time. Firms view their investments in terms of cost per unit of sales, rate of customer retention, and acquiring customers. CLV is, then, used as a convenient yardstick of performance. The concept of the lifetime value of a customer is well established in the theory and practice of database marketing. The lifetime value of a customer, defined to be the expected present value of the net cash flows from the firm's relationship with the customer over his or her lifetime, is often used as an upper limit on spending to acquire the customer (Pfeifer, 1999). Many firms agree that their efforts should be focused on growing the lifetime value of their customers. However, few have come to terms with the implications of that idea for their marketing management with focus on decision-making and accountability of customer values. The customer's lifetime value is constituted by three components—customer's value over time, length of customers association, and the services offered to the customer. Satisfaction is the customer's perception of the value received in a transaction or relationship and it helps in making repatronage decisions on the basis of their predictions concerning the value of a future product. Thus, it may be stated that the customer value paradigm is contemporary, which includes many elements of the customer satisfaction paradigm and is being more widely adopted and deployed by the firms (Rajagopal, 2012; Rust et al., 2004).

Information technology has been central to marketing since mid-twentieth century. It has played a significant role in revolutionizing products from domestic appliances to automobiles and providing higher convenience to consumers than before. These smart and connected products, with a combination of quality, structure, electronic measures, and ease of use, offer exponential customer values and opportunities for new functionality. The technology-led products and marketing processes have proved to be of greater reliability, low price, and high quality across consumer segments, and transcend traditional product boundaries (Paul, 1996). These products and services are conceived on consumer desires and are designed ergonomically to augment the use value. Wide applications of information technology have raised new strategic choices for companies about creating customer value and reworking with traditional partners to secure competitive advantage. As information technology has been in extensive demand, it has also become affordable for small and medium-size companies operating at the niche and regional levels. These companies are able to acquire new capabilities on automation of marketing functions like production, distribution, and sales, and reshape industry boundaries (Porter & Heppelmann, 2014). Consumer value generation concept gained prominence as companies began to involve them in the innovation process. IKEA, Amazon, and IBM are the contemporary examples of stakeholder involvement in business planning, performance, and augmenting perceived customer value.

The emergence of e-commerce has prompted consumer-centric companies toward adapting to 'direct-to-customer' (DTC) distribution strategy. This strategy has been successful over the years as it helps companies in minimizing the cost, time, and risk (CTR) effects in managing distribution. Lowering the CTR effects results in increasing the customer value, brand loyalty, market share, and profitability of the company. The DTC strategy, therefore, can be defined as a digital sales channel evolved as a convenience shopping outlet without a fixed retail location. Such technology-led distribution strategy is built by leveraging the consumers' engagement in social media, and the power of Internet shopping. The DTC practices are embedded in the social media as marketing through Facebook has become cost-effective for the companies on one hand, and also provides psychodynamics among the consumers on the other. The DTC distribution management involves social media as a driver of CTR-associated distribution strategy. In this strategy, companies improve customer relationships by developing skills in carefully listening, documenting, and responding to their concerns. The DTC transactions are done with transparency, consumer confidence, and within the ethical organizational cultures, which expands consumer communities and enhances customer value (Ferrell & Ferrell, 2012).

There are various consumer-related elements, which constitute 4C's of peripheral elements of the marketing mix. The 4C's consist of consumer relations, convenience, cost to customers, and consumer conflicts in the marketing of products and services. Successful consumer products companies develop satisfactory relations with consumers during the process of prospecting consumers and providing post-sales services to build consumer confidence. As marketing technology is growing rapidly, the expectation of consumers also grow up. Hence, most companies develop multiples routes to market to provide shopping convenience to consumers. Rapid expansion of e-commerce, m-commerce, and telemarketing practices of consumer products companies offer competitive shopping conveniences to consumers such as online product simulations, comparative market panorama, same-day delivery of products, and quick logistics for returns or exchange of products. However, cost to consumer is a sensitive determinant of managing consumers within the marketing mix strategies. Cost to consumer includes tangible (price and risk factors) and intangible (time, opportunity cost, and perceived value) costs. Companies manage the tangible costs by offering competitive prices and low-risk products to augment the customer value. In order to implement the tangible cost strategies, most consumer products companies like Nestlé, and Proctor and Gamble refine cost-cutting capabilities by economizing the consumer offers (get more and spend less). Value-conscious consumers demand cost-innovative pricing approaches in the mass markets in both developed and emerging markets. Competitive consumer products companies, therefore, enter into alliances with emerging Chinese companies to gain cost-innovation capabilities and deliver high customer value (Williamson & Zeng, 2009).

References

Bolton, M. (2004). Customer-centric business processing. *International Journal of Productivity and Performance Management., 53*(1), 44–51.

Bughin, J. (2014, December). *Three-ways companies can make co-creation pay-off*. McKinsey Insight. McKinsey & Co.

Cadbury, N. D. (1975). When, where and how to test markets. *Harvard Business Review, 53*(3), 96–105.

Casadesus-Masanell, R., & Ricart, J. E. (2011). How to design a winning business model. *Harvard Business Review, 89*(1–2), 100–107.

Chesbrough, H. (2010). Business model innovation: Opportunities and barriers. *Long Range Planning, 43*(2), 354–363.

Comstock, B., Gulat, R., & Liguori, S. (2010). Unleashing the power of marketing. *Harvard Business Review, 88*(10), 90–98.

Dawar, N., & Bagga, C. (2015). A better way to map brand strategy. *Harvard Business Review, 93*(6), 90–97.

De Meyer, A. (2011, September 15). Diving into the new innovation landscape. *IESE-Insight Magazine*.

Fedorenko, I., Berthon, P., & Rabinovich, T. (2017). Crowded identity: Managing crowdsourcing initiatives to maximize value for participants through identity creation. *Business Horizons, 60*(2), 155–165.

Ferrell, L., & Ferrell, O. C. (2012). Redirecting direct selling: High-touch embraces high-tech. *Business Horizons, 55*(3), 273–281.

Gourville, J. T. (2006). Eager sellers and stony buyers: Understanding the psychology of new-product adoption. *Harvard Business Review, 84*(6), 98–106.

Govindarajan, V. (2012). A reverse innovation playbook. *Harvard Business Review, 90*(4), 120–124.

Govindarajan, V., & Trimble, C. (2005). Building breakthrough businesses within established organizations. *Harvard Business Review, 83*(5), 58–68.

Hargadon, A., & Sutton, R. I. (2001). Building an innovation factory. *Harvard Business Review, 78*(3), 157–166.

Iansiti, M., & Lakhani, K. R. (2014). Digital ubiquity: How connections, sensors, and data are revolutionizing business. *Harvard Business Review, 92*(11), 90–99.

Kanter, R. M. (2011). How great companies think differently. *Harvard Business Review, 89*(11), 66–78.

Kirchherr, J., Reike, D., & Hekkert, M. (2017). Conceptualizing the circular economy: An analysis of 114 definitions. *Resource Conservation and Recycling, 127*(2), 221–232.

Klompmaker, J. E., Hughes, G. D., and Haley, R. I. (1976). Test marketing in new product development. *Harvard Business Review, 54*(3), Business Review products and competitive strategies of rival firms 128–138.

Kohler, T. (2015). Crowdsourcing-based business models: How to create and capture value. *California Management Review, 57*(4), 63–84.

Kohli, C., & Suri, R. (2011). The price is right? Guidelines for pricing to enhance profitability. *Business Horizons, 54*(6), 563–573.

Marques, D. P., Guijarro, M., & Carrilero, A. (2016). The use of customer-centric philosophy in hotels to improve customer loyalty. *Journal of Business and Industrial Marketing, 31*(3), 339–348.

McDonough, E. F., Zack, M., Lin, H. E., & Berdrow, I. (2008). Integrating innovation style and knowledge into strategy. *Sloan Management Review, 50*(1), 53–58.

Oakley, J. (1996),.Varietirs of virtue ethics. *Ratio, 9*(1), 128–152.

Paul, O. (1996). High Tech NPD success through faster overseas launch. *European Journal of Marketing, 30*(8), 75–91.

Pfeifer, P. E. (1999). On the use of customer lifetime value as a limit on acquisition spending. *Journal of Database Marketing, 7*(1), 81–86.

Porter, M. E., & Heppelmann, J. (2014). How smart, connected products are transforming competition. *Harvard Business Review, 92*(11), 64–88.

Prahalad, C. K., & Ramaswamy, V. (2000). Co-opting customer competence. *Harvard Business Review, 78*(1), 79–87.

Rajagopal. (2012). *Darwinian fitness in the global marketplace*. Palgrave Macmillan.

Rajagopal. (2013). *Managing social media and consumerism: The grapevine effect in competitive markets*. Palgrave Macmillan.

Rajagopal. (2016). *Innovative business projects: Breaking complexities, building performance* (Vol. 1)-fundamentals and project environment. Business Expert Press.

Rajagopal. (2019). *Contemporary marketing strategy: Analyzing consumer behavior to drive managerial decision making*. New York: Palgrave Macmillan.

Rajagopal. (2020). *Transgenerational marketing: Evolution, expansion, and experience*. Palgrave Macmillan.

Rajagopal, & Sanchez, R. (2005). Analysis of customer portfolio and relationship management models: Bridging managerial gaps. *Journal of Business and Industrial Marketing, 20*(6), 307–316.

Raghubir, P., Inman, J. J., & Grande, H. (2004). Three faces of consumer promotions. *California Management Review, 46*(4), 23–42.

Rashid, A., Asif, F. M. A., Krajnik, P., & Nicolescu, C. M. (2013). Resource conservative manufacturing: An essential change in business and technology paradigm for sustainable manufacturing. *Journal of Cleaner Production, 57*, 166–177.

Raymond, B. R. (1996). Virtual shopping: Breakthrough in marketing research. *Harvard Business Review, 74*(2), 120–131.

Ritzer, G. (2014). Prosumption: Evolution, revolution, or eternal return of the same? *Journal of Consumer Culture, 14*(1), 3–24.

Rust, R. T., Zeithaml, V. A., & Lemon, K. N. (2004). Customer centered brand management. *Harvard Business Review, 82*(9), 110–118.

Silvestro, R. (2016). Do you know what really drives your business's performance? *MIT Sloan Management Review, 57*(4), 28–34.

Stabell, C. B., & Fjeldstad, O. D. (1998). Configuring value for competitive Advantage: On chains, shops, and networks. *Strategic Management Journal, 19*(5), 413–437.

Thompson, J. D. (1967). *Organizations in action: Social science bases of administrative theory*. McGraw Hill.

Van Alstyne, M. W., Parker, G., & Choudary, S. P. (2016). Pipelines, platforms, and the new rules of strategy. *Harvard Business Review, 94*(4), 54–62.

Verganti, R. (2011). Designing breakthrough products. *Harvard Business Review, 89*(10), 114–120.

Williamson, P. J., & Zeng, M. (2009). Value-for-money strategies for recessionary times. *Harvard Business Review, 87*(3), 66–74.

PART II

Crowd Dynamics in Business

CHAPTER 4

Decision Space: Collective Intelligence

There are two-way and three-way decision spaces that involve multiple information taxonomy. In the three-way decision spaces, three basic elements: decision measurement, decision conditions, and decision evaluation functions are unified. The major challenges with collective intelligence are the screening, modeling, and measurement of information to make appropriate business decisions. This chapter discusses the ways of collective information decision process by involving the stakeholders and managers. The importance of stakeholder management and business governance in the decision process, interactive planning and governance, value chain management, and the pattern of market competition and growth in the crowd-based business ecosystems have been discussed in this chapter. The business governance, scaling, and performance management have been discussed in this chapter in the context of transformative relationship between data and people, which creates new forms of collective search for solutions and decision-making. This chapter argues that the crowd-based business model has emerged as voluntary open collaboration in the development of creative solutions that mobilize experience-led paradigms to improve the business performance of global–local firms.

Rajagopal, *Crowd-Based Business Models*,
https://doi.org/10.1007/978-3-030-77083-9_4

4.1 Stakeholder Management

Firms can categorize their stakeholders into primary and secondary segments. The primary stakeholders, which include value chain stakeholders comprising customers, suppliers, and service providers, can be external to an organization. Secondary stakeholders can be grouped into societal segments consisting of environmental groups, community organizations, and industry/trade associations. The collaborators in the governance of the firm may be categorized as regulatory stakeholders who are engaged in the monitor, evaluation, and control as authorities (Darnall & Henriques, 2010). The secondary stakeholders, who are not considered to be directly involved in the crowdsourcing or open-innovation process, belong to the government as a regulatory body or investor for specific activities and private investors who provide financial resources and seek financial returns by holding formal equities in the firm or negotiate the profit share. In addition, business incubators and accelerators, who support micro, small, and medium entrepreneurial growth and development constitute the segment of secondary stakeholders (Vanhaverbeke, 2017).

Most companies pay attention toward stakeholder engagement to manage innovation in entrepreneurial ventures. The open innovation based on crowdsourcing and crowdfunding concept appears complementary to the prospective collaborative efforts of micro, small, and medium enterprises with their primary and secondary stakeholders. The stakeholder engagement helps companies in cost and risk control, and in streamlining the sharing of knowledge and other resources for innovation management. Stakeholder engagement is implicitly understood as an umbrella concept for communication, collaboration, mutual understanding, and partnership between the firm and the collaborators. Effective communication and stakeholder participation contribute to the critical success factors in the crowd-based business models, and such practice widens the scope of collective or collaborative decision-making. The practice of stakeholder engagement in business modeling and decision processes inculcates stakeholder value and confidence. Stakeholder engagement bridges communication gap with the business, facilitates systems planning, and thereby improves business and investor alignments (Niemi & Pekkola, 2017). The following collaborative actions between firms and stakeholders drive the coevolution of business modeling process, which exhibits the following attributes related to collective intelligence and actions:

- Active involvement of stakeholders in the business modeling and decision-making,
- Active involvement in information dissemination and participation in the business creativity program,
- Participation of stakeholders in enterprise architecture actively through the crowdsourced business projects, and
- Building trust and confidence among stakeholders during the collaboration process.

Firms tend to improve the stakeholder value by introducing crowd-based business model sophistication strategies uncovering value-added benefits to stakeholders in business such as making them brand ambassadors and key social communicators. Stakeholders engagement provides opportunities to them in exploring strategic benefits for third parties and streamline the advantage of economies of scope. In addition, stakeholder confidence is boosted by continuous growth of the firm, utilizing cross-selling opportunities across geo-demographic segments, and increasingly involving users and the crowd. These strategies place a strong emphasis on stakeholder commitment. Google has coevolved over the years as a crowd-based company. The founders of the company realized that appearing on search result lists holds tremendous value for stakeholders with a willingness to pay as stakeholders (firms and investors) and other players incur high satisfaction in being found on the Internet. Toward both revenue and costs dimensions, the crowd-based business model strongly emphasizes on stakeholder involvement. Often, some stakeholders, who have been previously related to the firm in various roles, play a motivating role in business expansion and performance by serving as referrals. The advertisers, as stakeholders, enjoy traffic from Google's search engine even before the introduction of AdWords, and discretely benefit from positive externalities of the Google offer. Sophistication in the crowd-based business model involves these shareholders and starts a formal relationship with them in coevolving business (Kesting & Günzel-Jensen, 2015).

4.1.1 Consumer Value

Value perceptions among customers are induced by social, economic, and relational factors. The social learning theory explains this phenomenon as positive reinforcement, and it occurs when a behavior (response) is followed by a favorable stimulus (commonly seen as pleasant) that increases the frequency of that behavior. In the conceptual foundations of social learning theory, respondent conditioning and observational learning are the empirically supported approaches to understand the normative human development and the etiology of psychosocial problems. Social learning process is widely influenced by the manifold growth of social media, digital networks, and interpersonal communications. Information technology has dramatically changed the social communication inflow by the customers sharing their experiences, values, new product ideas, and complaints about companies and products. Online customer reviews extend word-of-mouth from new acquaintances and transform information from personal to public channels on social media platforms where interactions among experienced customers occur (Pfeffer et al., 2014).

Consumers increasingly expect brands to have a social purpose beyond mere functional benefits. As a result, companies are taking social stands in very visible ways. For example, TOMS's one-for-one program donates shoes and other goods for every product the company sells. Such programs can benefit society and the brand, but they may fizzle or actually harm the company if they're not carefully managed (Recall Starbucks's widely mocked Race Together campaign). Marketing professors Vila and Bharadwaj have developed an approach they call 'competing on social purpose,' which ties a brand's most ambitious social aspirations to its most pressing growth needs. An effective strategy creates value by strengthening a brand's key attributes or building new adjacencies. At the same time, it mitigates the risk of negative associations and threats to stakeholder acceptance. In order to create value for all stakeholders—customers, the company, shareholders, and society at large—managers must integrate the considered acts of generosity with the strategic pursuit of brand goals (Rodriguez-Vila & Bharadwaj, 2017). Brazilian insurer Real Tokio Marine Vida e Previdencia is a compelling example of how Experience Co-Creation can be used to develop a differentiated value proposition for a new player in a fairly commoditized industry. It is equally compelling as an example of the integrated use of three different, yet complementary, methodologies—the Balanced Scorecard, Value Innovation, and Experience Co-Creation—to achieve this aim (Luis & Santos, 2008).

Creating customer value has, therefore, become the contemporary benchmark to measure market performance of a company and building design-to-value-based businesses. The customer value propositions resonate in marketing models to lead the business by putting the customer first. Such marketing philosophy has enabled large companies like PepsiCo to conceptualize and implement the business strategy of performance with purpose. Co-created customer values help companies focus on customer-centric product offerings to gain competitive leverage. Upon understanding the perceptions, emotions, and values of customers, companies make smarter choices about allocation of resources in customer services, advertisement and communications, and implementation of marketing mix-driven strategies. The co-created and coevolved customer value constructs are able to deliver optimal benefits to customers by upholding their perceptions, choices, and self-esteem. Large companies with strategies focus on customers develop value dashboard to monitor customer touchpoints, which helps in co-creating customer value proposition. A good customer value dashboard helps firms not only in increasing sales and marketing professionals, but also in developing design-to-society and design-to-value business modeling (Villanueva, 2013).

Social learning process is oriented to individual's cognition and is beyond the socioeconomic profile of people. However, the geodemographic explosion of middle-income social segment comprises all types of customers. Gender polarization of customers in the marketplace has significantly affected the social value systems and lifestyle practices. Besides, urbanization, income inequality in the society, growing millennial trends, and shrinking corporate values have been the major factors influencing radical shifts in customer behavior. In addition, the attributes that stimulate experimentation and drive changes in the consumption patterns as the manufacturing companies and retailers enhance shopping conveniences like credit transactions, self-service return policies, and competitive promotions, and focus on wellness and green consumption. Customer behavior in the competitive marketplace is widely influenced by discretionary spending, buying low-cost products, and gaining value for money. Companies practicing incremental marketing technologies are able to understand the dynamics of customer preferences by using digital data analytics, social media-driven consumption patterns, and customer experience through virtual reality (Rajagopal, 2021).

Value creation is a derivation of conscious cognition, actions in subconscious mind, unconscious perceptions, and materialistic reasoning. The cognitive ergonomics of customers (emotions, perceptions, and memories and storyboards), knowledge, beliefs, and trust, and the abilities of information analysis constitute the conscious cognition, which embeds customer value perceptions. Companies following the design-to-value philosophy tend to put customers first in building and implementing competitive marketing strategies comprising push (resource-based marketing approach with all elements of marketing mix) and pull (psychodynamics and non-zero-sum game) approaches (Khurana & Nohria, 2008). Customer value-centric companies usually engage in knowing (exploring value perceptions), doing (implementing pro-customer strategies), and being (enjoying the state of win–win by serving the customers), which enables them to achieve performance with purpose. Companies tend to capitalize on social learning experiences and analyzing psychosocial dynamics of communities to deliver value to customers. Most customer-centric companies aim at providing desired value and lifestyle, self-actualization, and comparative self-esteem in the value creation process. Patterns of consumerism are changing in society, as there are shifts in the customer demography in the markets. The explosion of mass customer segments, urbanization, and increase in the size of the population of aging customers have contributed significantly to the shifts in customer preferences and overall consumption behavior. Co-creation and co-designing approaches of customer-centric companies like IKEA have established business philosophy of connecting customers and developing an emotion-based relationship with customers as the key to leveraging loyalty and advocacy behavior (Rajagopal, 2021).

4.2 Business Governance and Decision Process

Leadership plays a crucial role in business governance and influences the best practices that are co-created and coevolved within the organization. However, the governance patterns differ with the public (state), crowd (community), and privately funded business firms. The best practices in business governance irrespective of the size of the firm are largely affected by a collaged system of organizational culture, social conventions, regulations, and a mix of public and private policies. Such governance system in small and medium companies function with no accepted metric for determining the key performance indicators leading to measure success. Crowd-based businesses have collective leadership involving stakeholders and externally chosen business leader (as Chief Executive Officer), which serves as core decision-making unit. Collective governance is a social redesign built on the following maxims (Subramanian, 2015):

- The governing board is constituted by the stakeholder comprising customers and investors.
- Board exercises the right to manage the company for the long term.
- Business leaders collectively make decisions on business operations and systematically guide performance with purpose.
- Streamlining corporate earnings and inclusive growth provisions to contribute to business performance.
- Boards should explore and induct an organization to select the best possible people in the boardroom. This requires effective performance evaluations of directors and a consideration of shareholder proxy access.
- Boards should give shareholders an orderly voice. Instead of defending the corporate policies develop a reasonable process for shareholders to make decision on various issues.

One of the major challenges in managing stakeholder values in crowd-based businesses is to define long-term objectives and risk factors, and encourage stakeholders to invest with predetermined value propositions. Major investors in crowd-based business models focused on sustainability, consumer well-being, social innovations, and commercial frugal innovations set a multiyear time frame for payback and creating value. Accordingly, stakeholders decide how much underperformance they can tolerate in the short term in specific markets (niche or competitive markets) to align their investments with this business agenda of the firm. Effective stakeholder engagement drives an active sense of ownership of, or belongingness to the firm. Big investors cultivate ongoing relationships with the companies over time as they plan to invest more in diversified business projects and tend to collaborate with management to optimize corporate strategy and governance. Often investors demand strategic metrics from firms to improve their investment decision and value propositions. A collective structure of organizational governance in the crowd-based business projects usually support supports short-term approach; however, potential social and commercial intertwined business projects develop strategic vision and performance metrics to provide a precise growth-linked dashboard to the investors. Big investors gain confidence with competent board members who are committed to ensure long-term performance in business, as well as extend support in developing collaborative policies and governance to philosophy into action (Barton & Wiseman, 2014). The attributes of business governance by taxonomy are exhibited in Fig. 4.1.

The taxonomy of business governance has four broad categories comprising open system, social system, corporate system, and mixed system as illustrated in Fig. 4.1. The open system business governance is common in crowd-based businesses, which encourages proportional representation of customers, stakeholders, long-term investors, and crowd leaders in the collective governance process through a formal board set up. As most crowdfunded projects are initiated in the social businesses or social innovation projects, the social leaders engaged in the non-commercial (social value creation), transformational (driving social tasks from conventional wisdom to digital and automated technologies), and inspirational (spiritual and art of life) leadership practices contribute to the social businesses. Crowdfunded social businesses are encouraged to have total or partial community governance backed by non-governmental organizations or progressive youth leaders. Both the open and social business governance systems are influenced by the social value system. In these forms of business governance, social benefits of the business have higher priority as compared to revenue generation and profitability. The corporate governance system of crowdfunded business firms tends to follow bottom-up governance model by accommodating the customers, investors, and employees in managing the firm. In the bottom-up governance system corporate decision are initiated, processed, and endorsed by the governing body comprising the stakeholders, customers, alliance partners, and employees. Grameen Bank model of Bangladesh, dairy farmers' cooperatives in Japan and India, and microfinance institutions in Mexico are good examples of bottom-up governance. However, the boards of public enterprises, which constitute public equities and government capital resources, are headed by social and political representatives or civil servants. The recent shift in the business philosophy has influenced the companies operating on public and private resources to develop business models to integrate the governance system based

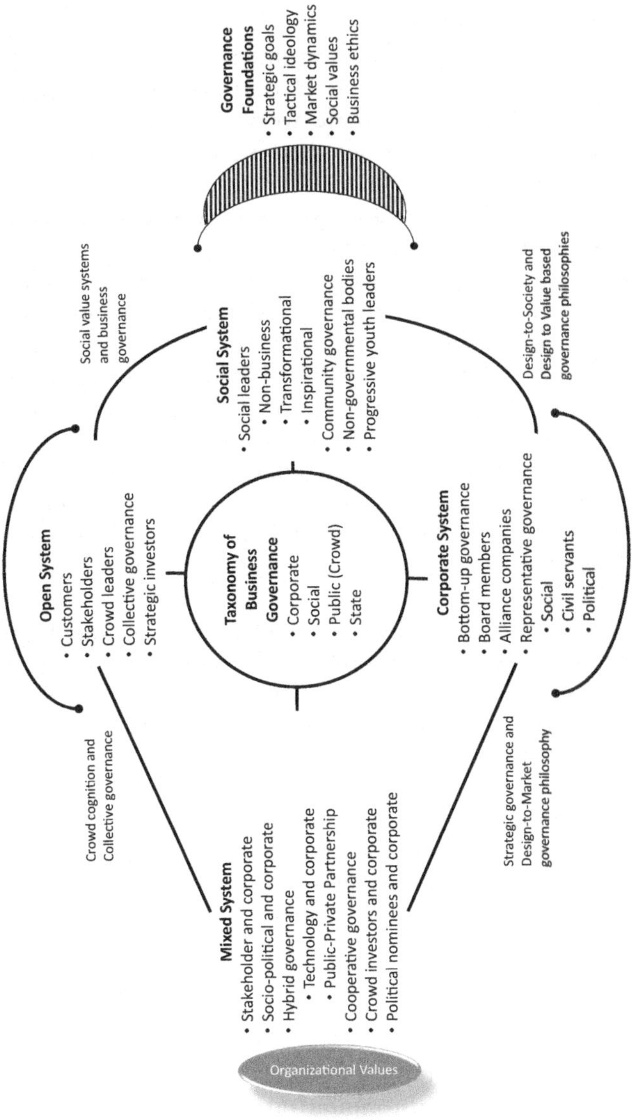

Fig. 4.1 Attributes and taxonomy of business governance system (*Source* Author)

on design-to-market, design-to-society, and design-to-value. However, there also exists mixed governance system in many regional and international companies which combines the representation of stakeholders, customers, employees, society, and government entities in the formal board structure as exhibited in Fig. 4.1. Hybrid governance model is an emerging phenomenon in the corporate world. In this model, a large number of representations from various groups (stakeholders, customers, technology experts, government, financial institutions, and social platforms) occupy the middle ground in the state-owned, public sector enterprises, and fully privatized companies operating in emerging markets. As sizable government stakes in leading industries in the form of ownership, management, subsidies, or other preferential forms are common in public companies. Such shifts are both market-driven and regulatory; and they lead to hybrid governance with a blend of human resources, technology, and regulatory framework. The hybrid governance helps firms in multi-stakeholder management, crowdfunded business projects, and publicly financed corporations that compete in the local and global marketplaces (Khanna, 2012). The hybrid governance encourages also public–private partnership in businesses, induces crowd cognition, and collective controls (commons), which operate with strategic goals and operational plans.

Nonetheless, corporate governance is not all about investment, power, and profit. Governance is about ensuring that decisions are made effectively and they contribute to business performance, create develop new alliances, and create corporate value. Good governance helps in building power relationships with stakeholders, key business players, employees, and customers. A good bottom-up governance (crowd-based, social, and customer-led governance) needs a system in which senior managers and the company's board collaborate on decision-making and regularly seek the input of shareholders to develop and implement co-created and coevolved strategies (Gilley et al., 2010). The key requirements in improving the governance system of a firm are to drive the collective role of directors and induce positive contributions of key players in business. They must have expertise on the corporate finance, administration, and technology management. The board, stakeholders, key collaborators, and customers should be aware of business procedures and be able to focus on new strategies through brainstorming on the business needs under the current market ecosystem. Only reviewing past performance will not be adequate to establish good business governance. In order to achieve effective governance outcomes in the firm, directors need better access to the company information so that they can devote substantial time to the corporation, and their compensation should be linked to equity performance. In addition, managers, board members, and shareholders must set up lines of regular and direct communication (Pound, 1995).

The social governance in crowd-based businesses is more effective than the conventional top-down governance model. Firms experience better performance through collective or coevolved business governance model by inducing customers and crowd-led investors in decision-making and building competitive strategies of the firm. Crowd-based firms aim at motivating behavioral change through collective leadership designed in a democratic pattern with design-to-society and design-to-value business philosophies. However, it is often difficult for firms to sustain the market competition due to lack of streamlined leadership and predetermined business philosophy. The major challenge with the crowd-based firms is uploading their performance and competitiveness for the long run. Often, firms growing with crowdfunding tend to develop alliance with social networks and engage in media advocacy to complement a social marketing program. Commonly, the crowd-based business operated through social marketing programs are intervened by social conventions, local politics, and community organizations to gain social support. For example, a health care company may involve social networks to disseminate knowledge about breast cancer, and diagnosis and treatments associated with it. Though this issue might be raised by the health care company as a social marketing debate, it also appears to be an issue to be addressed by the local non-governmental organizations and the local politics. Hence, this product of crowdfunded social health clinics in a social network could attract any of these behaviors—getting an annual mammogram as a mix of social–commercial issue, seeing a physician each year for a breast exam as a matter of social health care programs offered by the local public governance, and performing monthly breast self-exams as an issue associated with social education. As social media activities achieve a scale of returns over a period of time, the challenges of the company may center less around justifying funding and more on organizational issues such as developing the right processes and governance structure and identifying clear roles for all involved in social media strategy. Managers can identify the functions, touchpoints, and goals of social media activities, and craft approaches to measure their impact and manage their risks. However, companies may need to drive internal discussions on how to lead and to learn from social networks, competitors, and young consumers to stay competitive in the marketplace (Rajagopal, 2013).

Most developing nations have promulgated comprehensive public policies to streamline corporate governance on implementation of sustainability-driven business model in all industries. Public policies are focusing on macroeconomic disruption due to sustainability issues in developing economies (Béal, 2015). Therefore, large companies are developing alliances with local governments on public–private partnerships (PPP) in implementing sustainability norms and enhancing social value. The PPP initiatives in various geo-demographic sectors have generated social awareness among people and inculcated environmentally conscious consumption in the society. The core elements of crowdfunded business projects constitute stakeholders, society, innovation and technology, macroeconomic factors, sustainability, and corporate governance. Crowdsourcing or collective intelligence has emerged as a dynamic tool in the business ecosystem today, which is supported by the stakeholders. They support companies in co-creation and coevolution process with stakeholders through social interaction, social innovations, and social governance. Ecosystem of crow-based businesses linked with the sustainability goals drive public–private entrepreneurship (both upstream and downstream collaborations) to meet the sustainable development goals through social—and frugal innovations. Upstream collaboration refers to strategic alliances with national or international firms to have regional or global focus of business, while downstream collaborations are associated with the social business and community governance. Taxonomy of leadership and employee engagement largely drive the corporate governance practices as central to the business ecosystem (Rajagopal, 2021). In the context of an industry, business ecosystem is a community comprising various levels of interdependent firms that tend to coevolve in an ongoing business cycle and constantly renew their business configurations. The business cycle of a firm is largely affected by political, economic, social, technological, and legal subsystems. In view of the ecosystem discussed above, the coevolutionary process of business modeling consists of co-vision, co-designing, and co-creation as the domains of activities (Liu & Rong, 2015). Consumers also play a significant role in the innovation subsystem by co-creating products that add value to the social sustainability. End users share insights on low-cost innovations and the possible ways of their utility with the consumer communities. The consumer-led social innovations are supported by public policies and encouraged through non-governmental organizations and public–private participation. End users contribute to the innovation processes by contributing to the design perspectives and stimulating demand of the innovative product. Thus, stakeholders, corporate managers, and policymakers remain apprehensive about the potential of end users driving sustainable innovation (Nielsen, 2020).

Implementation and governance of sustainability-based business models are shared through public–private partnerships. In addition, stakeholder-driven governance forms such as cooperatives, public–private partnerships, or social businesses help companies develop strategic profit-maximizing models and simultaneously creating value. The business models are analyzed from a sustainability perspective to overcome the economic, social, and technological bias of sustainability approaches. Accordingly, business governance leading to performance with purpose is designed in improving social sector, and operates through interactive business models categorically in geo-demographic market segments (*e.g.*, Sánchez & Ricart, 2010). Business transformation in consumer-centric companies evolve over the years in reference to values-based governance. The necessity of creating hybrid business models infuses with local cultures and practices in global markets, leveraging strategic partnerships by encouraging co-creation with consumers (Gupta & Shapiro, 2014). The community creation model in managing renewable business projects across the downstream market comprising rural household and farm and non-farm sectors functions more as social governance than a corporate venture. The governance mechanism for managing green energy projects in rural areas lies between the hierarchy-based (closed) mechanism and the market-based (open) systems. Social behavior is built by attaining social needs through stakeholder governance and effective social governance. Sustainability projects lead to success as social behavior is strengthened by perceived social beliefs, values, and community consciousness. Psychosocial behavior, which is supported by the stakeholder education and experience, emotions, and motivations, also contributes to social behavior in general. Positive impact of public governance based on the public policies on sustainable goods and services set the consumption behavior among the stakeholders (Pahnke et al., 2015). The social leadership and working group on the sustainable projects not only generate awareness on the eco-innovation and technologies, but also boost social motivation among the stakeholders to adapt to the ecological products and services.

4.2.1 *Interactive Planning and Governance*

The CAGE framework comprising cultural variability, administrative factors, governance, economic system, and political ideology of the country also affects internationalization. The cultural factors can be analyzed in reference to religious beliefs, race, social norms, and language. Sociocultural interrelations in a region like Latin America, Caribbean, and South-east Asia; common currency; and trade arrangements (preferential and regional) influence the political ideology and business expansion of companies. Commonly, the governance and political ideology develop within the sociocultural norms in a country. However, disruptions in political ideologies are subject to the attributes of leaders, movements of political parties, external alliances, or internal pressures. In addition, consumer income, consumption culture, quality of life, and financial resources in the society also determine political consciousness and philosophy of business governance (Ghemawat, 2001).

The emphasis on interactive planning has become an applied perspective in organizational planning which was embedded in the planning theory (Ackoff, 1999). The Interactive Planning (IP) methodology has been developed as a conceptual tool to guide systematic and systemic (overall) development of organizations. Such an approach is idealistic and often considered as a guiding paradigm. IP offers a comprehensive layout for demonstrating a systematic, step-by-step, process of organizational development with focus on the design of an ideal organization (Haftor, 2011). Growing organizations use interactive planning models that are intertwined and interdependent, and tend to evolve as learning organizations involving stakeholders, customers, managers, and functional leaders. The interactive and reactive planning processes are able to predict collective outcomes within the organizational ecosystem. However, managers looking to navigate these difficulties need to adopt new approaches. Often reactive managers are typically dissatisfied with the way interactive decisions appear. They are quite satisfied with the way things were dealing with problems in a way to return to that state. They have a nostalgic longing for conventional wisdom. Large organizations use models that simulate the behavior of stakeholders within the organizational system. During the interactive planning process, risk mitigation is crucial in planning. Ackoff (2001) explained that planning consists of the design of a desirable present and the selection or invention of ways of approximating it as closely as possible. It creates its future by continuously closing the gap between where it is at any moment of time and where it would most like to be. It included parts of interactive planning as formulating the mess, ends-planning, means-planning, resource planning, design of implementation, and design of control.

Interactive planning directed at predicting organizational growth, which is based on the belief that an organization's future depends at least as much on what it does between now and then, as on what is done to it (Ackoff, 2001). Meanwhile, interactivity (crowd response, social networks, and grapevine communication) helps firms resolve organizational problems by altering complexities surrounding the customers and investors communities. It can be done by upholding desired design of the future and discover a way to realize it. Therefore, interactive planning methodology derives from interactivity concept and is a participatory method administering a set of problems correlated when believed that if a step is not taken, then desired future will possibly not happen; and that if the step taken it is the right one, and desired future can possibly be realized (Rachma-Fitriati, 2014).

Many industrial and customer-centric companies have shown interest in planning for their professional, managerial, and technical personnel to enhance their performance. However, foreseeing the organizational planning from the strategic perspective is a complex process due to non-controllable factors and the changing stakeholder value perceptions. Therefore, to get the leaders of the organization to make a paradigm shift is a major challenge. Designing and strengthening work programs, assessing the corporate culture, and modifying or reinforcing it from the top are among the ways human resource planners target performance objectives (Mills, 1985). In order to develop interactive business plans, firms rely on stakeholder and employee openness to generate new ideas. Accordingly, the need and opportunities can be explored through long-term planning.

Strategic planning is a long-term approach in managing various perspectives of organizational growth and administering managerial activities to reach prolonged goals. In strategic planning process, firms document managerial approaches and establish a direction to reach out the long-term goals by assessing various linear and discrete activities. The strategic plan helps firms build and refine organizational mission, vision, objectives, and values to achieve them collectively. The strategy determinants aim to evaluate how the company visualizes the activity integration within the broad organizational framework that embeds mission, vision, and objectives. In strategic planning, firms aim to create value through the following elements (Gomes-Teixeira & Junior, 2019):

- Approach—develops long-term mission, vision, and objectives of the firm in various business portfolios categorically,
- Objective—identifies the purpose of the growth and activity integration,
- Support—assesses senior managerial relationship to integration,
- Importance—evaluates the commitment and maturity that the company has to integration, and
- Decision-making—evaluates the degree of influence across the areas of work within the organization.

The organizational parameter focuses on evaluation how the values, beliefs, behaviors, and mission of the company are converged with organizational design, function and culture. A strategic planning system is a structured process, which helps firms in organizing and coordinating the activities of managers who plan. A strategic planning system develops an integrated, coordinated, and consistent growth through a long-term plan of action, and facilitates adaptation of the change management within the company. Among many factors, communication of corporate performance goals, the goal-setting process, organizational design, managerial roles, the corporate planner's tasks, and the linkage of planning and budgeting affect the strategic planning in an organization to carry out its administrative activities (Lorange & Vancil, 1976).

Over the years, strategic planning has evolved to build organizational culture, group dynamics, and leadership. Strategic planning originated in the management literature. It can be defined as breaking down a goal to achieve it into steps over predetermined time, formalizing those steps so that they can be implemented almost automatically, and articulating the anticipated consequences or results of each step (Mintzberg, 1994). By identifying basic trends and uncertainties, a manager constructs a series of scenarios that helps in overcoming the usual errors in decision-making. A strategic planning system develops an integrated, coordinated, and consistent long-term plan of action, and facilitates adaptation of the corporation to environmental change. Successful strategic planning requires analyzing managerial goals, diffusing strategic knowledge, and developing operational resources. It is argued that though operational effectiveness is necessary to superior performance, it is not sufficient, because its techniques are easy to imitate. In contrast, the essence of strategy is choosing a unique and valuable position in the systems of activities in an organization that can be synchronized with the goals of organizational growth (Porter, 1996).

Strategic thinking helps new entrants adjust the ecosystem with the socio-economic, cultural, and market-led factors that influence one another and stimulate the management of the design cube comprising design-to-market, design-to-society, and design-to-value. The business ecosystem is fundamentally based on these triadic design pillars. Large companies tend to radically explore new technology to disrupt existing markets, while the new entrants focus on pursuing value-adding improvement in the existing products and technologies on the frugal innovation platform. In this process of orchestrating business ecosystems, multinational companies and joint ventures follow integrative and long-term perspectives in business embedding business goals and strategic interests in decision-making. Such strategic business goals help these firms develop backward and forward linkages with suppliers and buyer groups to develop operational integration (Zahra & Nambisan, 2012).

Strategic planning occurs in large organizations in person, with a planned intensive leadership promoting shared dialogue and engagement between the stakeholders and employees, enabling collaborative and thoughtful strategic planning for the future. Such an interactive process leads to building greater connectivity and cohesion among the key enablers to organizational growth. Organizational leaders are brainstormed and polled to visualize the potential strategies which are believed to be of the highest priority for the future growth of the company. Implementation of strategic plan requires the organization to map resource allocations and the results of ongoing evaluation through vigilant and inclusive decision process to promote stakeholder and employee engagement. Organizations need to define achievable and measurable goals, address strategic issues, and formulate the roadmap to achieve the predetermined goals. Accordingly, it is necessary for the organizations to prioritize strategies and monitor performance through goal metrics (Uzarski & Broome, 2019).

The transformational leadership is charged with developing a strategic plan to implement the organization's goals, tactics, and progress. Within the context of its values and goals, a strategic plan steers the organization toward its mission. In strategic planning, board members need to be cognizant of their intent to implement the change leading to long-term effect through several new initiatives simultaneously. The over-arching decision need to be taken through interactive planning with stakeholders, customers, and corporate leaders to pursue strategic plans. Among many customer-centric companies, IKEA (Sweden), Samsung (South Korea), Nestlé (Switzerland), and Unilever (UK and India) largely rely on interactive planning to enhance long-term commitment and use social values in planning process with an attitude of 'things will get better' for both society and business.

4.3 Value Chain Management

The growing social awareness, peer motivation, and the experimentation about the crowdfunded and collective businesses ranging from renewable energy to organic food products consumption help in generating proactive green behavior among consumers. The growing interest of companies to involve customers in co-creation of customer-centric products and stakeholder knowledge play a dynamic role in inculcating proactive behavior in coevolving the collective intelligence-led businesses. The interest of people in investing in, and their conformity to, the adaptability of sustainable energy, water conversation, green products and services, and health and housing projects establish learned behavior. Such behavioral process is supported by the consumer's perceived value emerging out of the economic benefits and risk analysis in using the technology-based sustainability product and services. The stage of behavioral process leads to the defensive behavioral stage by critical evaluation of needs, awareness, and their fit into the values and lifestyle. The following stage of defensive behavior drives consumers to justify their perceptions and attitude toward collective decisions and optimize output. Most people at this stage seek social validation and reward for their decision to stay with the crowd-based businesses, and tend to lead customer and stakeholder advocacy at niche and regional levels of society. However, as the social consciousness grows, the self-actualization on public commitments increases. Further, the political ideologies, government support, and stakeholder engagement contribute to the definitive green behavior of people on sustainable products and services. Over the definitive state of behavior, most stakeholders enjoy the benefits of sustainable products and services and tend to push green goals as a social movement and stay as referrals to diffuse lessons and vision on the community business projects.

Sociopolitical approaches applied to the governance of urban transport and logistics services encourage human involvement to maximum limits and avoid mechanical interventions for improving sustainability. Service behavior, transport demand, cargo dynamics, and investment decisions are often explained by aggregating the supply chain behavior. The social and cultural resources interpret and analyze the dynamics involved in a system-wide transformation initiative to attain sustainability. Mumbai-based *Dabbawala*[1] organization achieves high service performance at par with the lean management and six sigma paradigm with a cost-effective simple operating system. The delivery system embodies mission, information management, material flow, human resource system, and operations processes to meet the growing requirements and challenges of home-cooked food delivery. It is a sustainable way of delivery system. As the city grew, the demand for Dabba delivery grew too. The conventional coding system is still prominent in the twenty-first century. Initially it was a simple color-coding but now since Mumbai is a widely spread metro with three local train routes, coding has also evolved into alphanumeric characters. An outside consultant proposes the introduction of new technologies and management systems, while the leading logistics companies (*e.g.*, FedEx) come to Mumbai to learn about the *Dabbawala* system (Thomke & Sinha, 2010). Digital *Dabbawala* is an initiative to combine technology and e-initiatives of the state government. This organization has six sigma certification (Forbes Magazine) that engages over 5,000 human resources working in Mumbai to deliver over 200,000 lunch boxes each day. The e-deliveries are managed by registering clients in the organizational system, which enables a delivery person (*Dabbawala*) to come with a laptop and a biometric device, and register the client's agreement through the validation of social security card. The service begins after the registration is successful. This logistics and transportation organization has been ISO 9001:2000 certified by the Joint Accreditation System of Australia and New Zealand.

The value proposition of both customers and social communities contributes significantly in the sustainable business modeling process.

[1] In Mumbai, one of the largest cosmopolitan cities in South-east Asia, *Dabbawala* (lunch-box delivery person) is a conventional logistics and transportation system for delivering the food packs to the thousands of employees working in various organizations within the city. *Dabbawala* organization use bicycles, motorcycles, delivery vans, and public transport to deliver food packs.

Value proposition describes the attributes of product/service offering, the customer segments, and their relationship in the social deliveries; whereas value creation and delivery describe how value is provided to customers (the channel efficiency and value delivery process), including the structure and activities in the value chain (Osterwalder & Pigneur, 2010). There are various layers of business value creation in crowdfunded businesses. At the bottom of the pyramid, the value chain model includes mainly informational, emotional, esteem, and commitment factors, which positively influence the value creation process. The intermediate level of social value creation is developed by establishing relationships with stakeholders that enables sharing of information, co-creation, and coevolution process of social innovation and business projects. The apex level of social value creation has been identified as the sense of belongingness among stakeholders of sustainable business projects. In addition, collaborative projects promoting stakeholder engagements in managing sustainable projects, innovations, and technologies contribute to social value creation (*e.g.*, Liu et al., 2020). The value chain management, and deliveries of sustainable business projects show effective results when organizations follow collaborative work culture with autonomy and employee engagement. The corporate social responsibility projects of most multinational companies are implemented as the pilot to test the sustainability-based business model. Such business philosophy emphasizes stakeholder and customer needs; and defines ways through which companies deliver value to them, invests in value creation, and co-creates resources through the proper design and operation of the various elements of the value chain (Teece, 2010).

Although most consumers tend to experiment with low-priced products and substitute the products that deliver satisfactory experience, they fail to develop sustainable perceptions and build attitudes toward repeat buying. However, industry attractiveness describes competition among traditional pipeline brands, which succeeds by optimizing the activities in their value chains. In addition, as a globalization effect, the platform brands co-created together with the consumers and producers; such as Uber (transport service), Alibaba (e-commerce), and Airbnb (urban housing); are growing in the market by improving the consumer chain and delivering satisfaction (Van Alstyne et al., 2016). Substitute products in the market adversely affect the industry potential, and pose threat to customer preferences. Bargaining power of buyers refers to the direct or indirect pressure tactics to force the industry to reduce prices or increase product features, in view to optimize the customer value. Buyers gain power when they have choices, and when their needs can be met by a substitute product or by the same product offered by another supplier (Rajagopal, 2019).

Large firms engaged in multidimensional business optimize their value chain activities and competition to leverage valuable capabilities and to acquire sustainable competitive advantage. Effectively performing value chain activities allows firms to develop capabilities to outmaneuver competitors and gain strategic advantage in enhancing their market share. However, value chain activities are not of equal significance to all firms due to varied specific goals. In order to understand the elements of the value chain, it is important to first understand the resources and abilities that create these underlying elements of the chain. The resource-based view of the firm indicates that firms can achieve sustainable competitive advantage by implementing value-creating strategies with their valuable, uncommon, inimitable, and non-substitutable resources (Prajogo et al., 2008). Most multinational firms are targeting bottom of the pyramid market segments to acquire higher market share in the mass market, and these firms are fostering to develop sustainable value chain by building local capacity through 4As comprising awareness, acceptance, adaptability, and affordability. Firms also invest in educating local market players and alliance partners, developing the infrastructure, and providing basic community services. Large firms also create shared value opportunities by improving products and reorganizing market segments, redefining productivity in the value chain, and enabling local cluster development. As discussed in the pre-text, large and emerging firms also aim at co-creation of products and business models to upgrade the shareholder value and enhance the value creation process. Social entrepreneurs offer lower costs, strong social networks, and deep insights into potential customers and communities, and set up hybrid value chain. This framework may be defined as the hybrid value chain. For example, Elektra, a consumer durables retail company in Mexico, initially aimed at the customers at the bottom of the pyramid, and is now expanding and monitoring its market by associating social networks. The company expanded its business in the USA and other countries in Latin America. It is operating as an innovative project aimed at meeting the needs of families of relative lower sociodemographic profiles (Drayton & Budinich, 2010).

4.4 Market Competition and Growth

Operating on economies of scale may also have a significant competitive advantage for a large firm as it may enjoy a large volume of production at lower costs, which may further lead to price leadership with low retail prices. Such strategy would also prevent the potential competitors from entering in the business. A new entrant firm may make it hard for a would-be entrant by incurring huge sunk costs with high-budget advertising. In view of such strategy, any new entrant may match its products and services to compete effectively but may lose the market share if the attempt to compete fails. Sunk costs are the costs that have been incurred and cannot be reversed, such as spending on advertising or researching a product idea. They can be a barrier to entry. If potential entrants would have to incur similar costs, which would not be recoverable if the entry failed, they may be scared off. Another radical strategy used by the powerful firms to discourage entry is by raising exit costs, for example, by making it an industry norm to hire workers on long-term contracts, which would build escalated cost barriers for rival companies. Thus, firms can earn some excess profits without a new entrant being able to compete to bring prices.

Crowdfunded businesses have grown in social and customer-centric sectors under the predominant business environment of big manufacturers and survived with marginal options. Most crowd-based businesses are successfully serving the niche markets beyond the oligopolistic competition. The focus of consumer products companies within the niche has shown increasing the sales by gaining customer trust. The low-cost consumer products from India, China, and other developing markets have been promoted through the e-commerce strategies, collective intelligence, and social networks. The principal business goals in crowd-based businesses are set around the strategic profiteering over the other consumer-centric indicators, though the pace of growth of these firms is slower than the firms with private capital base. Over time, as the markets evolved to grow in an advanced competitive environment, emergence of crowd-based firms significantly altered the niche business models of small manufacturers and retailers. Since the late twentieth century, such crowd-pushed business-move has helped the potential companies and prospecting retailers break the conventional marketing paradigms and attract open investments in building customer-centric business models to expand their markets. Crowd-based businesses operating in the niche markets set short-term goals to be achieved by developing strategies on basic marketing mix elements comprising product, price, place, and promotion. The competitive strategies of the companies also cover driving territorial expansions and acquiring new customers. These companies tend to deliver value for money and other tangible competitive advantages across the brands of competing companies based on product attractiveness. The outgrowth of crowd-based firms in emerging markets, and penetration of multinational companies into the local markets, had set tough competitive norms. Various elements influencing the market competition and business growth are exhibited in Fig. 4.2.

Understanding the nature of market competition is important for the firms to develop appropriate marketing strategy. Crowd-based business firms often face upstream market competition in the context of product attractiveness, pricing, distribution and services, and value-based promotions as illustrated in Fig. 4.2. These firms usually survive in the niche markets; however, they turn weak while competing with other firms for a single buyer in monopsony conditions. The major competitive forces that affect the growth of an infant crowd-based firm include unforeseen disruptions in the market (technology-based diversifies products), new incumbent firms with similar or identical product portfolios, and substitute products. Nonetheless, the bargaining behavior of customers and suppliers also affects the performance of crowd-based products and services in the market as they are often lack validation from a large segment of customers in the initial stages. The rapidly changing market trends and vogue (product design, ergonomics, and collective values) also affect the growing crowd-based companies favorably to sustain the market competition. Most companies with crowdfunding observe austerity measures meticulously, which restricts their capabilities toward investing in technologies with prolonged lifecycle. Consequently, these companies adapt to frugal innovation and face major challenges in commercializing it. Enhancing customer value by understanding the behavioral dimensions of existing and potential customers is the major strategy challenge for small and medium companies. Most companies tend to exhibit competitive advantages among customer by co-creating customer value. Therefore, interactivity among customers on face-to-face and digital platforms contribute significantly to inculcate positive values among them.

Over time, oligopolistic competition caused congestion of companies, and slow growth of markets in this phase of evolution of competition. Successful companies invested resources in developing brand loyalty and

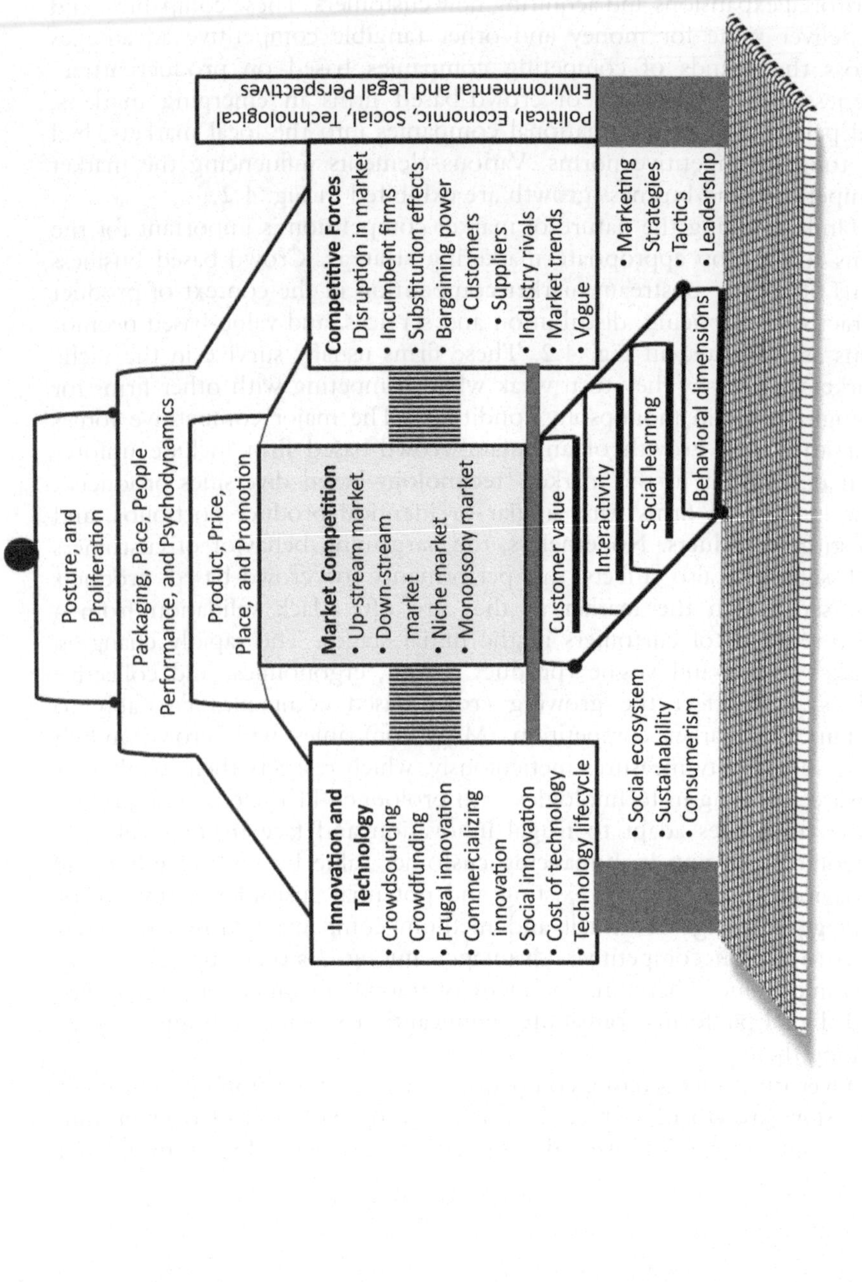

Fig. 4.2 Ecosystem of market competition (*Source* Author)

took extensive measures to control customer defection until the end of the century. Most companies invested huge resources in product, distribution, promotion, and packaging to attain first-mover advantage. Crowdfunded firms in niche markets rely on continuous innovation with increased customer value to survive and tend to dominate the market with their less-known brands. These companies behave monopolistically within the niche as they get social recognition and try to develop social dominance in the competitive marketplace. Some firms occasionally innovate, but fail to prevent competitors from replicating the products as they fail to patent them. This implies that only some firms invest continuously in research and development, and each one chooses the investment differently (Etro, 2019). The high-performing crowdfunded companies create cross-functional teams drawn from strategy, marketing, and finance to ensure the assumptions underlying their long-term plans, which reflect both the real economics of the company's markets and its actual performance relative to competitors. Oculus Rift, a firm developing virtual reality (VR) game is based on crowdfunding in 2012; and after the campaign was over, the firm had more than 9,500 backers that raised over $ 2.4 million making it one of the biggest crowdfunding success stories at the time. Later on, in 2014 Facebook acquired *Oculus VR* for two billion dollars. Today Oculus Rift is known as a member of Facebook Family of apps and services. Overall revenue from Oculus Rift is forecasted to amount to 4.95 billion US dollars worldwide in 2019 and that's only from hardware.[2] Similarly, *Allbirds,* a crowdfunded footwear company of New Zealand, launched its fundraising campaign in 2014 and quickly became one of the most successful crowdfunded businesses in the world. With their Kickstarter campaign, the firm could raise 120 K US dollars in a short time with over 900 backers. The brand has collaborated with the likes of Nordstrom, Outdoor Voices, and even Shake Shack. The logo-less unisex merino wool shoes have emerged in the market in one of the promising athletic styles with a newer slipper-like iteration and priced at the competitive edge of $95. After two years of the start, the company was valued at $1.4 billion and generated $50 million revenue in 2017.

It has been observed that the high-performing companies use rigorous analytic frameworks to analyze the collective intelligence data. Such companies ensure that the dialogue between the corporate office and the

[2] For details see https://www.oculus.com/.

business units about market trends and assumptions is conducted within a rigorous framework, such as that of *profit pools*. Emerging companies in the competitive marketplace find it challenging to manage the price competition and reinforce low prices to take on rivals whose strategies, strengths, and weaknesses can be easily turned down. Large companies are often susceptible to threats from disruptive and low-cost competitors in the local markets. Slashing prices usually lowers profits for incumbents without driving the low-cost entrants out of business. Companies take various approaches to compete against cut-price players. Some differentiate their products—a strategy that works only in certain circumstances. A careful analysis of a microenvironment indicates whether a company can successfully enter a specific market. It may be hypothesized that prosperity of a nation depends on the productivity with which it uses its human, capital, and natural resources. This is manifested in the way a nation's firms compete. Productivity, in turn, is a function of the interplay of many factors including political, legal, and macroeconomic context; the quality of the microeconomic business environment; and the sophistication of company operations and strategy. Low-priced products and crowdfunding have proved to be a worthy combination in the niche market evolved around price-conscious, gender-based, and millennial consumers segment. The crowdfunding campaign on *Indiegogo* and other fundraiser platform was initiated in 2013 for MVMT fashion watches, which raised around $300 thousand with the help of over 3850 investors. The firm extended its product portfolios to various fashion accessories including eyewear and jewelry focused on millennial consumers.

Competition in disruptive products has emerged in reference to the characteristics of products as breakthrough, competitive, and improved. A *breakthrough product* is a unique innovation that is mainly technical in nature, such as the digital watch, virtual reality games, and fashion accessories. A *competitive product* is one of many brands currently available in the market and has no special advantage over the competing products. An *improved product* is not unique but is generally superior to many existing brands. Both companies and customers experience the tangible market competition as customers rely on 'touch, feel, and pick' emotions across brands in the competitive marketplace, while the intangible competition grows over the social media and informal blogs on Internet. Customer interactions on the digital space drive intangible competition across brands and companies on the online marketplace. The smart and connected products developed under the concepts of Internet of Things offer exponentially expanding opportunities to companies. Such products are attractive for their new functionality, exhibit far greater reliability, and hold capabilities that cut across and transcend traditional product boundaries. Smart, connected products raise a broad set of new strategic choices for companies about how value is created and captured, how to work with traditional partners and what new partnerships will be required, and how to secure competitive advantage as the new capabilities reshape industry boundaries (Porter & Hepplemann, 2014).

The buying power of customers determines the extent to which they retain most of the value created for themselves. The threat of substitutes determines the extent to which some other product can meet the same buyer needs, and thus places a ceiling on the amount a buyer is willing to pay for an industry's product. The power of suppliers determines the extent to which value created for buyers will be appropriated by suppliers rather than by firms in an industry. The intensity of rivalry acts similar to the threat of entry. It determines the extent to which firms already in an industry will compete away the value they create for buyers among themselves, passing it on to buyers at lower prices or dissipating it at higher costs. Buyers gain power when they have choices—when their needs can be met by a substitute product or by the same product offered by another supplier. In addition, high buyer concentration, the threat of backward integration, and low switching costs add to buyer power. Similarly, the bargaining power of suppliers refers to their ability to force the industry to accept higher margins or reduced services, in the interest of augmenting or securing their profits. The factors influencing supplier power are the same as that of buyer power. In this case, however, industry members act as buyers (Rajagopal, 2012). The buying power of customers determines the extent to which they retain most of the value created for themselves. The threat of substitutes determines the extent to which some other product can meet the same buyer needs, and thus, places a ceiling on the amount a buyer is willing to pay for an industry's product. The power of suppliers determines the extent to which value created for buyers will be appropriated by suppliers rather than by firms in an industry. The intensity of rivalry acts similar to the threat of entry. The fundraising and marketing campaigns that are close to the quality of life gain perceptual leverage among investors and consumers. Brooklinen, a bed sheet manufacturing crowdfunded firm kickstarted the fundraising campaign as 'If you're ever having troubled sleeping, feel free to ask one of us our thoughts on different textile constructions.' Brooklinen started a crowd-funding campaign back in 2013 and raised over US $236 thousand with the viral strategy of big and bold images of pets on the bed with their sheets.[3]

The generic strategy of crowdfunding and crowd-based business model to boost marketing specifies the fundamental approach to competitive advantage a firm is persuasive and provides the context for the actions to be taken in each functional area. In practice, however, many strategic plans are the lists of action steps without a clear articulation of what competitive advantage the firm has, or seeks to achieve, and how. A firm's strategy is the route to competitive advantage that will determine its performance. Build, hold, and harvest are the results of a generic strategy or recognition of the inability to achieve any generic strategy, and hence, of the need to harvest. Business leaders try to gain significant advantages in combating low-end competition, but they often hesitate because of the hidden risks and adverse effects on their current profit margins. The solution may be to find the response that is most likely to restore market calm in the least disruptive way. A business leader driven by collective intelligence could choose to ride out the challenge by ignoring, blocking, or acquiring the low-end competitor; or it could decide to strengthen its own value proposition by adding new price points, increasing its level of benefits, or dropping its prices. Such tactics can be effective in the short term, but the industry leader also needs to consider strategic retreat, particularly when certain conditions make future, low-end challenges inevitable.

A majority of such low-end firms fall into the categories of strippers, predators, reformers, or transformers in sustaining the market competition. Such categories of firms are defined by the functionality of product and the convenience of purchase. Stripper firms, for instance, typically enter a market with skeletal offerings and limited functions, and usually offer convenience services. Large firms have significant advantages for combating low-end competition, but they often hesitate because they're afraid their actions will adversely affect their current profit margins. Thus, new and growing firms in the competitive market environment need to find the response that is most likely to restore market calm in the least disruptive way. The market leader firms could choose to

[3] For details see https://www.brooklinen.com/.

ride out the challenge by ignoring, blocking, or acquiring the low-end competitor; or decide to strengthen its own value proposition by adding new price points, increasing its level of benefits, or dropping its prices (Potter, 2004). In a competitive marketplace ecosystem, companies coevolve around co-created innovation, technology, and products and services that have high value for money. Successful companies amidst rivals in the marketplace work cooperatively and competitively to support new products and satisfy customer needs. In a large business environment comprising multiple niches and geo-demographic market regions, several small and localized ecosystems exist for survival and dominance of local companies. Such market destinations drive competition among business ecosystems but not across companies. Such business scenarios are observed in geographic segmentations within a large region. For example, in Europe, Baltic region, Nordic segment, Benelux states have evolved through small ecosystems with their own market culture (Moore, 1999).

Most companies with a clear, concise strategy statement emphasize on business expansion by converging internal and external sources, collaborations, and long-term involvement of stakeholders in developing strategic plans. Perhaps successful business-to-consumer and business-to-business companies need to have a clear sense of advantage of strategic planning, as long-term planning leads these firms to define and determine the objectives, scope, and advantages in managing trade-offs in business over time. If a firm pursues to enhance its growth or expand the organizational size, strategic planning appears to be a key business requirement (Collis & Rukstad, 2008). However, firms without strategic planning descend into underperformance because they are unable to bridge the gap between their strategies, capabilities, behaviors, and their business plan. Often organizational hierarchy, work culture, and values deter the implementation of strategic planning. In addition, managers do not engage in truthful conversations about the problems due to the lack of internal communication within the organization. These factors determine the success and failures in planning and implementation of long-term strategy. Indeed, the dynamics in almost any organization determine the strategic planning process (Beer & Eisenstat, 2004). Formal strategic planning follows a rationalist view that top management develops a vision of the company and translates it into a formal plan of goals and activities that are systematically implemented throughout the firm over time (Grant, 1991). Competitiveness is an end-product of a successfully developed and implemented strategic plan. Such planning efforts effectively inputs various stakeholders within dynamic networks and organizations.

References

Ackoff, R. L. (1999). *Re-Creating the corporation: A design of organizations for the 21st century*. Oxford University Press.

Ackoff, R. (2001, May 31). *A brief guide to interactive planning and idealized design*. Interact Consulting, Lancaster.

Barton, D., & Wiseman, M. (2014). Focusing capital on the long term. *Harvard Business Review, 92*(1/2), 44–51.

Béal, V. (2015). Selective public policies: Sustainability and neoliberal urban restructuring. *Environment and Urbanization, 27*(1), 303–316.

Beer, M., & Eisenstat, R. A. (2004). How to have an honest conversation about your business strategy. *Harvard Business Review, 82*(2), 82–89.

Collis, D. J., & Rukstad, M. G. (2008). Can you say what your strategy is? *Harvard Business Review, 86*(4), 82–90.

Darnall, N., & Henriques, I. (2010). Adopting proactive environmental strategy: The influence of stakeholders and firm size. *Journal of Management Studies, 47*(10), 1072–1094.

Drayton, B., & Budinich, V. (2010). A new alliance for global change. *Harvard Business Review, 88*(9), 56–64.

Etro, F. (2019). Monopolistic competition for the market with heterogeneous firms. *Economics Letters, 179*(1), 9–12.

Gilley, K. M., Robertson, C. J., & Mazur, T. C. (2010). The bottom-line benefits of ethics code commitment. *Business Horizons, 53*(1), 31–37.

Ghemawat, P. (2001). Distance still matters: The hard reality of global expansion. *Harvard Business Review, 79*(8), 137–147.

Gomes-Teixeira, G. F., & Junior, O. C. (2019). How to make strategic planning for corporate sustainability? *Journal of Cleaner Production, 230*, 1421–1431.

Grant, R. M. (1991). The resource-based theory of competitive advantage: Implications for strategy Formulation. *California Management Review, 30*(3), 114–135.

Gupta, S., & Shapiro, D. (2014). Building and transforming an emerging market global enterprise: Lessons from the infosys journey. *Business Horizons, 57*(2), 169–179.

Haftor, D. M. (2011). An evaluation of R.L. Ackoff's interactive planning: A case-based approach. *Systemic Practice and Action Research, 24*(4), 355–377.

Kesting, P., & Günzel-Jensen, F. (2015). SMEs and new ventures need business model sophistication. *Business Horizons, 58*(3), 285–293.

Khanna, P. (2012). *The rise of hybrid governance*. McKinsey & Company.

Khurana, R., & Nohria, N. (2008). It's time to make management a true profession. *Harvard Business Review, 86*(10), 70–77.

Liu, G., & Rong, K. (2015). The nature of the co-evolutionary process: Complex product development in the mobile computing industry's business ecosystem. *Group & Organization Management, 40*(6), 809–842.

Liu, S., Xiao, W., Fang, C., Zhang, X., & Lin, J. (2020). Social support, belongingness, and value co-creation behaviors in online health communities. *Telematics and Informatics, 50,* 101398. https://doi.org/10.1016/j.tele.2020.101398.

Lorange, P., & Vancil, R. F. (1976). How to design a strategic planning system. *Harvard Business Review, 54*(5), 75–81.

Luis Eduardo de Carvalho, & Santos, Z. (2008). *Co-creating a new value proposition at real Tokio Marine Vida e Previdencia.* Harvard Business School Publication.

Mills, D. Q. (1985). Planning with people in mind. *Harvard Business Review, 63*(4), 97–105.

Mintzberg, H. (1994). The fall and rise of strategic planning. *Harvard Business Review, 72*(1), 107–114.

Moore, J. F. (1999). Predators and Prey: A new ecology of competition. *Harvard Business Review, 71*(3), 75–86.

Nielsen, K. R. (2020). Policymakers' views on sustainable end-user innovation: Implications for sustainable innovation. *Journal of Cleaner Production, 254.* https://doi.org/doi.org/10.1016/j.jclepro.2020.120030.

Niemi, E., & Pekkola, S. (2017). Using enterprise architecture artefacts in an organisation. *Enterprise Information Systems, 11*(2), 313–338.

Osterwalder, A., & Pigneur, Y. (2010). *Business model generation: A handbook for visionaries, game changers, and challengers.* Hoboken, NJ: Wiley.

Pahnke, E. C., Katila, R., & Eisenhardt, K. M. (2015). Who takes you to the dance? How partners' institutional logics influence innovation in young firms. *Administrative Science Quarterly, 60*(4), 596–633.

Pfeffer, J., Zorbach, T., & Carley, K. M. (2014). Understanding online firestorms: Negative word-of-mouth dynamics in social media networks. *Journal of Marketing Communications, 20*(1-2), 117–128.

Porter, M. E. (1996). What is strategy. *Harvard Business Review, 74*(6), 61–78.

Porter, M. E., & Heppelmann, J. (2014). How smart, connected products are transforming competition. *Harvard Business Review, 92*(11), 64–88.

Potter, D. (2004). Confronting low-end competition. *Sloan Management Review, 45*(4), 73–79.

Pound, J. (2015). Promise of the governed corporation. *Harvard Business Review, 3*(2), 89–98.

Prajogo, D. I., McDermott, P., & Goh, M. (2008). Impact of value chain activities on quality and innovation. *International Journal of Operations & Production Management, 28*(7), 615–635.

Rachma-Fitriati, A. (2014). Applying interactive planning on leadership in the organization: The case of transforming public transport services in Banjarmasin. *Procedia—Social and Behavioral Sciences, 115*(3), 283–295.

Rajagopal. (2012). *Darwinian fitness in the global marketplace*. Palgrave Macmillan.

Rajagopal. (2013). *Managing social media and consumerism: The grapevine effect in competitive markets*. Palgrave Macmillan.

Rajagopal. (2019). *Contemporary marketing strategy: Analyzing consumer behavior to drive managerial decision making*. New York: Palgrave Macmillan.

Rajagopal. (2021). *Sustainable businesses in developing economies—Socio-economic and governance perspectives*. Palgrave Macmillan.

Rodriguez-Vila, O., & Bharadwaj, S. (2017). Competing on social purpose. *Harvard Business Review, 95*(5), 94–104.

Sánchez, P., & Ricart, J. (2010). Business model innovation and sources of value creation in low-income markets. *European Management Review, 7*(1), 138–154.

Subramanian, G. (2015). Corporate governance 2.0. *Harvard Business Review, 93*(3), 96–105.

Teece, D. J. (2010). Business models, business strategy and innovation. *Long Range Planning, 43*(2–3), 172–194.

Thomke, S., & Sinha, M. (2010). *The dabbawala system: On-time delivery, every time*. Harvard Business School Press.

Uzarski, D., & Broome, M. E. (2019). A leadership framework for implementation of an organization's strategic plan. *Journal of Professional Nursing, 35*(1), 12–17.

Vanhaverbeke, W. (2019). *Managing open innovation in SMEs 35*(1), 12–17.

Van Alstyne, M. W., Parker, G., & Choudary, S. P. (2016). Pipelines, platforms, and the new rules of strategy. *Harvard Business Review, 94*(4), 54–62.

Villanueva, J. (2013). Reading the signs of your customer value. *IESE-Insight Magazine, 17*(2), 24–29.

Zahra, S. A., & Nambisan, S. (2012). Entrepreneurship and strategic thinking in business ecosystems. *Business Horizons, 55*(3), 219–229.

CHAPTER 5

Crowd-Based Business Leadership and Strategies

Capturing customer value, expectation, and co-creation options from collective information leads business model sophistication for exploring new opportunities in the marketplace. Sophistication of business strategies is of critical importance toward refining the pool of resources for the firm's development. The collective intelligence drives critical thinking and helps managers in developing semantic perceptions of ideas, interventions, and implications (3Is). The semantics induce lead thinking in firms for involving crowd to set new business order. These intricacies are categorically discussed in this chapter. This chapter categorically discusses the attributes of co-creation, and the role of wisdom of crowd in the context of brainstorming, perceptual semantics, and design thinking. In addition, the role of stakeholder contributions in transformative leadership, strategies and tactics, and social branding is discussed significantly in the core discussions in this chapter.

5.1 Co-Creation

Co-creation has emerged as an outgrowth of crowdsourcing and crowdfunding practices in most firms engaged in commercialization of innovative customer-centric products and services. Collective brainstorming to generate new ideas and coevolving the business with innovative products,

Rajagopal, *Crowd-Based Business Models*,
https://doi.org/10.1007/978-3-030-77083-9_5

which have the potential for market disruptions, often provide competitive leverage to crowd-based businesses. Stimulating ideation process in crowd is effectively channelized through the social networks by creating portfolio-based groups to allow conscious participation. Crowdsourcing has become a dynamic tool in the business ecosystem today, which stimulates collective ideation, critical thinking, and investor prospects. The crowd-based ideas are largely customer-centric and based on cost-effective technologies. However, there remains challenges on branding crowd-based products and developing competitive marketing strategies to commercialize them. Often crowd-based business ideas portray strong disruptive attributes and drive product attractiveness against the existing brands. The collective intelligence embeds social emotions and strong psychodynamics that have the potential to disrupt the demand of existing brands in the competitive marketplace. Crowd-based ideation supports companies in co-creation and co-evolution process with stakeholders through social interaction, social innovations, and social governance. In the context of crowd-based businesses ecosystem, customer, and potential investors constitute the core of crowd to contribute ideas and resources. Social entrepreneurship is therefore, a community comprising various levels of interdependent innovation-driven business projects, which coevolve in an ongoing business cycle and constantly renew their crowd configurations. The business ecosystem of crowd-based firm is affected by extrinsic factors comprising political, economic, social, technological, environmental, and legal subsystems in a given region. The coevolution process of business models based on crowdsourced ideas envelop collective-vision, co-designing inputs, and co-creation potential as the triadic activities in a business domain (Liu & Rong, 2015). Public policies encourage co-creation of social innovation and potential competitive business projects through crowdsourcing, crowdfunding, and public–private partnership in developing countries. However, crowdfunding regulations are yet to take a mature shape in many emerging markets. In India, crowdfunds can be raised for a social cause to support public health, education, ecological housing, and rural transport in the form of donations. Equity Crowdfunding in India is illegal. To issue equity shares in India, companies need to comply with the provisions of The Companies Act, 2013. The Companies Act, 2013 provides detailed provisions and rules regarding the issue of equity shares through public and private placement. The crowdfunding policies focus on improving the sociocultural conditions by ensuring higher social and economic gains in managing social innovation and sustainability projects. Such public policies emphasize pooling of crowd capital resources within the approved financial outlay of the business projects, develop cooperation strategies, and encourage community business governance or proportionate share in the firm's governing board. Crowd-based companies tend to explore different types of alliances that combine productivity, spontaneity, and tangible outcomes in the context of managing sustainability projects, eco-innovations, management, and marketing. In this process, relationships among the customers, potential crowd investors, social entrepreneurs, and firms contribute significantly in promoting cooperative networks engaged in developing attractive strategies for improving performance (Lin & Jin, 2016).

Collective information boosts social values in various layers. At the bottom of the pyramid, the values from collective intelligence (ideation, reviews, and investment proposals) not only pool information but also inculcate emotions, esteem, and commitment among the people and entrepreneurs. These factors positively influence the value creation process. The crowd-based businesses rely on value creation to develop and strengthen relationships with the customers, stakeholders, and potential investors (donors) that enable co-creation, and coevolution of social innovation and business projects. The crowd investors, donors, and equity holders have a sense of belongingness in crowdfunded firms, and they intend to have community governance of such firms. In addition, collaborative projects promoting stakeholder engagements in managing sustainable projects, innovations, and technologies contribute to the social value creation (e.g., Liu et al., 2020). Business-to-consumers and Business-to-business markets are driven by consumer demands, because they are perceived as more value oriented and of added benefits. Locally integrated strategies of business-to-consumer companies of micro, small, and medium sizes exhibit the current trends of consumer engagements and co-creation. Such crowds-based business model explains the current trends from economic perspectives, and the new crowd-based organizational theory is beginning to examine the organizing principles of such firms at the bottom of the pyramid (Tallman et al., 2002). In the customer-centric business models, firms often assure product quality and services, and tend to overcome the administrative complexities on cost control, environmental technologies, and chaotic social issues. The co-creation and co-designing approaches of customer-centric companies like IKEA have established business philosophy of connecting consumers and developing an emotion-based relationship with consumers as the key to leveraging loyalty and advocacy behavior (Rajagopal, 2019).

Entrepreneurs in crowdfunded firms are engaged mostly in developing social innovations by exploring the social resources comprising, social capital, skills, capabilities and competencies, stakeholders' values, and expected returns. These firms are engaged with their crowd-based collaborators in improving existing business practices and acquired competencies to integrate crowdsourced ideas and corporate goals to co-design and co-create business models for niche segments (Arena et al., 2020). Effective social innovators stimulate external stakeholders to meet the existing social needs and build strategies business initially focused around the bottom of the pyramid market segment with a scope to penetrate the mass market. The right market for a social innovation depends on whether the entrepreneur or the firm has a clear social purpose and mapping of targeted problems. Creating social businesses and sustainable innovation, therefore, are aimed at delivering cost-effective and long-term solutions through social marketing approaches. Most multinational firms are targeting bottom of the pyramid market segments to acquire higher market share in the mass market, and these firms are fostering to develop sustainable value chain. These firms in association with small and medium enterprises tend to build local markets and augment the scope of markets considering the 4A elements comprising awareness, acceptance, adaptability, and affordability toward the crowdfunded social brands. Firms growing with the collective business approaches also invest in educating local market players and alliance partners, developing infrastructure, and providing value-added community services. The alliance firms also create shared value by improving products and reorganizing market segments, redefining productivity in the value chain, and enabling local cluster development.

In crowd-based firms, consumers and potential investors are considered as valuable source of innovation; they effectively engage in co-creation activities such as the generation, design, refinement, and testing of ideas and building new product concepts. Crowd collaboration helps firms develop new products and services with customer focus. The voice of customers, projections on investments, and crowd-based business strategies help firms to provide effective solutions to decrease the high failure rates among new products. The recent shift of businesses from private to cloud capital is toward integrating conventional wisdom of customers and market integration to gain wider customer recognition for disruptive products. Crowd-based firms not only explore the opinions, desires, and needs of consumers, potential investors, and social leaders, but also motivate them to contribute their creativity and problem-solving skills to design, develop, and deliver (3D) disruptive products. Consequently, consumers serve as co-creators. Crowdsourcing has also become a common practice among large multinational companies to increase the proximity with customers and inculcate brand value. With the growing success of crowdsourcing contribution, most companies have developed virtual platforms to collect information. However, the transfer of tacit knowledge that enables consumers to innovate with the firms needs high level of stimulation focused on returning benefits. Competitively strong customer-centric companies have focused on the development of superior crowdsourcing tools for concept evaluation through virtual prototypes and product testing (Füller, 2010).

In 2012, Heineken, A Dutch beer company, asked designers in different destinations about how should be the future of nightclubs in Europe. Many volunteer product designers, customers, and product critiques joined the campaign, and their semantically mapped opinions were presented at Milan's Design Week in 2012, with a live recreation of the space. Apart from being a co-creation success story, the co-creation initiative of the company has attracted considerable media impact and it has also become a reference campaign in terms of advertising and marketing. In addition, Heineken launched its co-creation platform in 2012, asking game lovers, beer drinkers, and environmentally conscious consumers for ideas that would make its packaging more sustainable. Similarly, Threadless, a fashion e-commerce company that manages and sells crowdsourced T-shirt designs, built a sustainable model by producing high-quality shirts in limited quantities to create the sense of a premium brand. The company pushed co-creation by inviting users to suggest designs and buying preferences. Consumers posted their design in the website while other users voted on the design options and the creations that received the most support from the community were produced. Threadless is an artistic creation and has become a profitable business. The crowdsourcing, therefore, raises an evident example of sustainable payoff among both large, small, and startup ventures (Boghin, 2014).

Companies engage consumers in knowledge co-creation and collaborative knowledge diffusion processes to support an interpretative model of consumer knowledge. The knowledge co-creation process encourages diffusion of customer-generated content on the social media, and helps in strengthening the community learning design. Consumers learn about products, services, and new consumption patterns through community resources. The community learning process prompts co-shopping and co-viewing of brands in the marketplace, and also stimulates consumers to review the referrals and conform to community decisions. Hence, most referral programs of the consumer products companies focus on diffusing brand awareness among the family or community as a source of knowledge hub of consumers (Rajagopal, 2019). Most social-centric companies develop new products as 'design-to-value' by involving consumers in co-creation process. Such consumer and stakeholder engagements in new product development help companies effectively manage seasonality of products in the marketplace and develop sustainable consumer attitude and consumption behavior. Therefore, it is observed that like social needs, consumer behavior also turns value-oriented over time. The consumer value chain often supports sustainability and social consciousness.

Co-creation with customers has evidenced a wide success among some brands of customer-centric companies. However, the challenges that practitioners need to overcome in building and sustaining online collaboration in design and product development process include hypothetical ideas, high project costs, market risks, and the expected time to prepare market in adapting to the products based on the collective intelligence. Since 2001, Procter and Gamble (P&G) has successfully been bringing outsiders into its research and development process and motivating them to speak out their ideas on new product development. The company has also targeted senior citizens with specific skillsets, ex-employees, and retired technical specialists of airline companies. The co-creation platform of the company—'Connect + Develop'—has supported many products across portfolios, improved product development process, and effectively doubled the number of employees engaged in the research and development area of the company without adding to payroll costs, though incentives were given to external collaborators (Boghin, 2014).

Successful innovation leads to customer involvement and profits, which can be achieved through co-creation by aligning consumers and market players in the innovation process. Some multinational companies have invested in sustainability projects by taking advantage of social media to diffuse new ideas and stimulating co-creation of innovative products and services. For example, the role of co-creation has become central to sustainability management in the social initiatives of twenty-first century.

Energy market transition, which is enabled by new affordable energy technologies and digitalization, opens novel opportunities for developing innovative energy solutions through collective intelligence and public–private co-creations. The new technologies emerging through co-creation enable stakeholders to buy low-cost renewable energy. The process of co-innovation is stretching the ideation process through extensive use of digital platforms and stakeholder involvement. Co-innovation is an ecosystem-wide activity that involves multiple stakeholders who collaborate toward a shared social goal and explore niche strategies to commercialize eco-innovations. However, in active societies like Chinese sociological and business culture, the co-innovators simultaneously compete with one another across geo-demographic segments to market their innovative products and services (Kotilainen et al., 2019).

Social innovation integrates social entrepreneurship and cooperative network by investigating the product attractiveness, technology, and process innovation investments of social enterprises on social and environmental outcomes. Social innovation central to understanding the market, in the context of needs different stakeholders and expected benefit from co-creation. It fosters cooperation and social engagement by the enterprises and the social actors with whom firms intend to co-create a social outcome and business impact (Cajaiba-Santana, 2014). Social innovation has evolved in convergence with social entrepreneurship and cooperative network innovation. The distinctiveness of social innovation focuses on social needs and solutions through continuous innovation, and implies cooperative and network innovation based on crowd cooperation involving a wider range of stakeholders such as customers, investors, and strategic partners (Ge et al., 2019). Social enterprises are community-conscious organizations evolved within the social framework, which addresses co-creation of solutions to a predetermined social need or a problem. Among many social problems in the urban–rural environment, sustainable housing, green energy, natural resources management, transportation and logistics, and poverty alleviation are some primary areas for social enterprises to work with. Social marketing is an approach to develop socially beneficial behavior for community-oriented products and services. In this context, social marketing is a concept of co-creation, and has been explored in a number of social marketing examples from marketing of birth-control contraceptives to renewable energy and water conservation products for social benefit. Co-creation is the process of customers and producers determining value together, where customers are engaged at all levels of value proposition and market transaction. Value, co-created in the social products and their marketing to customers, relies on the belief that customers are proactive to the social innovations and their applications (Desai, 2008).

5.2 Wisdom of Crowd

Soliciting new ideas from existing and potential customers have set a new trend of customer engagement among firms. Most customer-centric firms rely on collaborative decision-making through crowdsourcing, as the wisdom of crowd not only contributes to the utilitarian design-thinking process, but also leverages market competitiveness of the firms by providing collective decisions on pricing, promotion, and psychodynamics (social networking) perspectives. Crowd thinking helps in creating user-generated content and maintaining brand reputation by demonstrating the quality of high-end products and services. The growing popularity of the sharing economy has stimulated customer-centric firms to explore crowd ideas in business, which has changed the business dynamics over time and encouraged any individual (professional or non-professional) to share business ideas and get involved in the decision-making process of crowd-funded firms. Such individual contributor, who owns an underutilized resource, can contribute to the new product development process. Consumer feedback in businesses today encompasses the whole social experience rather than just the product or service usage (Roma et al., 2019). Collective intelligence, or the wisdom of crowds, refers to the contribution of groups of individuals who tend to render accurate judgments based on community needs and desired solutions. Exploring wisdom of crowd has become a phenomenon, which yields prolific ideas, decision dynamics, and growth perspectives under the right conditions combined with right communication and selection of crowd communities. This phenomenon has long played an important role in developing economics, where understanding of individual and group behavior has explained positive business and economic outcomes (Epp, 2017). Collective intelligence is built around the triadic conditions comprising liberal thinking, diversity, and personal judgment with the homogeneous crowd communities, which contributes to rewarding, rationale, and responsiveness in group behavior. Liberal thinking indicates that participants in the group think without peer influence and develop individual cognitive semantics which is not ratified or coordinated by the group. Diversity in the crowd wisdom exhibits that participants bring obscure knowledge to stimulate their decisions while personal judgments tend to maintain privacies and not broadcast their decisions to influence the crowd and bias the community's point of view (Surowiecki, 2004).

5.2.1 *Brainstorming*

The brainstorming is a group discussion approach intended to inspire collective creativity and thinking. It embeds circular and discrete attributes of using multiple ways of thinking, overcoming conventional thoughts, associating new concepts, expanding existing thoughts, and seeking applied problem-solving. The principal concern in brainstorming is to carry out icebreaking exercises on a given topic within the existing conditions. In the brainstorming process, participants are encouraged to contribute their thoughts without criticizing any idea or interrupting the threads of thoughts. In this process, the group members push and force themselves to think of any possible ideas and array of emerging thoughts within a broad conceptual framework (Hsu et al., 2018).

Brainstorming has a major role in the idea generation process. Contemporary methods for ranking the relative merits of ideas generated by brainstorming sessions rely on comparing average scores across members of the group. The average is a measure of the overall merit assigned to an idea but it does not measure unanimity or the concentration of opinion across members of the group with respect to the idea under consideration. The standard deviation of responses is the accepted measure of group consensus, but is rarely used in brainstorming possibly because the ranking of ideas is a more complex cognitive procedure when the two statistics—mean and standard deviation—are considered separately, or because most voting schemes are very simple (Walsh & Wood, 1992). Industrial organizations largely implement direct management control and influence the activities of employees leading toward improving their efficiency. The extent of monitoring sales managers, directing, evaluating, and rewarding activities in an organization intend to guide sales team behavior through team control processes to achieve favorable results to the organization and the employees (Anderson & Simester, 2011). Team control in a sales organization is, thus, recognized as an important performance indicator of the task performed by the salespeople. The innovation teams should be constituted with autonomy and enough scope for brainstorming on various task-related issues in the project. Constitution of teams should include the following attributes:

- *Warming*: Educating the team members about the project and respective tasks of the members. Effective warming up sessions would encourage members of the project team to conceive the goals, objectives, tasks, and modalities of the innovation project.
- *Forming*: Attract like-minded people to get into the task and project management process. Members exhibiting similar interests in the project and demonstrating capability and competence in conducting tasks in the innovation projects should be pooled to form an efficient project team in a company.
- *Storming*: It is a healthy practice to allow the member of the team to use their space in the team for loud thinking, discussions, debate over the issues, and present their point of view on managing the various tasks to be performed in the innovation projects.
- *Norming*: Though brainstorming exercises result in arriving at common approaches, solutions to the problems, and taking preventive measures; there is a need to determine the rules and standards for open discussions on the innovation project activities. This would streamline the participation of members within the team and keep them on track for carrying out the tasks in the project.
- *Performing*: Teams constituted with the above attributes should be given autonomy or flexibility in decision-making to conduct various tasks and enhance the performance of the project. However, the performance of teams should be monitored and evaluated on a task-by-task basis to fix any advertence in the project operations process.

The contemporary trend of collective intelligence meets the challenge of satisfying the growing need for creativity and innovation through brainstorming, especially in product designing and prospective product ergonomics contexts such as space saver products, small automobiles, and multi-utility products. The wisdom of crowd helps designers and ergonomists to come up with products through crowd-consensus to make appropriate decisions. Promoting creativity through brainstorming is becoming more challenging for firms with increasing knowledge on technology, market competition, and disruptive business trends. Therefore, creativity needs to be fostered through the combined efforts of society and business firms in order to produce an agile creative workforce to tackle complex tasks (Miller & Dumford, 2014). The strategy orientation would drive the brainstorming discussion to a result orientation effort and the measurability would count on the success of the deliberations (Rajagopal, 2006). Rapidly changing work culture and complexities of organizational problems demand a quick and judicious managerial decision to drive toward a win–win situation. Fast-cycle decision-making is not just about making decisions more quickly; it is rethinking of the decision-making model, where managerial intuition is combined with employees performing brainstorming discussions, carrying out task simulations, and sharing information among the peers. Experiences of project managers drawn from several companies and leading management studies suggest that the manager's ability to act quickly and wisely depends on his or her personality traits, problem-solving abilities, and managerial relations with the employees (Prewitt, 1998). In the progressing companies with the practices of bottom-up decision-making and relying on crowd wisdom, brainstorming has been a key tool to generate ideas. The brainstorming exercise is often configured around the following norms (Paulus & Brown, 2003):

- Liberal thinking,
- Refraining from interpersonal criticism,
- Compressive documentation of all the things that come to mind,
- Unrestricted steering of contextual ideas,
- Generating multi-stream and multi-utility ideas,
- Pooling of ideas and later screening with quality indicators, and
- Encouraging development of intertwined and relevant ideas

Open and active communication with employees, for example, earns their trust and engagement. In order to develop participation in the developing innovation project plan and budgeting, project managers should go beyond brainstorming among the stakeholders and sponsors. Project team should link strategy and purpose with project and initiative development by implementing a process of idea generation, selection, and conversion, known as 'front-end innovation.' Once the project charter is complete, debate on project budgeting can be initiated by assessing the adequacy of financial resources, people, and competencies to execute new innovation plans. The project team can make changes accordingly in hiring people, cost estimations, and contingency planning with required skills (Joan and Joaquim, 2015). As discussed earlier, the wisdom of crowd leading to collective intelligence can be broadly networked with three process factors comprising brainstorming, semantics, and design thinking. The attributes of these factors are illustrated in Fig. 5.1.

Wisdom of crowd is a broad-spectrum cognitive pool, which contributes to the collective intelligence with liberal thinking, hybrid knowledge (a blend of conventional and technology-oriented knowledge), and group behavior has emerged as the principal source for firms to learn the perceptions of customers and stakeholder at large. Figure 5.1 exhibits that wisdom of crowd is motivated by the firms by creating a free space for thinking together on a predetermined topic. The digital networks and the enhanced scope of interpersonal meetings among peers have helped collective intelligence grow manifold over the years. The brainstorming in the crowd-cognition process categorically exhibits individual and group behavior. However, teams are able to manage the tasks with precision provided proper strategy orientation is given to the team members. Consequently, brainstorming on digital platforms and physical workstations drive dynamic thinking on multiple streams and enable the participants contributing to ideation pool, which builds the prevailing knowledge foundation. The most complex task observed by the participants during the barnstorming exercise is synchronizing the overriding thoughts with the principal stream of discussions. In addition, resolving intermittent conflicts across divergent ideas appears to be a major challenge in managing the brainstorming to reach consensus and core outcome. The perceptual semantics spread across various variants contributes to the value-based thinking. The design-thinking attempts to screen the inputs from brainstorming and perceptual semantics contributed to develop the collective intelligence. Accordingly, the crowdsourced designs are developed as design-to-market strategies for commercialization and launching in the market. The design thinking is intensively and extensively supported by the co-creation and coevolution processes through the shared values.

Companies often explore innovation ideas either by activating the crowdsourcing tools, outside-the-box thinking, or by collecting information from the consumers in the existing market and financial data on innovations in reference to the cost and time. The major problem with

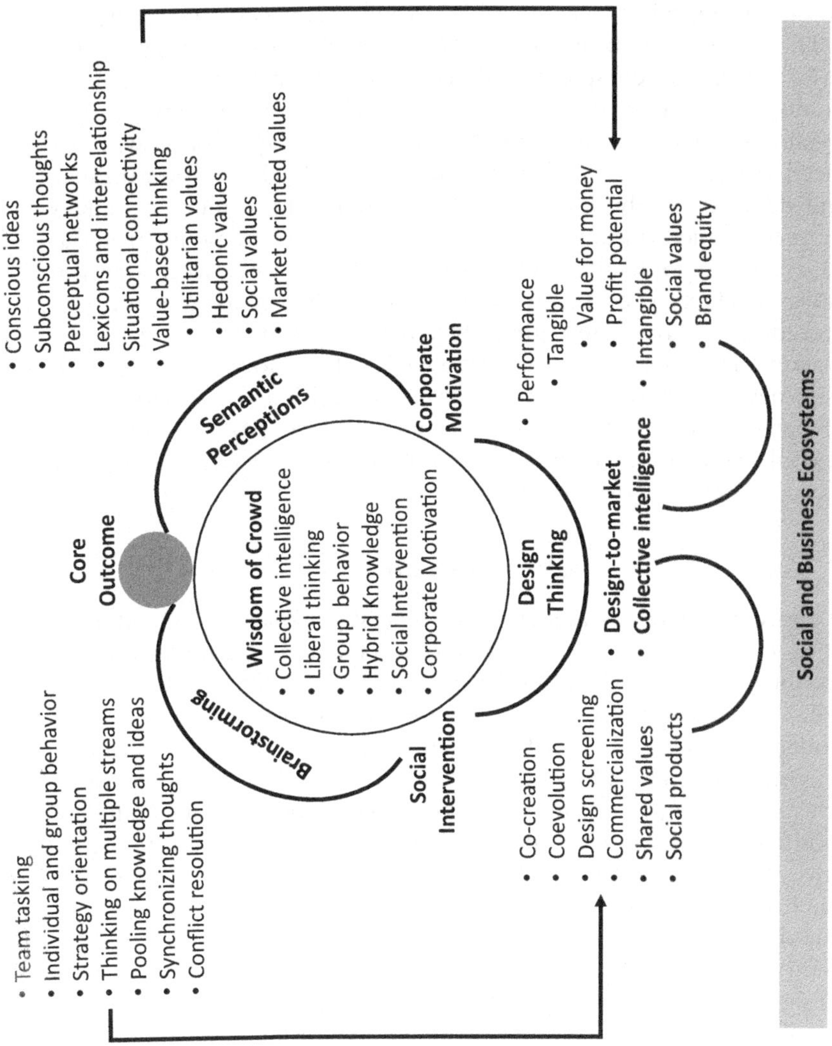

Fig. 5.1 Converging brainstorming, semantics, and design-thinking attributes (*Source* Author)

crowdsourcing of ideas is that few people are very good at unstructured, abstract brainstorming; however, it is often difficult for the project teams to ensure as to how to fit these ideas into the canvas of economic viability, technological feasibility, marketability, product services, and customer value. The problems with the process of outside-the-box thinking are that databases are usually compiled to describe current market requirements and do not offer strategies for the next generation products. Hence, there are possibilities that customers rarely come forward to express whether they need or want a product they have never seen. Such situation triggers creating demand for the innovation and would require more resources for the project and consume longer time, which at some point may also be risk-averse as competitors may penetrate the market with identical or similar products. The secret of new innovations is to generate lots of good ideas, whereas some great ones may occasionally appear simple and marketable. In doing so it is necessary for the innovation companies to create new boxes for innovation players comprising consumers, trend gatekeepers, product critiques, researchers, employees of the company, which could generate new ideas in the context of knowledge, skills, and previous experience (Coyne et al., 2007).

5.2.2 *Semantics*

Social and cultural values influence customers' personal values and alter cognitive dynamics comprising attention, semantics, memory, perception, problem-solving abilities, creativity, conscious thinking, and decision rationale. The cognitive value assessment is a major task in understanding the underlying personal, social, and cultural values among customers in the conscious and subconscious states of mind. Value co-creation and consumer-brand engagement are integrated brand-building strategies that positively influence customers' behavior. The value-based strategies influence customer satisfaction building, consumer–brand relationships, customer retention, brand equity, and competitive advantage. The design-to-value business strategies embed the value-based strategies to gain competitive advantage in the market, converging the design-to-society and design-to-market business philosophies (Pansari & Kumar, 2017). Periodical analysis of the following attributes helps firms in understanding behavioral dimensions of customers:

- Perceptions (awareness, self-image congruence, and perceptual semantics),
- Preferences (product attributes, perceived use value, initial knowledge, and motivation),
- Purchase intentions (competitive leverage, price and promotion benefits, buying outlets, and point of sales stimulus), and
- Propensity of buying (volume and frequency of buying).

Analysis of the above attributes contributes to developing design-to-value business strategies by the firms through enhancement of personal and lifetime values of consumers. Personal values of consumers include anthropomorphism, self-actualization, and self-esteem. The design-to-value strategies of the companies enable them to resolve the dilemma in decision-making and loyalty standpoints of the customers. Customer-centric companies develop customer engagement not only to enhance their participation in product development and promotions, but also to develop the design-to-value strategies in businesses. Design-to-value strategies of the firm enhance the scope of creation and capture of value by engaging customers and stakeholders. Co-creation of products and services provide opportunities to generate value, enhance customer relationships, and cultivate loyalty. Most customer-centric companies tend to create customer value by delivering distinctive values in the niche markets (Yoo & Park, 2016). Most companies open up their design-to-value thinking based on experience sharing of customers with products, services, or the consumption chain. It is a co-creation process where customers and firms both uncover opportunities to vail competitive leverage

Semantics exhibits connectivity of thoughts, perceptions, and values among customers on any given object, situation, or within an existing business ecosystem. Cognitive semantics is the continuity of the thought process that occurs in human mind. The cognitive semantics emerges as a process of thoughts and communication that connects to a core thought or mental state addressing the specific ecosystem (Brandt, 2005). Customers tend to develop compositions of contextual meaning and senses of a given word, phrases, situations, concepts, or acquired information that affect the processing of complex thoughts, perceptions, and emotions. However, research on embodied cognition demonstrates that perceptual semantics is more than just synchronization of thoughts on lexical meanings rather perceptual experience. The semantic thoughts are extensions of a principal thought leading to contextual interpretations and decisions. Therefore, perception-based information such as key terms in communication, advertisements, social media messages, and corporate announcements need to be meticulously drafted and posted. Customers sensitive to the critical appraisals of words and their meaning engage in wooing perceptual semantics to arrive at cognitive synthesis and decisions.

Using cognitive semantics customers tend to bread contextual meaning of words and perceptions on specific communication keywords. For example, the word 'green' might have the semantic expansion to explore the contextual terms such as sustainable, organic, fertilizer, permaculture, natural cultivation, renewal sources, energy, public policy, social consciousness, and the like. Necessarily, the perceptual semantics act as decision drivers in developing awareness, comprehension, conviction, and action (ACCA) paradigm. However, the question of how the meanings of words are conceived in the mind is complex as the development of semantics to a specific word or concept is connected with the existing knowledge and past experience of the customers in building semantics. Commonly, the meaning of words depends not only on how words are defined (Sanford, 2006). The growing concepts in social psychology and neuromarketing experiments endorse that cognitive semantics has been vibrant among the customers today due to updated knowledge and analytical vigor to build appropriate perceptions and buying intentions. The cognitive process, neural network, and social behavior moderate the cognitive semantics process among customers in making buying decisions. Semantics is more frequently associated with language skills, which comprehends cognitive thought process and perceptual manifestation; and portrays non-verbal behaviors including action perception, object interaction, and a range of socio-cognitive processes. The non-verbal behavior, which broadly constitutes semantic representational system within hub (desire and need)-and-spoke (perceptual semantics) model. Non-verbal cognition is expressed as empathy, emotions, and communications (Rajagopal 2021a).

Cognitive semantics play a significant role in value creation among customers. Managers with large multifunctional teams in customer-centric companies monitor customer perceptions; map variation in their perception to identify the origin of information contributing to the thought process; and modify the affecting words, phrases, or information accordingly (Govindarajan & Gupta, 2001). The strategic and tactical market approaches of companies play a significant role in driving the market thrust, which include co-creation and coevolution (customer collaboration in innovation, strategy development, and managing communications), and competitive push (product attributes, pricing, delivery of products, promotions, packaging, and proliferation of products within the portfolios). In addition, social pull through community values also contributes to customer values. The factors driving market thrust moderate the perceptual semantics and cognitive semantics. Accordingly, emotions keep changing, which affects the customer values. The value foundations are based on the convergence of the corporate value-based goals and customer personality. Nonetheless, collective intelligence derived from the social networks and market behavior also affects the customer value in the short term.

The journey of thought process among customers is complex and interrelated to the causes and effects, events, motivations, experiences, and self-learning. The perceptions of customers on any tangible or intangible object or process have vast expansion over the temporal and spatial dimensions, which significantly contribute in building the cognitive ergonomics of customers. Therefore, mind mapping has emerged as a neuromarketing experimental science to understand customer psychology and develop marketing strategies to align with the state-of-the-mind of customers. Mind maps track the natural progression of through process and perceptual semantics by connecting end-to-end thoughts with intermittent moderating thoughts in a linear or discrete path. Mind maps of customers are used in learning the customers' perceptions on tangible (products) and intangible (services) domains. It is a continuous learning process for the companies to analyze perceptual semantics and customer thought process to develop the right customer-centric strategies.

5.2.3 Design Thinking

In large organizations, design perspectives are becoming central to the process of business modelling and strategy implementation. The concept of business design has emerged as a collective approach in an organization involving customers, stakeholders, key functional partners. Most organizations have realized today that staying in business as learning organizations helps them grow competitively and consistently in the marketplace. Such business maxim has been described as 'systems thinking' that leads to the design principle in business, known as 'design thinking.' Companies pursue this concept as a response to the mounting complexities in business operations. Design thinking in business has been conceived as an essential tool for simplifying the business operation by interlinking organization, society, and stakeholders, and more comprehensively humanizing the business. The extended principles of design thinking in business converge with the market attributes (market players, ethics, and business growth), social responsiveness (marketing with purpose), and customers' (stakeholders') value propositions.

Consumer behavior is growing complex with the advancement of frugal and disruptive innovations and affordable technologies such as social, domestic, and light industrial robots that influence customers. The rapid and abrupt shifts in consumer behavior have thrown major challenges of achieving market competitiveness and consistent lead to the customer-centric companies. Therefore, the design thinking has become a popular tool to develop customer-centric marketing strategies. The design-to-market strategies have helped companies co-create products for customers with high-perceived use value. IKEA home décor, furniture, and fixtures based on the need and design suggested by the customers, LEGO Creation from static models to power-driven creations, and simplified Oral-B electric toothbrush from P&G, which has reduced from many functions to two for customer convenience, set the right examples of the use of design thinking to induce consumer behavior. Conventionally, design has been a downstream perspective in the product development process for the high-value customer segment. Over time, with the convergence of collective intelligence and customer research, firms have focused on developing new products with perceived aesthetics, and inculcating brand perception among customers. The digital and reminiscent advertising of products has helped firms in making customers understand the design attributes in products and co-create value. Consequently, the design thinking has gone public today, and is known for its contributions in marketing with customers. The design and innovation encompass collective intelligence that exhibits not only the customer demand, but also the emotions associated with the products and buying decisions. The emotions and personality of customers associated with the products are evolved around the creative ideas, product attributes, complementarity, and user-oriented designs. These factors significantly contribute to the design-to-market concepts of developing and managing new products rather than simply managing them with a conventional marketing strategy. Design thinking has emerged as a method to deliver needs and desires of customers through streamlined solutions, which could attain high market share. The design process is carried out in a technologically feasible and strategically viable (cost-time-risk-profit) manner. The most challenging situation in the design-thinking process is the radical change in cost-time-risk factors combined with customer brainstorming and rapid prototyping. Most design-to-market products are developed using innovative processes and software that radically streamline information exchange between the companies, stakeholders, and key partners (Brown, 2008).

Companies tend to reach customers and offer them competitive benefits through co-created organizational practices and design. Shifts in the market processes in the society are induced by fundamental beliefs and shared assumptions, and resemble elements of social culture-defining norms of markets, expected behavior, and thought. Most firms know their customers sketchily, and the marketing strategies are based on their innate assumption, competitive response, and rapid guesswork than scientific analysis of customer insights and strategic requirements. The rapid and abrupt shifts in consumer behavior has thrown major challenges to the customer-centric companies in achieving market competitiveness and consistent lead. The elements of marketing mix have evolved over the years in reference to the changing business environment, shifts in industry focus, and government regulations. Advances in digital technologies have augmented the scope of outsourcing of business activities beyond geographic boundaries through several independent contributors. The collective insights develop co-created business models to drive an impact in emerging markets through popular attributes of products, pricing, promotions, packaging, and managing customer psychodynamics based on collectively generated contents. Innovation of new products is a complex process that needs to be carried out meticulously in the firms integrating the business and customer use values in the marketplace.

In large organizations, design thinking is becoming central to enterprise performance and a key indicator in achieving market competitiveness. Such design orientation intensely supports the marketing strategy of firms than holding merely the aesthetics values and product development process. Crowdsourcing of design ideas is an emerging process of design thinking throughout the organization. The crowd-design approach is time taking and it piles up information in an unclassified bin unless carefully segmented on digital platforms. The crowd-design ideas deal with huge responses and meet the complex challenges for many products, services, and processes. However, crowd-design projects need programmed interactions with technologies and other complicated systems as a design project and stimulate the participants to be intuitive and pleasurable. Therefore, design thinking is an essential tool for simplifying and humanizing the collective ideas for crowd (mass customers). The principles of crowd-based design thinking include many attributes, of these some are as listed:

- Focus on customer experiences,
- Exploring emotions,
- Creation of physical models, such as diagrams and sketches,
- Manifesting ideas to resolve social or consumption problems,
- Use of prototypes to experiment with solutions,
- Critical success factors, expected problems, and a tolerance for failure, and
- Limiting product features to avoid complexities and ensure ease of use of technology.

Creating a design-centric culture involving crowd requires continuous motivation to promote quality designs so that the returns on investment in design can be ensured, though it is difficult to measure. Quantifying and allowing people to contribute to designs, and appreciating how designs can stimulate returns is a complex crowd campaign to get design thinking (Kolko, 2015).

Crowd-based design thinking has become popular in many customer-centric firms and this practice has been pioneered by IKEA, Samsung, and Harley Davidson. These firms have tried to explore customer perceptions through crowd-based designing and evoke designers' problem-solving techniques to innovate products. Key elements of the design-thinking methodology include exploring and applying user-generated contents, carrying our early and frequent interaction with customers, developing agile process design with low cost and hierarchy; and a learning-by-doing approach. The crowd-designing process involves not only sharing ideas but also building prototypes and creating mock-ups of any kind at the quickest possible time to launch in the market. The design-thinking initiatives have been floated through the social media frequently by the startup companies and such initiatives rarely proceed according to a prescribed business model. Such crowd initiatives are focused on agile and frugal innovation concepts, which are initially targeted to a niche market. Crowd-based innovation is initially an unfiltered process with hidden conflicts and complications on design processes and structures. The raw data on crowd design may not be congruent with the corporate objectives and cultures. Therefore, firms critically analyze the crowd-design data and measure the cost, time, and risk factors in adapting to the ideas from the crowd information pool. The design-thinking methodology encourages democratic and self-organized teams. However, most large companies work with the hierarchical decision-making process. In fact, the design-thinking teams work for outsourced ideation process with the clear project charter defining processes and expected outcome. Such projects are managed by senior managers who constitute small crowd groups and supervise design-thinking projects on spatial and temporal dimensions (Kupp et al., 2017). The design-thinking process embeds the following steps:

- Effective coordination between managers and users (crowd groups) in managing design-thinking initiatives,
- Developing balance between emotions, intuitions, and analytical thinking among design-thinking teams,
- Establishing ground rules to systematically draft the design process,
- Providing adequate autonomy to the design-thinking teams to operate with liberal cognitive space integrating design-thinking process into the product development processes,
- Encouraging design thinking as a continuous learning project rather than an isolated exercise, and
- Measuring profits as metrics for design-thinking projects upon commercializing the designs.

In large organizations, design perspectives are becoming central to the process of business modeling and strategy implementation. The concept of business design has emerged over time as a collective approach in an organization involving customers, stakeholders, key functional partners. Most organizations have realized today that staying in business as learning organizations helps them grow competitively and consistently in the marketplace. Such business maxim has been described as 'systems thinking' that leads to the design principle in business, known as 'design thinking'. Companies pursue this concept as a response to the mounting complexities in business operations. Design thinking in business has been conceived as an essential tool for simplifying the business operation by interlinking organization, society, and stakeholders, and more comprehensively humanizing the business involving the crowd in innovation and ideation process. The extended principles of design thinking in business converge with the market attributes (market players, ethics, and business growth), social responsiveness (marketing with purpose), and customers' (stakeholders') value propositions. Design thinking has emerged as a method of delivering needs and desires of customers through streamlined solutions, which could attain high market share. The design process is carried out in a technologically feasible and strategically viable (cost-time-risk-profit) manner. The most challenging situation in the design-thinking process is the radical change in cost-time-risk factors combined with customer brainstorming and rapid prototyping (Rajagopal 2021b).

Most organizations manage individual design teams through the initial stage of idea generation to its commercialization process. In this process it is important to establish a clear rational and objective, choose the right design-thinking methods, and integrate key partners and resources to market the designed product. The above stages are the sensitive touch-points in design thinking and outsourcing of design activities. One of the critical requirements for crowd-based design projects is communicating clear directions on the process and simultaneously managing the cost, time, and risk factors associated with the design process. However, incremental prototyping and testing of design are internal marketing projects, which call on employees to measure the success and failure of designs by markets and customer segments (Bason & Austin, 2019). Consequently, firms need to manage the design processes at both ends—in internal and external ecosystem. Employees, market players, and stakeholders need to be provided with continuous guidance and support from corporate and social leaders to manage product designs in a competitive and profitable manner. Though the role of crowd-group leaders and investors is primary in crowd-based designing process, executives of the firm stay on top of such innovation projects and lead them to success. Diverse businesses like PepsiCo and Airbnb have successfully implemented the design-thinking process using collective intelligence to launch products and services, respectively. The design thinking is refined over time in many firms, and is integrated with stage-gate process to implement checks and balances effectively in the design process. The stage-gate process is an integrated part of project management and is used today to create innovations. Many firms today have installed the Stage-Gate (SG) innovation system which is a process of phased project reviews to develop new products and services (Nakata, 2020).

The rapid and abrupt shifts in consumer behavior has thrown major challenges of achieving market competitiveness and consistent lead to customer-centric companies. Therefore, the design thinking has become a popular tool to develop customer-centric marketing strategies. The design-to-market strategies have helped companies co-create products for customers with high-perceived use value. IKEA home décor, furniture, and fixtures based on the need and design suggested by the customers, LEGO Creation from static models to power-driven creations, and simplified Oral-B electric toothbrush from P&G, which has reduced from many functions to two for customer convenience, set the right examples of the use of design thinking to induce consumer behavior. Conventionally, design has been a downstream perspective in the product development process for the high-value customer segment. Over time, with the convergence of collective intelligence and customer research, firms have focused on developing new products with perceived aesthetics, and inculcating brand perception among customers. The digital and reminiscent advertising of products have helped firms in making customers understand the design attributes in products and perceive values. Consequently, design thinking has gone public today and is known for its contributions in marketing with customers. Successful companies like Nestlé, Whole Foods, and Apple bring business and society back together by creating shared value and generating economic value, using collective intelligence. Companies deliver value through collective designing of social products for society by addressing its challenges.

Wearable products like the Nike FuelBand are transforming the idea of branded activity through social consciousness. The *FuelBand* allows customers to set goals, track progress and celebrate achievements. The information from the wristband is then integrated into existing online networks like Facebook. Simply by wearing the band, consumers' fitness activity is now branded 'Nike.' This is an example of convergence of social and commercial product designed through collective intelligence. As digital sharing is becoming a part of our daily experience, the brands will benefit most through socially conscious lifestyle. The social and value-oriented business designs tend to reconceive products and markets based on social needs, redefine productivity in the value chain, and build social innovation clusters at their business hubs. Social collaborations focus on improving business processes and performance. Social orientation of a business starts from a niche, links corporate-interest to shared interest, encourages productive competition, co-creates values, and builds trust among customers.

5.3 Crowd Leadership

A new model of Enterprise 2.0 is focused on establishing interactive communication with the stakeholders; developing cognitive association with the stakeholders through listening to them; and creating, sharing, and capitalizing knowledge. The internet technology of Web 2.0 in support of new marketing models led to enhancement in customer relationships and supports advertisement, stakeholder participation, and social networking to mobile communication. Marketing 3.0 paradigm emphasizes on vision and values associated with each of its stakeholders in order to make a company a successful marketer. The Marketing 3.0 scholarship suggests that a company gets better profits by creating superior value for its customers and stakeholder partners than by benchmarking its profit and setting its path to market leadership. Family businesses are co-created with stakeholders to cater to the community needs, and grow around cultural and geographical context. The ecosystem of family business integrates the pedigree of knowledge, business skills, leadership, innovation proneness, and redefining the scope of business. These businesses face generational gaps in management as the new generations are guided by the contemporary market competition, innovation, and technology. However, limitation of resources and family's willingness to realign the business ties with new-generation companies have appeared as major obstacles in improving business performance (Rajagopal, 2020).

Individual leadership governs the firm through asymmetric business plans which are outlined informally. Family firms initially grow in a niche market with public relations and profit-high business values domain founded on welfare business philosophies. However, individualism in leadership often turns subjective in family firms. As the entrepreneurs take over the family firm in its second generation, they review the experience of the previous generation and revise the business model from value orientation to profit-centric approach. The transgenerational gap between the first and second generation usually requires moderate changes in business process. The leaders in the immediate next generation to owner-founder tend to modify family-centered control, and encourage incremental innovation to improve the market performance of products and services of the firm. Streamlining financial flows, documentation of business activities, and decentralizing the business controls are taken up on priority by the second-generation leadership of family firms. The leaders in the immediate next generation to owner-founder tend to modify family-centered control, and encourage incremental innovation to improve the market performance of products and services of the firm. Streamlining financial flows, documentation of business activities, and decentralizing the business controls are taken up on priority by the second-generation leadership of family firms. The transgenerational gap between the second and third generation stimulates business leaders for diversifying business and following multi-brand, multi-market strategy in the existing and new markets. These companies also develop strategic alliances on production, distribution, technology, and finance with large companies. The transgenerational firms also carry out corporate restructuring and stakeholder management during transitions in business. The size of the market for the new products may also be determined by analyzing the microeconomic variables. It is necessary to build the strategic business mindset to outwit the competitors and gain competitive advantages over the segmented markets. The following factors need to be considered for achieving strategic business leadership:

- Develop a plan capable of delivering outcomes that will add significant value to a state of affairs.
- Explore internal and external fit for the innovation and technology-led products.
- Capitalize on market needs and behavioral change in the markets in order to turn them to advantage.
- Stay future-focused.
- Plan the implementation of business strategy in both sequential and parallel direction to accomplish goals and sustain the impact thereof.
- Develop a win–win platform at an acceptable cost to launch the technology-led innovation products.

Thinking of an innovation is easy, but making the same work is a challenging task. A cost-effective innovation in consumer products sector is reaching its popularity in developing countries and emerging markets, where entrepreneurs face global challenges amidst paucity of resources but hold high market potentials. Such innovations offer low-cost solutions but exhibit attributes of being robust, consumer-friendly, and having high sales potential at the large and bottom of the pyramid market segments. Such innovations are grown locally and are positioned initially in a niche. Scaling low-cost innovations gives rise to various financial and managerial challenges. However, once such innovations are successful in large-scale operation, they could pose major threats as disruptive innovations to the established commercial brands of multinational company. Bringing local innovations to commercial scale is subject to successfully managing various operational factors including cost, active demand, developing a sustainable business model, diffusion of innovation, social networking and demonstrating use value, effective entrepreneurial leadership, and managing corporate reputation (Soman et al., 2012).

At the core of every company, there exists crowd-based group of varied sizes consisting of customers, investors (emerging out of crows, regular, and potential investors), and key partners who raise the voice on design, process, performance, and profit goals and achievements. Broadly, the voice of customers is critical to design quality and marketing strategies. Firms need to nurture these groups as the think tank of knowledge and provide liberal space to share their emotions, experience, and egalitarian values. They contribute to the collective intelligence over time, which encourages firms to adapt to the organizational behavior of *knowing* (acquiring and analyzing information), *doing* (adapting to practical recommendations of the group), and *being* (growing as customer-centric company with competitive differentiation). Long-standing crowd communities (such as Microsoft user communities, Kindle self-publishing communities, and Amazon prime communities) grow like an institution which comprises the people whose perceived interests and needs are considered as decisions are made throughout the organization. In large customer-centric organizations, the core group constituted out of a larger segment of stakeholders and customers (may be defined as crowd segment) is supported by the organization to grow as a collective intelligence resource). The members of the core group share unique values and knowledge that support corporate decisions toward new designs, product development, and developing competitive marketing strategies; and induce independence, creativity, and power, across the employees of the company. Such behavior of key partners, stakeholders, and customers create sustainable value, and boost-up the practice of taking collective decisions and adapting to bottom-up organizational strategies in developing new innovations and managing strategies (Kleiner, 2003). Business environment today is hierarchically arrayed within industry with transitional multimodal business systems across large firms. Large firms within industries (such as pharmaceuticals) develop business consortiums and focus on collaborative strategizing, and expanding the key partners geographically. The changing business ecosystems today drive greater flexibility in strategic partnership by allowing firms to develop collaborations contextual to the collective intelligence, social values, and benefit spread across the stakeholders (Reeves et al., 2015). Such shift in the business philosophy has encouraged the role of collective intelligence in building customer-centric strategies and co-creating customer-centric innovations to develop stand-alone posture in the competitive marketplace. The growth of virtual commerce (electronic and mobile commerce) has emerged as the most popular outgrowth of marketing-with-customer philosophy.

It is observed that if individualism–collectivism in business is adequately balanced, they serve as a good source of intercultural fit while building shared leadership to protect mutual values. Such managerial perspectives help firms in reconfiguring individual and cultural orientations and styles of persons of different origin in the design of management teams to build high levels of social effectiveness in the work environment (Carlos, 2005). However, managing the cross-cultural challenges in the workplace may be made easy by developing a strategic fit of values in the organization with flexibility in individual values and shared personality traits. In the low-trust cultures, the interpersonal relationship remains obscure and business dealings are largely bureaucratized and tagged with evidences. Such negotiation approaches slow down the process of getting the work done and may cause retrenchment from the business scenario over time. Thus, it is necessary to identify the right and responsive people, who can be relied upon and who qualify on organizational parameters, to build a future relationship continuum.

References

Anderson, E. T., & Simester, D. (2011). A step-by-step guide to smart business experiments. *Harvard Business Review, 89*(3), 124–132.

Arena, M., Azzone, G., & Piantoni, G. (2020). Shared value creation during site decommissioning: A case study from the energy sector. *Journal of Cleaner Production, 251*, (in press) https://doi.org/10.1016/j.jclepro.2019.119587.
Bason, C., & Austin, R. D. (2019). *The right way to lead design thinking*. Harvard Business School Press.
Boghin, J. (2014). *Three ways companies can make co-creation payoff*. McKinsey & Company.
Brandt, P. A. (2005). Mental spaces and cognitive semantics: A critical comment. *Journal of Pragmatics, 37*(10), 1578–1594.
Brown, T. (2008). Design thinking. *Harvard Business Review, 86*(6), 84–92.
Cajaiba-Santana, G. (2014). Social innovation: Moving the field forward. A conceptual framework. *Technological Forecasting and Social Change, 82*(1), 42–51.
Carlos, M. R. (2005). Emergence of a third culture—Shared leadership in international strategic alliance. *International Marketing Review, 22*(1), 67–95.
Coyne, K. P., Clifford, P. G., & Dye, R. (2007). Breakthrough thinking from inside the box. *Harvard Business Review, 85*(12), 70–83.
Desai, D. (2008). Role and relationship management and value co-creation in social marketing. *Social Marketing Quarterly, 15*(4), 112–125.
Epp, D. A. (2017). Public policy and the wisdom of crowds. *Cognitive Systems Research, 43*(1), 53–61.
Hsu, C. C., Wang, T. I., Lin, K. J., & Chang, J. W. (2018). The effects of the alternate writing and sketching brainstorming method on the creativity of undergraduate industrial design students in Taiwan. *Thinking Skills and Creativity, 29*(19), 131–141.
Füller, J. (2010). Refining virtual co-creation from a consumer perspective. *California Management Review, 52*(2), 98–122.
Ge, J., Xu, H., & Pellegrini, M. M. (2019). The effect of value co-creation on social enterprise growth: Moderating mechanism of environment dynamics. *Sustainability, 11*(250), 1–20.
Govindarajan, V., & Gupta, A. K. (2001). Building an effective global business team. *MIT Sloan Management Review, 42*(4), 63–71.
Joan, B., & Joaquim, V. (2015). An innovation management system to create growth in mature industrial technology firms. *International Journal of Innovation Science, 4*(4), 263–280.
Kleiner, A. (2003). Are you in with the in crowd? *Harvard Business Review, 81*(7), 86–92.
Kolko, J. (2015). Design thinking comes of age. *Harvard Business Review, 93*(9), 66–71.
Kotilainen, K., Saari, U. A., Mäkinen, S. J., & Ringle, C. M. (2019). Exploring the microfoundations of end-user interests toward co-creating renewable energy technology innovations. *Journal of Cleaner Production, 229*, 203–212.

Kupp, M., Anderson, J., & Reckhenrich, J. (2017). Why design thinking in business needs a rethink. *MIT Sloan Management Review, 59*(1), 42–44.

Lin, F. J., & Jin, Y. H. (2016). The effect of network relationship on the performance of SMEs. *Journal of Business Research, 69*, 1780–1784.

Liu, G., & Rong, K. (2015). The nature of the co-evolutionary process: Complex product development in the mobile computing industry's business ecosystem. *Group & Organization Management, 40*(6), 809–842.

Liu, S., Xiao, W., Fang, C., Zhang, X., & Lin, J. (2020). Social support, belongingness, and value co-creation behaviors in online health communities. *Telematics and Informatics, 50*, (in press) https://doi.org/10.1016/j.tele.2020.101398.

Miller, A., & Dumford, A. (2014). Creative cognitive processes in higher education. *Journal of Creative Behavior, 50*(4), 282–293.

Nakata, C. (2020). Design thinking for innovation: Considering distinctions, fit, and use in firms. *Business Horizons, 63*(6), 763–772.

Pansari, A., & Kumar, V. (2017). Customer engagement: The construct, antecedents, and consequences. *Journal of Academy of Marketing Science, 45*(3), 294–311.

Paulus, P. B., & Brown, V. R. (2003). Enhancing ideational creativity in groups: Lessons from research on brainstorming. In P. B. Paulus & B. A. Nijstad (Eds.), *Group creativity: Innovation through collaboration* (pp. 110–136). Oxford University Press.

Prewitt, E. (August, 1998). Fast cycle decision making. *Harvard Business Publishing Newsletter*. 1–2

Rajagopal. (2006). Innovation and business growth through corporate venturing in Latin America: Analysis of strategic fit. *Management Decision, 44*(5), 703–718.

Rajagopal. (2019). *Contemporary marketing strategy: Analyzing consumer behavior to drive managerial decision making*. Palgrave Macmillan.

Rajagopal. (2020). *Transgenerational marketing: Evolution, expansion, and experience*. New York: Palgrave Macmillan.

Rajagopal. (2021a). *Sustainable businesses in developing economies—Socio-economic and governance perspectives*. Palgrave Macmillan.

Rajagopal. (2021b). *The design cube: Converging markets, society, and customer values to grow competitive in business*. Business Expert Press.

Reeves, M., Haanaes, K., & Sinha, J. (2015). Navigating the dozens of different strategy options. *Harvard Business Review, 93*(6), 1–17.

Roma, P., Panniello, U., & Nigro, G. L. (2019). Sharing economy and incumbents' pricing strategy: The impact of Airbnb on the hospitality industry. *International Journal of Production Economics, 214*, 17–29.

Sanford, A. J. (2006). Semantics in psychology. In K. Brown (Ed.), *Encyclopedia of language & linguistics* (2nd ed., pp. 152–158). Elsevier.

Soman, D., Kumar, V., Metcalfe, M., & Wong, J. (2012). *Beyond great ideas: A framework for scaling local innovations*. Rotman School of Management, 50–55.

Surowiecki, J. (2004). *The wisdom of crowds: Why the many are smarter than the few and how collective wisdom shapes business, economies, societies and nations*. Anchor Books.

Tallman, S., & Fladmoe-Lindquist, K. (2002). Internationalization, globalization, and capability-based strategy. *California Management Review, 45*(1), 116–135.

Walsh, P., & Wood, J. (1992). A new rule for assessing ideas from brainstorming. *Total Quality Management, 3*(1), 47–54.

Yoo, J., & Park, M. (2016). The effects of e-mass customization on consumer perceived value, satisfaction, and loyalty toward luxury brands. *Journal of Business Research, 69*(12), 5775–5784.

CHAPTER 6

Technology and 'Generation Next' Business

Information technology is increasingly changing, which is providing more options in business modeling and the implication of strategies involving stakeholders and market players. Crowdsourcing is emerging as a customer-centric tool through which firms develop and commercialize innovation. In view of the attributes of collective intelligence, this chapter discusses the critical role of social media and the digital interactions in collective business modeling using various technology platforms. This chapter discusses critically the role of social media in developing crowd-based business projects by explaining the transitions of crowd-based information to drive corporate decisions. Effects of emotions and personality of customers and investors in the crowd-based businesses are also discussed in this chapter. The discussions in this chapter also focus on the crowd-based innovation approaches in the context of transferability of innovations, ambidexterity, and commercialization of frugal innovations. Discussions on organizational design and digital transformation are also central to this chapter.

Consumer behavior is continuously and rapidly evolving with the advancement of information technology. The technology-driven marketing strategies have not only offered convenience-led buying resources but also provided a wide array of products and services, which encourage variety seeking tendency of consumers on digital platforms. The growth of Internet-based social media in the twenty-first century

Rajagopal, *Crowd-Based Business Models*,
https://doi.org/10.1007/978-3-030-77083-9_6

has made it possible for one person to communicate with unlimited friends and peers about products and consumer experiences. Most companies also get connected to social media platforms on the Internet and offer opportunities to share consumer experiences. The second generation of Internet-based applications enhanced customer interactivity on digital networks and crowd-based marketing efforts pushed firms to implement innovative forms of communication that could co-create influential user-generated content. Such efforts of firms have promoted psychodynamics among customers, which has not only increased the demand for innovative products, but has also helped firms in reducing the cost of marketing. Consequently, most firms like Coca-Cola, Pepsi, and Lays could create crowd motion in marketing for their products by lowering the expenditure on advertisements in print media and televisions, reducing promotions, and narrowing down the in-store customer entertainment expenses. Such crowd-based practices resulted in a significant profit contribution of the company.

6.1 Social Media and Crowd-Based Business Projects

The successful impact of crowd behavior in promoting products and services through effective psychodynamic approaches like electronic word-of-mouth, digital community meets, and webinars has induced the emerging firms to adopt a digital presence in social media platforms. The digital marketing engagement firms can be categorized according to perceived benefits and digital marketing usage. The rule of thumb for crowd-based businesses (and other private businesses also) is that the involvement of a firm on social media is directly proportion to the customer engagement on digital networks. In other words, if most customers engage with social media, firms should engage with social media as well. Most customer-centric companies like IKEA, Nike, Apple, and Kellogg's have developed market-synchronized, relationship-based interactions with their customers (Borges-Tiago & Cristóvão-Veríssimo, 2014). Accordingly, the impact of consumer-to-consumer communications is magnified manifold in the marketplace through their participation on social media. Social media is a hybrid element of the promotion mix because, in a traditional sense, it enables companies to interact with their customers, while in a nontraditional sense it enables customers to interact directly among the peers. Firms use digital platforms significantly to boost their business, post marketing messages through page views, and advertise on the Internet channels to enhance their outreach in a short time. Such push strategies on social media serve as an advertising tool that could share net-surfer behavior. However, it is difficult for the companies to precisely target the communications to a specific audience, as this kind of marketing strategy is too broad to effectively target connectors, referrals, and salespeople. Most crowd-based firms tend to develop long-term digital relationships using value-driven promotional strategies that emphasize co-creation and grow in user experiences and user-generated contents. To this end, electronic word-of-mouth communication appears to be a trendy, convenient, and cost-effective solution (Whitla, 2009). The content, timing, and frequency of the social media-based conversations occurring between consumers are often beyond the control of a firm, as the communication process takes its independent interactive path in the social media. This stands in contrast to the traditional integrated marketing communications paradigm whereby a high degree of control is present. Therefore, firms must learn to shape consumer discussions in a manner that is consistent with the organization's mission and performance goals. Methods, by which this can be accomplished, include providing consumers with networking platforms, and using blogs, social media tools, and promotional tools to engage customers (Mangold & Faulds, 2009).

Most companies have driven lots of friends and followers on social platforms such as Facebook, and few have succeeded in generating profits there. That is because they merely deploy their digital strategies into social environments by broadcasting their commercial messages or seeking customer feedback. However, firms need to develop social strategies that are consistent with consumers' expectations and behavior as over a period, people want to connect with other people but not with companies. Interactivity among customers and stakeholder in crowd-based projects stimulates informal and meaningful conversations which enable the ideation process between customers and firms, involving customers in content generation and value creation. The continuity of dialogues on the crowd platforms helps in building long-term relational exchanges. With an increasing usage of the Internet, the social media has changed the word-of-mouth landscape in developing nations, transforming the target from one or a few friends to the community and the entire world (Duan et al., 2008). The successful social strategies reduce search costs or increase customers' willingness to get associated with the company and its brands through the various social media platforms. With the success of integrated social networks with the customer relations policies at Zynga (online Poker and games web-platform), eBay, American Express, and Yelp, it has been observed that social strategies can generate profits by helping people connect in exchange for tasks that benefit the company such as customer acquisition, marketing, and content creation. A systematic way to build a social strategy and process path, to know how a major credit card company banked on social networks to build customer relations and brand value of its products, is to use the proactive consumer communication within the peers (Piskorski, 2011).

With growing social media consciousness among consumers and stakeholders, most consumer-centric companies, irrespective of whether they have crowdfunding, tend to invest increasingly on brand communication using the social media channels. Consequently, firms allocate enormous budgets to establish their new and flagship brands and maintain a social media presence. Firms have discovered many interactive ways on social media, which not only motivate crowd movements on customer preferences, but also generate user-generated contents. New experiments on crowd-based brand communications on prominent channels like Facebook and Instagram rapidly affect customers' behavior. The 'likes' on a brand drive customers to discretely follow it and allure people more likely to purchase it. The number of 'likes' not only affect family and friends but also drive the community at large to lean toward making buying decision. Interactions on the social media inculcate crowd cognition, collective intelligence, and conscious consumption behavior in the long run among users of social media channels, while the 'like' and 'follow' options affect their short-run purchasing. For example, social media may persuade people to engage in social health and well-being behaviors in the long run. However, the 'likes' need to be checked for manipulations and unethical disruptions to influence people adversely (John et al., 2017).

As the competition is increasing in the global marketplace, most firms are reorienting their marketing communication strategies through customer-to-customer networking, as the customer-driven communication is found to be more trustworthy and decisive. Consequently, consumers are adopting increasingly active roles in co-creating marketing communication with companies and their respective brands. Most of the emerging firms are working hard in developing online social marketing programs and brand campaigns to reach consumers where they 'live' virtually. However, the challenge faced by many companies is apparently the way to be active in social media, as most firms do not have clear understanding of how to manage the social networks effectively and what performance indicators they should be measuring, and how they should measure them. Further, as companies develop social media strategies, platforms such as YouTube, Facebook, and Twitter are too often treated as stand-alone elements rather than part of an integrated system. Firms should invest in building strategies in a systematic way to understand and conceptualize online social media as an ecosystem of related elements involving both digital and traditional media (Hanna et al., 2011). As re-communication in social networks like Facebook and Twitter is becoming common, many companies take advantage of such grapevine communication trend. Recent research identifies the factors that increase the likelihood of retweeting of communication, so that a firm's tweets will be shared with social networks among peers. Retweeting is desirable both because the original tweet reaches more people and a retweet is essentially an endorsement from recipients to their followers. Opening a communication with an attention-grabbing headline is important to post the communications on social networks. Socializing the brand may drive enormous scope for retweeting, as peers can use and act on the message, and save time and money on information search. The best practice of all communication strategies is when organizations combine several of these practices to get the most out of their marketing messages (Malhotra et al., 2012).

In the initial digital drive, most firms assumed that Facebook, YouTube, and Twitter would let them bypass mainstream media and connect directly with customers. However, as the above media channels became popular for social interactions and grew manifold with the membership, they pulled businesses to use these channels to communicate with customers and stakeholders. Over time, these social media channels turned to be the hubs for crowdsourcing, opinion building, and co-creating innovations. Firms with the goals to attract huge customers to their brands, made high investment on advertisements developed with their own creative content but the response of customers has been less than estimated. In fact, social media seems to have made such brands less significant. The social channels stimulated crowd-cultures and promoted the alternative approach of cultural branding (Holt, 2016). The attributes of diffusion of crowd-based information and its adaptation to the business ecosystem are exhibited in Fig. 6.1.

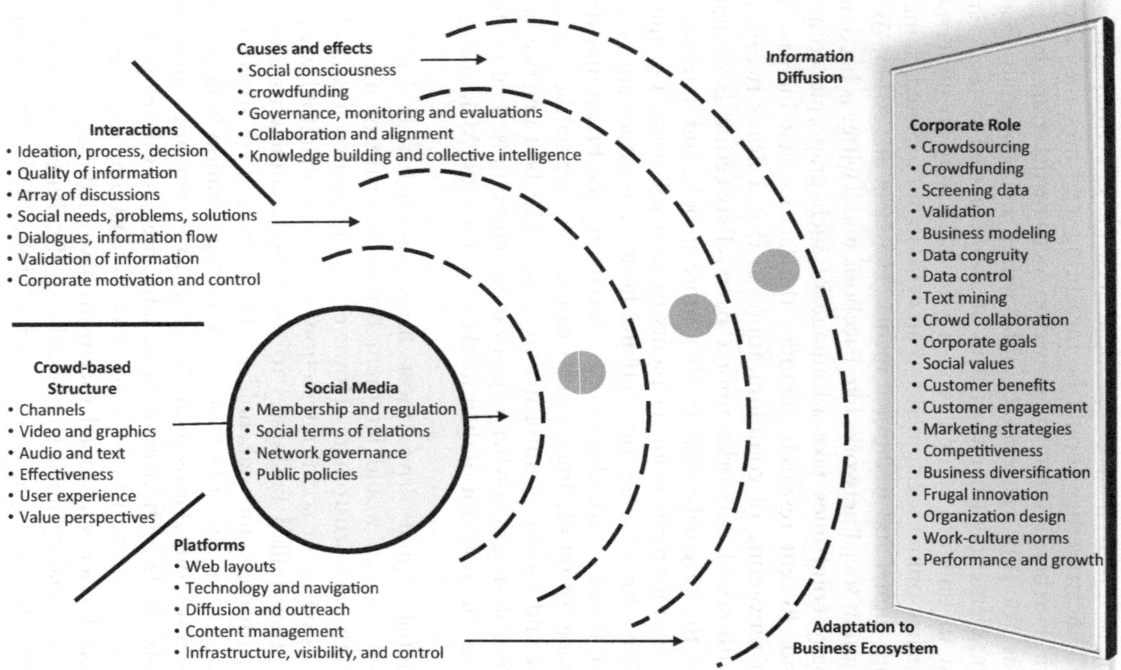

Fig. 6.1 Crowd-based information path to corporate decisions (*Source* Author)

Social media has bidimensional attributes of being informative and vulnerable to controversies as well. Therefore, businesses working with the social media need to ensure the membership terms and regulations on communications. Figure 6.1 illustrates that firms participating in social media must ensure the relationship contracts between the member of social media channels and their role in the business administration of a firm. However, safe public policies on social media make it more business friendly than merely being a platform for social interactions. The crowd-based media structure operates through videos and graphics as a powerful resource to acquire customers and reinforce confidence among the existing customer on brands and reputation of firms. The effectiveness of the social media channels is built through the user experience and customer value perceptions on dialogue space and quality of interactions. The channel excellence is experienced in the dissemination of ideas, debate on social and business processes, and guiding pro-customer and pro-society decisions to the crowd-based or crowd-leaning companies. Some corporate social media channels on public platforms like Facebook and Instagram (e.g., IKEA, Hershey, and Nestlé), systematically organize the information by arraying topical discussions, future perspectives, and critical reviews of customers. Consequently, these firms motivate discussions, take control of information inflow, control influx, and validate the user-generated contents. As exhibited in Fig. 6.1, most social media channels operative independently and backed by the business corporations have embedded causes which include broadly on generating social consciousness, prospecting business projects for crowdfunding, collaboration, or building collective intelligence on macro socio-economic perspectives.

Technology platforms for social media commonly include Facebook, Twitter, YouTube, instant messaging, video conferencing, and web meetings. These and many other techno-communication collaboration and social media platforms have now become the lifestyle of people around the world. Firms are continuously exploring their way to enterprise communications and management strategies using the above social media technology platforms. However, the efficiency of firms in using these social media applications and technologies poses a greater challenge and raises one of several questions as to how successful the companies are in navigating business changes through social media platforms. Though the efficiency of firms in using social media applications vary, many firms drive through multiple talents and organizational elements in driving business communication effectively across consumer and peer segments. In this process, firms work on creating a shared vision, gaining buy-in across locations and levels, and dealing with consumer expectations and streamlining consumer preferences in the day-to-day competition. Social networking and collaboration applications are extremely effective ways of converging the bidirectional flow of information among the firm, consumers, and market players (suppliers, service providers, retailers, etc.). The convergence of crowd communication helps firms in performing new processes together and to share experiences on the innovations, improvements, and the temporary setbacks.

Interactive marketing experience contributes to the collective intelligence to support crowd-based decisions in the emerging customer-centric companies. Online interactions have expanded the customer outreach and refined the value perceptions and co-creation perspectives in managing disruptions in business and competitive leverage for growing firms. The growth of interactions and dialogs between the firm, community, and the consumer through online social networks like MySpace.com and Facebook.com are just the prominent examples of these conversational platforms. Such interactions and dialogue exchanges help firms in penetrating business into the society by understanding the customer values and social needs to deliver the most appropriate solution. Firms embrace and listen to the customer-community dialogs to understand their views and suggestions to improve the business strategies. Most customer-centric companies like Kellogg's, Nestlé, and IKEA have customized their websites and installed digital device interfaces to learn customer views, needs, and proposed solutions. Most firms are opening up the opportunities to interact across multiple channels to stay customer-centric, crowd-focused, and competitive in the marketplace. The Internet, remote communication devices, large consumer databases, and advances in mobile information technology have introduced new forms of direct-to-consumer marketing approaches. However, as companies seek more outreach and customer accountability from their advertising, they rely on customer-generated contents and interactive means to develop communications customer friendly. Consequently, crowd-driven companies are investing rapidly on interactive marketing platforms. It is evident from crowdsourcing and crowdfunding practices in business that demand for interactive marketing is continuous seamless and sustainable (Shankar & Malthouse, 2007). There is a new computer-based experimental platform called dialogue marketing, which is, to date, the highest step on an evolutionary ladder that ascends from database marketing to relationship marketing to one-to-one marketing. The major advantages of dialogue marketing over conventional communication approaches are that it is completely interactive, and it runs on multi-communication channels. This platform continuously tracks every nuance of the customer's interaction with the business. Thus, dialogue marketing responds to each transition in that relationship at the moment the customer requires attention (Kalyanam & Zweben, 2005).

Firms may find effective ways in working with the social media applications to deliver personalized learning experiences to the consumers related to the brand equity, promotions, and comparative advantages. Firms should not use the social media just for general broadcasts of information. Business organizations should use social media linked innovative collaboration platforms in a variety of ways to encourage effective company–consumers–suppliers coordination in information sharing and knowledge building opportunities. Social media and collaboration solutions allow information to flow in multiple directions rather than only from the top-down. For example, using wikis and micro-blogs applications for sharing short bursts of information, marketing firms can crowd-source ideas and involve employees more directly in the innovative strategies. Firms can build greater internal loyalty by actively soliciting continuous feedback on issues related to the change. Social media is an important addition to a traditional change management program, one that can dramatically increase the acceptance of change and advance an organization more predictably toward its business goals. Collaboration and social media tools can reduce the time an organization needs to navigate large-scale change programs and deliver a better solution for consumer-related marketing issues in the future. The exponential growth of social media has been observed from the beginning of the twenty-first century with manifold channels booming around the world. Besides, independent and company-led blogs have also been able to attract stakeholder interactions and build categorical resources (society, technology, sustainability, innovation, green consumerism, and consumer electronics). The increasing contribution of collective intelligence also percolates from video informatics and journalism published on Facebook, Twitter, LinkedIn, Instagram, and YouTube, which offers firms to explore the user-generated contents in creating customer-centric communication and stay competitive. Both the extensive and intensive use of social media channels by the customers and stakeholders have trusted companies to use it as a tool for mass customization by motivating crowd-based design thinking for their own products in a democratic way manifesting the philosophy of 'by the people and for the people.' Consequently, the social media has nearly democratized most businesses by empowering people not only to gain stakeholder and customer confidence, but also to focus the company's business explicitly to the target customers (Hildebrand et al., 2013).

The advancement of information technology in global business has resulted into the prevalence of online communities to drive the virtual business of many firms. The online communities are connected through the social network platforms that allow consumers to exchange information about products or services virtually. The social network platforms are used by the consumers to compare prices among competitors. These platforms have also opened freeways to exhibit products online and share opinions or experiences on the products and services. Consequently, marketers have lost control over how and where their products are presented to potential customers. Social media has widened the opportunities for the consumer-oriented firms to expand their market beyond the brick-and-mortar stores. The consumer networks are used by most firms to supplement traditional sources of buyer insights with a wealth of information gathered by listening in to community sites such as Facebook, LinkedIn, and Twitter, as well as customer forums and product review services. Monitoring the information flow on social media gives firms unique access to unfiltered feedback from customers, which may not be possible to obtain through other means such as focus groups and surveys. Firms intending to experiment with monitoring the web can outsource the entire process to third parties, or build the capabilities internally. However, as the information technologies are evolving rapidly, firms need to carefully choose some of them to reach their consumers and avoid locking themselves into a solution that constrains their future capabilities (Rajagopal, 2020).

New insights of firms on marketing and sales to gain competitive advantage continue to use the consumer online support besides advertising of their products and services. The social networks also drive traffic to firms' retail websites. Firms can engage employees, customers, suppliers, and other third parties as active participants in the innovation process, expanding the range of ideas and gathering real-time feedback on their potential take-up. For example, Nokia operates an online lab that allows users around the world to download beta applications and provide feedback to its product development teams. This strategy provides an early opportunity to identify potential problems and alerts customer differences across geographic markets. Social media has embedded in the business culture and has drawn the attention of large as well as a small firms. More and more people are getting connected with their computers and mobile devices to build relationship with family and friends to post their opinions and engage in conversations. Social media is vital for managers to understand this phenomenon and to learn how to prepare their organizations to thrive when customers exercise more power and influence over businesses than ever before. Some companies have made major strides in leveraging social media to develop more effective growth strategies (Wollan et al., 2011).

Though, there exists a minor difference in marketing and sales; the collective intelligences play a significant role in motivating customers toward making buying decisions and supporting sales strategies. Most companies use social media to implement sales strategies; however, some succeed in putting the SMART (strategic, measurable, attractive, responsive, and timely) sales strategies on social media in a productive way by generating psychodynamics among customers. Previous research studies reveal that the social media has enormous potential to promote sales of innovation, social health, sustainable, disruptive consumer electronics, and organic products. It could boost short sales cycles and create quick opportunities through the e-commerce business calls. The social media tools are also valuable for maintaining relationships with post-sales customers and pursuing new sales projects (Giamanco & Gregoire, 2012).

The social media backed by the Internet has changed the style of communication among consumers, companies, and the associated market players. Social media websites are designed to carry verbal and nonverbal communication with stimulus contents to attract millions of users, many of whom integrate the sites into their daily lives and business practices. Thus, social media allow users to connect with peers, companies, and brands irrespective of individual familiarity by adding them to the networks of friends (Zhang & Daugherty, 2009). Social media websites provide a public forum that gives individual consumers the opportunity to present their observations, and access to product information that facilitates their purchase decisions. User-generated online reviews on products and services have proliferated among the peer consumers through social media that drives a great impact on marketing (Trusov et al., 2010). The word-of-mouth, which percolates down the neighborhood, not only increases guiding messages for the consumers, companies, and marketers toward converging better value chains, but also alters processing of consumer information in building customer-centric marketing strategies. In particular, peer communication through social media has emerged as a new form of consumer socialization which is driving the consumer decision-making and helping companies to develop value-added marketing strategies (Casteleyn et al., 2009).

Consumer socialization among peers is driven by the dynamism of the social media, which encourages market-based interactions among the peers. The blogs, instant messaging, and social networking sites all provide communication tools that make the socialization process easy and convenient. The virtual communities easily socialize new incumbents into common and special interest groups and help them quickly learn task-related knowledge and skills through their interactions with other members. Beside quick inductions of members in the virtual groups, the inflow of consumers to social media websites is increasing and helping them communicate with others and find information to help them make various consumption-related decisions. The grapevine effect of the social media also facilitates education and information analysis among the members as the socialization agents within the informal groups provide vast product information and evaluations quickly (Taylor et al., 2011). Some studies reveal that peer communications influence consumers to such an extent that they convert others into virtual shoppers, while some retailers also encourage social media communication by setting up tell-a-friend functions on websites.

6.2 Consumer Emotions and Personality

Crowd interactions on social media channels have become the major source of cognitive manifestation among customers and stakeholders. Customer interactions on the crowd platforms manifest emotions to streamline their possible association with the businesses and brands. As most customer-centric firms connect with the social media to stimulate crowd and build customers' emotions, they intend to reap huge benefit in the long run. Among many types of leverages emerging out of the customer emotions include the contribution of user-generated contents, brand endorsements, loyalty, and volunteering in the co-creation process.

The combination of crowd engagement through the social media channels derives huge payoff over time, which helps firms in building market competitiveness and augmenting business performance. Yet building customer connections on social media to stimulate emotions and loyalty is often a conjecture and an art than science. Firms encourage referrals and gatekeepers including bloggers to reinforce confidence among customers and investors and benefit from such motivators to maximize their competitive advantage and business performance. In order to initiate the crowd interactions and induce customer motivations, firms need to conduct research to analyze the behavioral dimensions of consumers and provide liberal space for their expressions and security on public identity. In addition, firms need to motivate high-value groups so that values and motivations can percolate down to the bottom of the pyramid customer segment. Firms also need to ensure commitment to protect emotional connection of customers with the firm and brands for continuous growth with customers in the competitive marketplace (Magids et al., 2015).

Consumer emotions are largely set through verbal and nonverbal market communications extended by the companies. Advertisements play a critical role in stimulating the consumer emotions. Since the late twentieth century, as the usage of computers has rapidly grown, the Internet has been the prime anchor of the marketing communications and stimulant of consumer emotions. The increased participation of people on the social network platforms has brought the emotions associated with the products, services, and companies very close to the market players. Compared to offline media communications, social network platforms possess unique characteristics that affect the likelihood of generating emotions and reactions to the experience of the brand among fellow customers and employees of the firm. The emotions online are largely driven by the vividness of social networks, interactivity, challenge, interaction speed, machine memory, and allowable social interactions. Depending on how a social network platform performs on these dimensions, positive or negative emotions on the products, services, or on the image of the company may emerge. For example, using machine memory to automatically generate purchase recommendations based on prior consumption patterns may be perceived as pleasantly surprising, while a firm sending unsolicited emails based on a user's cookie trail may be annoying. Such feelings are generated and shared by the consumers get attached to the brand and build its equity in the market. Thus, the challenge of brand managers is to get consumers to develop positive emotions with a brand, and to manage company sponsors' social network websites by understanding the consumer emotions and their ramifications (Jones et al., 2008).

Driving consumer arousal and merriment as a major influencing factor in making buying decision is a recent strategy and an innovative concern of retailers, as these factors reveal personalized enjoyment during shopping. Arousal during shopping may be seeded through multifaceted activity that may be performed in various ways and embodies different consumer feelings. However, firms at times fail to recognize that what influences buyers' satisfaction is not the same as what engenders store loyalty, and consequently does not effectively develop the retail ambiance to stimulate buying decisions. Hence, they need to vigilantly manage the quality of arousal by developing adequate customer involvement in the buying process and retain young consumers (Miranda et al., 2005). The three distinct dimensions of emotions including pleasantness, arousal, and dominance have been identified as major drivers for making buying decisions among adolescent consumers. The retail point of purchase is the time and place at which all the elements of a sale—the consumer, the money, and the product—converge. Marketers must make the most of the communications possibilities at this point to increase their sales (Rajagopal, 2006). There are some common strategies adopted by retailers to overcome the problems of fickle consumers, price-slashing competitors, and mood swings in the economy. Such wishful thinking holds that retailers will thrive only if they communicate better with young consumers through in-store amusement, recreation, and collaborative product demonstrations involving consumers, to help their purchase decisions. Most customer-centric firms also offer buying incentives to develop conviction on buying such tried-out products (Berry, 2001).

Crowd platforms are commonly considered as good tools to drive individual and community emotions through brainstorming, sustained interpersonal relations, and bargains on common interests. However, moderating the crowd interactions to generate focused discussions and streamlined outcomes has been a growing challenge for most emerging and large-size companies. Often crowd interactions lean toward vested interests of the participants and community-driven problems, as participants in brainstorming sessions are thrilled and animated with the semantics of thoughts. Consequently, crowd discussions are influenced by various extrinsic factors like web layout of digital platforms and intrinsic factors such as cognitive ergonomics of the participants. Often, mob emotions like anger, happiness, fear, disgust, and trust influence the outcomes of crowd discussions and affect the collective intelligence. Firms, engaging customers on crowd platforms for brainstorming and collective decisions, need to moderate the abrupt rise and fall of the following emotions among the participants (Brooks, 2015):

- Pacifying the growing *anxiety* among consumers and stakeholders about the product, services, technology, company, or the products and services to be debated upon within the crowd community. Anxiety reduces the quality of information contributes and affects the precision in negotiation.
- *Anger* creates cognitive imbalances and causes behavioral irrationality. Sometimes anger intimidates participants and firms and helps in bargaining a better deal, but most often, particularly while involving in long-term relationships, it damages trust and goodwill and creates an impasse.
- *Disappointment* among the participants in delivering the crowd information needs to be channeled to reach a more satisfactory outcome by fixing technical flaws and navigating problems on the crowd platforms.
- *Excitement* is a good sign of participation but often it makes the participants to overoptimistic and unrealistic while debating the specific topics like price and promotion. However, if feelings of excitement, like other emotions, are well managed, may lead to a win–win feeling.

Consumers are increasingly using the Internet to search for the products and services, evaluate competitive advantages, and make purchases. Online consumer decision processes have many cognitive drivers that set emotions of consumers. Hence, websites must not just be created, but must be carefully managed, and should offer live experiences involving customers. Significantly, emotions can be attached to the products and services and inculcate perceptions, attitudes, and behavior among consumers (Lindgaard et al., 2006). Consumer satisfaction with the decision-making process leading to the expected level of satisfaction is measured by the firms, which may be expressed as one of a number of cognitive and affective responses that may result from a clearance sale. The retail sales performance and the customer value approach are conceptually and methodically analogous. Satisfaction is the customer's perception of the value received in a transaction or relationship and it helps in making re-patronage decisions on the basis of their predictions concerning the value of a future product. Hence, many retailers develop innovative approaches to prospect new customers for new products by strengthening customer relationship and value management strategies (Ganesh, et al., 2000).

On crowd platforms, customers' assessments on quality, pricing, value for money, buying decisions, and general community recommendations are influenced by emotions. However, customer emotions rely more on user experiences than community referrals. Such cognitive attributes are especially true for high-emotion services such as insurance businesses, sustainable consumer products, public transport, and hospital services-based organizations. Firms need to manage the emotions of customers by identifying right emotional clues, early response to emotions, and supporting customer loyalty attitude (Berry et al., 2015). A company may also need to consider emphasizing an integrated promotion strategy for new brands in reference to attributes, awareness, trial, availability, and repeat (AATAR) principle. One of the challenges for the manager of a retail store is to enhance the in-store ambiance to influence the young consumers for prolonged stay in the store for shopping and explore the zone of experience of new products. An augmented and sustainable customer value builds loyalty toward the product and the brand. Systematically explored customer preferences and arousal-driven retailing approach toward new products would be beneficial for a company to derive long-term profit optimization strategy over the period. This needs careful attention and the application of managerial judgment and experience to generate consumer arousal and develop appropriate point-of-sales strategies for stimulating the buying decision. Appropriate promotional strategies considering the economic and relational variables discussed in the study may be developed by the managers upon measuring the intensity of leisure shopping and the scope of expanding the tenure of leisure shopping in view of maximizing consumer satisfaction and increasing the volume of sales. On a tactical level, managers need to consider the optimum spread of consumers on a matrix of product attractiveness and sales. This needs careful attention and application of managerial judgment and experience to measure the customer value-driven performance (Rajagopal, 2019).

6.3 Crowd-Based Innovations

Digital advances have encouraged crowd-based ideation process to enable customer-centric innovations in the first two decades of the twenty-first century. Crowdsourcing approach has enabled more people than ever before to express their experience, values, and ideas to contribute to creative intelligence. The growing social media mobile applications have also contributed in encouraging crowd ideas and powered transformation of ideas to a well-defined innovation process in large firms. The breakthrough ideas emerging from brainstorming at the crowd platforms are focused on new and amateur innovation concepts, social perspectives, radical and nonconventional ideas, and hybrid combinations to gain potential leverage in the competitive markets (Bouquet et al., 2018). Innovations have bidirectional dynamics. They evolve ambidextrously in global and local marketplaces. Multinational companies are exploring a combination of frugal and reverse innovations managed by the small and medium enterprises to elevate its demand in the global marketplace, while most local firms or SMEs are engaged in working with cost-effective incremental innovations. The innovations developed in local markets are based on consumer needs and marketed within niche at an affordable price to the consumers. These enterprises do not adapt to 'design-to-market' innovation approach. However, innovations with the utilitarian values tend to drive high demand in local markets as they match with the socio-cultural and ethnic values.

6.3.1 Innovation and Transferability

In small and medium enterprises, innovative ideas are largely triggered by the owner–managers. Some enterprises also involve consumers and stakeholders in co-creating innovations. Frugal innovations are an increasingly important source of competitive advantage in the local and regional markets. Growing SMEs in emerging markets also develop similar innovations that have been successful in the overseas markets. The owner–managers of small companies translate new ideas into action in their organizations as *Idea-practitioners* who keep scouting for ideas continuously. Once the local companies, which hold promise, identify the frugal ideas, they are tailored to fit into the specific needs of consumers. Small companies actively build selling ideas for comprehensive innovations, and make efforts to either develop alliance with large companies to incubate or negotiate to transfer the ownership rights (Majchrzak & Shepherd, 2021). Finally, SMEs get the ball rolling by participating in small-scale experiments (Davenport et al., 2003). There are variety of innovations driven by the firms in global marketplace. Innovations are not limited to consumer-centric or market-oriented products and services.

Social innovation and social entrepreneurship are widely supported by the crowd ideation, crowd funding, and social governance. Most firms doing business in green innovation products and services tend to rely on crowd resources to go customer-centric and build crowd-based business models. Whenever a need emerges to find solutions for social products or consumer goods, the crowd ideation triggers quickly to brainstorm on the problem and develop products or services concepts. Crowd-based technologies involve investors as a first step to develop and implement the innovation project. Such technology-based innovations help to build user community, mobilize crowd resources including funding and social infrastructure for initial start of the project. The crowd-based business projects magnify entrepreneurial responsiveness and facilitate collective learning. Social or customer contingencies often trigger compassion venturing stimulated by the crowd movement demanding quick resolution to the problem. Such crowd drive helps entrepreneurs in creating and running a new business venture, for example, developing the low-cost water filters to provide clean potable water after natural calamities. The idea of treated rice husk ash as a novel biosorption process for developing a low-cost water filter has been tested in the social communities with a prototype, and later commercialized by Tata Chemicals in India. Incremental innovation is a common phenomenon in all types of consumer products ranging from toothpaste to an automobile. It is a process of continuous innovation over the existing products. Most firms prefer to engage in a series of small improvements to an existing product or product line that usually helps in maintaining or improving their competitive position over time in the industry or against rivals. Companies that need to continue to improve their products to include new features increasingly desired by consumers regularly use incremental innovation within the high technology business. However, radical innovation is about making major changes in the existing products moving few stages ahead of the routine incremental innovation. A radical change can represent a radical innovation at a technological level, but the impact may show an incremental trend from an organizational perspective. The term radical often refers to the level of contribution made to the efficiency or revenue of the organization (McLaughlin et al., 2008).

Most micro, small and medium enterprises largely depend on the crowdsourced ideas to develop frugal innovations through crowd-funded business model to penetrate niche markets and later move to the wider competitive markets. The frugal innovations are defined as low-cost differentiators toward simplifying product attributes by optimizing its functions, components, and processes while maximizing its perceived use values. As consumers today have to live with complex products such as automobiles and smartphones, the frugal innovations do provide competitive leverage to them in view of its value for money. Consequently, the concept of frugal innovations emphasizes a relatively complex but less expensive product to cater to the unserved low-end of the mass market and bottom of the pyramid segments (Lim & Fujimoto, 2019). Innovative products tend to fail in the market not only due to technical inadequacies, but also because of lack of enough groundwork in market. These products are launched in the market with point-of-sales information, which fails to attract consumers, as the company generates no awareness prior to the display of products. Small firms should consider managing 4As comprising awareness, attributes, affordability, and adaptability determinants before launching the innovative products. Innovative products perform better in the market, provided the companies generate enough awareness on the attributes of products and their adaptability from the utilitarian or hedonic perspectives. In order to achieve a quick acceptance of innovative products, successful companies generate timely and reliable knowledge on products by understanding customer preferences and requirements. This is the single most important area of information, which serves as mainstay information necessary for developing and launching new products.

6.3.2 *Innovations and Ambidexterity*

Ambidextrous innovations are of various types ranging from the low-cost to disruptive innovative products focused in either lower or upper niche markets. It is developed with the ability of an organization to both explore the customer- and community needs and exploit the existing market with need-based solutions. However, in order to compete with mature technologies and markets, ambidextrous innovations need an adequate brand support that ensures efficiency, value determination, and incremental improvement. Such ambidextrous innovation strategies are co-created and coevolved on crowd platforms, and attain market competitiveness through the collective intelligence inputs. These innovations are socially rewarded and crowd-supported to compete in new technologies and markets that have business agility, organizational autonomy, and liberal crowd-based experimentation and experience sharing possibilities (O'Reilly & Tushman, 2013).

Ambidextrous innovation is a valuable addition to the incremental innovation that refers to dexterity of an organization to be efficient in its management and adaptable to THE shifts in market behavior. The recent global economic recession (2007–2011) has driven most firms including large multinational companies toward concentrating on small improvements in the product line instead of investing resources in new product developments of working with innovation afresh. irrespective of their size, firms, must be capable of managing different innovation streams to be successful in the global marketplace. The incremental innovations help firms to leverage their posture in the marketplace, while the architectural innovations reconfigure firms' technology in reference to future business growth in the marketplace (Gary, 2003). As the market competition is increasing manifold in the domestic and international markets, firms need to build abilities to explore the changing consumer preferences and the potential and dormant markets to ensure long-term survival and prosperity. However, in this process, firms often face difficulties to accommodate the unforeseen business factors including cost, time, and risk. To achieve dynamic ambidexterity, firms need to develop marketing designs for both premier and mass-market consumer segments. The notion of dynamic ambidexterity and its managerial practices can help firms in exploring new consumer segments and ensure long-term survival and prosperity of innovative products (Chen, 2017). A firm that simultaneously engages in innovation and efficiency follows ambidextrous strategy. However, few firms are able to balance their business operations on these two parallel platforms. Small and medium firms often face challenges in developing marketing efficiency on the innovative products and services due to internal resources limitations. However, pursuing ambidextrous strategy to push innovative products may be risk averse to small companies. Despite the risk, firms push innovative products in competitive markets through this dual approach for longer-term success (Sarkees & Hulland, 2008).

Dynamic capabilities of crowd-based businesses have been evidenced over time through the effective crowdsourced ideas to develop value-driven affordable innovations using the long lifecycle technology and markets. The collective intelligence has driven firms, which are able to generate dynamic capabilities and competence to manage the innovative products in competitive markets, to stay in close proximity of customers and stakeholders, and take competitive decisions. However, the convergence of dynamic capabilities and ambidexterity is a complex discipline of organizational management, which has not yet been able to derive specific mechanisms through the blend of crowd cognition, decision-making, operations management, and adaptation to changing technology (O'Reilly & Tushman, 2011). Process innovation signifies the implementation of a new or improved production, or product or service delivery method. Process innovation may drive an increase in production or service capabilities through the addition of manufacturing or logistical systems, ceasing to use a low-cost economic process. Firms carry out process innovations to improve a conventional production or services process, which may result into changes in the factor prices, customization, regular seasonal and other production cycles, and improve the revenue streams of the firm.

Stakeholders and customers are the foundation of small and medium firms that help innovations to grow in the competitive marketplace. These firms focus on building customer profiles and attempt to develop innovative products fitting to customer preferences. In order to develop purchase intention among consumers, firms tend to co-create products. Consumer communities exhibit powerful social and emotional dimensions that have the potential to push the business of small firms (Christensen et al., 2016). Innovative products are design-oriented and reveal the sense of aesthetics to consumers. Large companies create new trends in the society through aesthetic and ethnic products. The new products are developed imparting the principles of design collectively, which is a form of design thinking. Innovative products are evaluated through social interactions of consumers, which helps in learning and experimenting among innovations and technologies, and derive utilitarian or hedonic values. Though the focus of firms on improving the quality of existing services certainly marks difference in the competitive marketplace, firms should also make efforts on overcoming the gaps in innovation capabilities by delimiting new ideas. Multinational firms focus on improving service capabilities to address the fundamental needs of their customers and developing service innovations through shared solutions with customers. Firms with co-creation strategies are able to create effective breakthrough products and processes. Such process of service innovation results into value co-creation, which makes a significant difference to customers and competing services products in the marketplace (Bettencourt et al., 2013).

6.3.3 *Frugal Innovations*

Business model innovation is critical to the success of the competitive growth of the firm. The economic value of an innovation remains latent until it is commercialized in some way via a business model. Successful commercialization of an innovation leads to breakthrough in two different ways—in some instances an innovation can employ a business model, which is already familiar to the firm, while in others, a company can have a business model that can make use of the innovation by licensing to third parties. The business model in a competitively dynamic firm can be improved or a new model can be innovated in reference to the following considerations (*e.g.*, Chesbrough, 2010):

- Crowdsourcing the value proposition in reference to the value created for users through new technology, process, or services,
- Social or private governance of innovative products with significant public representation,
- Exploring and exploiting new markets for frugal innovation products,
- Identify dynamic capabilities to support continuity of revenue streams,
- Co-creating value chain structure to diffuse innovation concept through multichannel strategies,
- Diversifying sustainable revenue streams for low-cost social innovations through collective intelligence,
- Estimating the cost structure and profit potential on given value proposition and value chain,
- Building an effecting customer relationship and customer services management strategies,
- Building a posture of the firm within the value network linking suppliers and customers, and

- Developing market competitiveness through value-added benefits on frugal innovative products.

Sustainable innovation is an outstanding way of achieving both competitive advantage and differentiation. Sustainable innovations are not limited to technology-led innovations, but generate higher perceived use value and social accountability. Sustainable innovations are strategic and slow growing in the market but stay for long term in the market. The innovation is not necessarily a new product or product advancement, it also entails new ways to communicate products, operate in new market or consumer segments. Firms pursue sustainable innovations to demonstrate social responsiveness, and expect that the efforts will only add to their costs instead of delivering competitive advantages. However, sustainable innovations have a long-term yield in both top-line and bottom-line market returns. Hence, large multinational firms have begun to transform the competitive landscape by redesigning products, technologies, processes, and business models by moving through the following stages (Nidumolu et al., 2009):

- Exploring innovation opportunities,
- Making value chains sustainable,
- Designing sustainable products and services,
- Developing new business models, and
- Building next-practice platforms by co-creating with strategic alliances and consumers.

Frugal innovation is the process of reducing the complexity and cost of products by taking cost-effective measures in manufacturing and following economies of scale. Usually, this refers to removing conspicuous features from products such as an automobile in order to market it at bottom of the pyramid and emerging markets. Designing products for such markets may also call for an increase in sustainability of innovative products and selling through modern routes to market. However, profits earned on frugal innovations are much lower than high value-high technology innovative products targeted to up-front or premier markets.

Commercializing new ideas and turning them into innovative products is one of the many challenges faced by small and medium enterprises. Commercializing crowdsourced ideas and realizing profits from them are different for every company. Small firms may excel at finding good ideas but have weak design-to-market and operations systems for commercializing them in the competitive marketplace. However, complex organizational design and unclear decision-making process in ideation, resources management, manufacturing process, and marketing make the commercialization of innovative products less market competitive. Companies using the innovative approaches and tools without pilot testing and understanding their technology-specific innovation systems damage the market performance of such products and services. In managing any innovative products in the market, the innovation value chain needs to be carefully developed and implemented for consumers, market players, and stakeholders of the company. The value chain comprises the main phases of innovation which include idea generation, conversion, and diffusion. Besides determining the appropriate innovation management strategies, firms need to evaluate the consistency of the ideas and their anticipated perceived values among consumers. Therefore, selecting ideas, investing on them, and converting and marketing ideas are complex. Using the value for money framework, managers can evaluate an end user view of their innovation efforts before launching them in markets. Companies must attend to understand the weaknesses of innovative ideas and tailor them appropriately to reconstruct those links. Companies typically succumb to one of three broad 'weakest-link' scenarios comprising economically nonviable ideas, inefficient transformation of ideas into products or services, and low value for money perspectives. Many large companies like General Electrics (GE), Haier, and Unilever that bank on small ideas of bottom of the pyramid and transform effectively to high-value innovation such as portable electro-cardiogram machine (GE Mac400), and non-compressor cooling machine (Haier). These companies follow best innovation practices, and measure their economic value from the perspectives of consumers' needs and associated values of products (Hansen & Birkinshaw, 2007).

The theory of disruptive innovation has emerged in the market as a powerful tool for predicting the success of new business incumbents in an industry. Over time, such companies with the innovative market outlook gradually move upmarket to challenge the industry leaders. Disruption is a gradual process, which may gain near monopoly benefit for a short term as the competitors copy the innovative disruptions and parallel competition begins in due course in a market. In the emerging markets, Uber stayed as a disruptor in the beginning, but today it has become a competing service in many countries such as India (Ola *vs* Uber), Mexico (Didi *vs* Uber). The disruptive innovation leads incumbents to ignore significant threats and blindly accepting the disruptive power of a company. It is hard for the existing companies to do core business as they try to defend against disruptive competitors (Christensen et al., 2015). A disruptive innovation creates a new market and value network for the close substitutes, and eventually disrupts an existing market and value network of established commercial brands displacing the current technology. Disruptive innovation-led products are typically positioned in the market for a relatively lower consumer segment by designing quality products at lower prices with high-perceived value for consumers in the existing market (Christensen & Overdorf, 2000). Disruptive innovation is linked to reverse innovation that drives the firms back to the consumers' buying behavior in reference to 4As paradigm comprising awareness, acceptability, adaptability, and affordability. Reverse innovation refers to developing ideas in an emerging market and persuading them in the existing markets, which drives tough challenges. Such innovation requires a company to overcome the institutionalized thinking that guides its actions and acquires ideas through the social media. Firms following reverse innovation develop a radically simpler and cheaper way of creating products in emerging markets and then position them in the desired consumer segments (Govindarajan, 2012).

6.4 Organizational Design and Innovation Performance

Companies in the twenty-first century are adapting to learn administrative processes by streamlining the employee engagement, reducing process time, and narrowing the decision complexities. Linear approaches used to derive the cause–effect relationship are generally focused on the gaps in the administrative process. However, performance improvement approaches such as lean thinking in the business organizations focus more on improving the production along with the streamlining administrative processes by reducing the cost and time frame (Belayutham et al., 2016). Developing systems thinking, and planned layout of business strategies by firms to enhance growth and competitiveness drive managerial symphony. Firms offer a variety of tactical strategies to achieve business growth in a short time, measuring economic and social risk. However, companies with long-term vision develop cross-cultural marketing expertise through building brand image, competitive management, sharing and analyzing market information, and developing intimacy with customers to lead in the market (Rajagopal, 2012) Organizing and planning management ideas in a schematic manner leads to systems thinking and is said to hold great promise. The systems approach, which is also synonymous to the managerial symphony, is viewed as taxonomy to gain sustainable growth in the competitive marketplace. For a manager to become a systems thinker and symphony organizer, he or she needs to spend years learning competitive strategies and apply them appropriately to witness transformative results (Cabrera et al., 2008).

Performance of a business organization can be viewed from many perspectives. However, the performance does not necessarily endorse growth of business in a competitive marketplace. The financial performance of a firm may unveil a different scenario of growth as compared to the performance of various brands with a product category in the overall product mix. Achieving good organizational performance requires more than the will of a single person; indeed, it requires the united commitment of an organization's members. This commitment must also move beyond mere talk, and encompass concrete action (Adler, 2010). The strategists may contribute toward improving the performance of the firm by linking expectations to the capability and competence of managers and employees of the firm, and providing necessary support to improve the capability and competency at the first stance.

Employee autonomy is one of the critical elements for motivating employee engagement and creativity in a company. Team culture in organizations encourages functional autonomy among the employees to express their ideas, learn voluntarily, and experiment innovation in management on pilot basis. However, employee autonomy needs a strict accountability for results, and for the actions and behaviors that deliver those results. Therefore, organizations enforce tough monitoring and evaluation practices with measurable objectives for the employees to work in teams and enjoy autonomy. The results of the autonomous team work culture should be consistent with the measurement of progress toward those goals, feedback systems, and reporting parameters along the stages of the task management. Alongside the benefits of workplace autonomy, most organizations also employ appropriate consequences for failing to reach the goals (Mankins & Garton, 2017).

Organizational design is contextualized as an employee-oriented phenomenon that arises through interaction between employees and organization. It depends on a mix of autonomy, top-down directives, and bottom-up or democratic approach of employee administration in an organization. The dignity of work involves recognition and trust, autonomy and self-efficacy in employees. In autonomous work relations, employees tend to achieve their goals through innovative approaches within the framework of administrative norms and avoid vulnerability of the employment relationship and power differentials in the organization. In large organizations, autonomy among employees works when they carry out tasks with clear objectives, commitment, and work processes regardless of their position in an organization or in the area of their operations. They respectfully disagree to the direction of their superiors, and rationally adapt to work through new approaches as they deem fit. Employees in an autonomous organization expect that they would be heard in an organization to work with innovative management trends, without fear of reprisal. Employees, who contribute to the change initiatives, believe that workplace autonomy would increase creativity and team responsiveness, and reduce control in their work environment. Employees contribute most actively in the shared leadership work culture and express high trust in management (Valcour, 2014).

Employee autonomy has been one of the important elements in organizational performance of the multinational companies. Large companies like Apple, 3 M, and Google have shown the worth of employee empowerment in organizational growth, performance, and competitiveness. These companies have developed internal environment of the organization supportive to help employees engage in the innovative activities by using organizational autonomy in a right perspective. The dimensions of internal policies, monitoring, evaluation, and control standards need to be streamlined and simplified to promote and support workplace environment for organizational innovation. Japanese philosophy of organizational performance emphasizes on *Kaizen* as a tool for continuous improvement caused by empowering employees by providing a conducive internal environment. The organizational performance is also improved by strengthening the employee engagement and measuring the employee productivity. Such policies of employee autonomy drive organizations to successfully implement an innovative strategy, and define employee engagement in increasing employee contribution to the organization (Kuratko et al., 2014). An appropriate administrative support from top management, workplace autonomy, rewards, enforcement of team culture in carrying out tasks, project planning and scheduling the output delivery, and defining organizational goals and norms help employees exercise autonomy in a positive manner, and orient their goals without conflicts. Effective workplace autonomy in an organization generates corporate entrepreneurship, which motivates employees to lay innovative projects that help in improving organizational performance.

6.5 Digital Transformation

Information technology has been central to marketing since 1980s and played a significant role in revolutionizing products from domestic appliances to automobiles, and providing higher convenience to consumers than before. These smart and connected products, with a combination of quality, structure, electronic measures, and ease of use of technology help firms to explore opportunities for new functionality. The technology-led products and marketing processes have proved to be of greater reliability, low price, and high quality across consumer segments and transcend traditional product boundaries. These products and services are conceived on consumer desires and are designed ergonomically to augment the use value. The information technology infrastructure helps in offering services and value to consumers for the products they prefer. Information technology has driven companies to go innovative and enhances their market competitiveness in the global and regional markets. SMART companies can be explained as strategic, multichannel, accessible to consumers, responsive to consumers, and technology-oriented that are connected with consumer products and services in the competitive marketplace. Wide applications of information technology have raised new strategic choices for companies about creating consumer value and re-working with traditional partners to secure competitive advantage. As the information technology has been in extensive demand, it has become affordable for small and medium size companies also, which are operating at the niche and regional levels. These companies are able to acquire new capabilities on automation of marketing functions like production, distribution, and sales, and reshape industry boundaries (Porter & Heppelmann, 2014).

Digital transformation of backward and forward linkages in business are reaching critical firms across the most conventional industrial segments. The automation of marketing processes is creating an array of improvements in services and generating competitive advantages. Digitization of various operations including packaging, distribution, logistics, and inventory management has become an essential move among the large companies in order to gain competitive advantage. General Electric, for example, was at risk of losing many of its top customers to nontraditional competitors IBM and SAP on one hand, and big data startups on the other. These companies offer data-intensive analytics-based services that could connect to any industrial device. In a retaliatory competitive strategy, GE added digital sensors to its machines, by connecting them to a common cloud-based software platform. The company invested in software development capabilities and built advanced analytics capabilities, which could embrace crowd-based product development. With such automation strategy, GE has not only evolved as business model, but also emerged as an automation leader in marketing functions (Iansiti & Lakhani, 2014).

Often, digital transformation process in firms is internal, but collective intelligence plays a significant role in driving customers to adapt to such changes in businesses. Abrupt digital transformations in business fail as customers are not prepared for adapting to such changes. It has been observed that unnoticed changes on transactional platforms in the banking firms are frustrating to most customers as no proper customer education is associated with changes. However, the users' reviews and user-generated contents help customers in gradual adaptation to the changes. The technology adaptation in firms demands not only a marketing-driven approach but also require adequate crowd support to gain confidence in the new operations environment. Consequently, firms need to drive the campaign of digital transformation in marketing of products and services than relying on assumptions. Managers need to analyze competitors, collaborators, and customers prior to getting approval from the board to implement the digital commitment (Villanueva & Ferrandiz, 2017). The use of marketing technology by large marketing companies in the retail industry has made significant impact on consumers. Brand simulations, do-it-yourself kiosks, and order—and delivery tracking have offered value additions in motivating purchase decisions. Marketing technologies have proved to be a precious source of new solutions in various product categories and, by introducing convenience marketing. Such technological growth in marketing has helped companies in implementing the shifts in market instruments, strategies, and consumers' behavior. Information technology connects marketing activities with customers as systematic interactions to make quick decisions at a low cost. However, empirical evidence regarding the actual diffusion of web-based tools supporting collaborative innovation remains weak (Prandelli et al., 2006). However, technology-based marketing might cause significant market uncertainty, technological uncertainty, and issues of compatibility within multichannel marketing system. Most emerging companies struggle to orchestrate network effects and navigating ecosystem complexities in the competitive marketplace. The inherent risks of making choices between technology-led marketing and conventional wisdom in marketing (Dhebar, 2016).

Business analytics has risen into prominence in the twenty-first century, as it offers solutions that benefit a variety of disciplines in business like marketing, new product development, innovation, and customer services. Interestingly, business analytics is not just primarily an extension of information technology or business intelligence or a business function, but a convergence of information technology (IT) capabilities and competencies, and business performance measures in a company. Business analytics demands an increased collaboration across organizations on issues relating to information selection and screening the datasets, and to warn managers about the data intricacies, risks, and teams for the information oversights. The software tools that companies consider as a part of business analytics span across various areas, including analytics, data integration, querying and reporting, and managing information technology projects. As business analytics is designed to enable fact-based real-time decision-making, it may be one of the expensive tools to work with for the companies that have paucity of resources. The key benefits of business analytics functions are currently derived from using business analytics software encompassing various areas of business analytics, with the following benefits related to improving and speeding up the decision-making process:

- Aligning market information and corporate resources with strategic decision process,
- Managing cost-effective and real-time business decisions,
- Enabling customer-centric decisions to be implemented by the companies,
- Improving the market competitiveness and business performance of the companies,
- Producing a unified enterprise-wide business information,
- Synchronizing financial and operational strategies, and
- Supporting corporate decision to increase revenue and reduce financial risk.

In reference to the changing scenarios of market economy and information technology, most companies are leaning toward reaching the cost efficiencies, improving market competitiveness, and increasing revenues as the principal objectives of their companies. Driving through the business analytics experiences, every organization gets different outcomes, as the appropriateness of the decisions taken and implemented varies by companies toward realizing the benefits (Rajagopal & Behl, 2017). The major challenges observed in acquiring and analyzing market information include data integration with multiple systems or information channels, data quality, and finally building integration with other enterprise applications. In the global marketplace, companies tend to invest in business analytics to access the right information at the right time in order to empower fact-based real-time decisions at every level of the enterprise, to achieve key objectives and to gain maximum return using the IT tools appropriately.

References

Adler, R. (2010). Enhancing business success: The role of performance management. *Business Horizons, 53*(4), 331–333.

Berry, L. L. (2001). The old pillars of new retailing. *Harvard Business Review, 79*(4), 131–137.

Berry, L. L., Davis, S., & Wilmet, J. (2015). When the customer is stressed. *Harvard Business Review, 93*(10), 87–94.

Borges-Tiago, M. T. P. M., & Cristóvão-Veríssimo, J. M. (2014). Digital marketing and social media: Why bother? *Business Horizons, 57*(6), 703–708.

Belayutham, S., González, V. A., & Yiu, T. W. (2016). Clean–lean administrative processes: A case study on sediment pollution during construction. *Journal of Cleaner Production, 126*, 134–147.

Bettencourt, L. A., Brown, S. W., & Sirianni, N. J. (2013). The secret to true service innovation. *Business Horizons, 56*(1), 13–22.

Bouquet, C., Barsoux, J. L., & Wade, M. (2018). *Bring your breakthrough ideas to life*. Harvard Business School Press.

Brooks, A. W. (2015). Emotion and the art of negotiation. *Harvard Business Review, 93*(12), 57–64.

Cabrera, D., Colosi, L., & Lobdell, C. (2008). Systems thinking. *Evaluation and Program Planning., 31*(3), 299–310.

Casteleyn, J., Mottart, A., & Rutten, K. (2009). How to use Facebook in your market research. *International Journal of Market Research, 51*(4), 439–447.

Chen, Y. (2017). Dynamic ambidexterity: How innovators manage exploration and exploitation. *Business Horizons, 60*(3), 385–394.

Chesbrough, H. (2010). Business model innovation: Opportunities and barriers. *Long Range Planning, 43*(2), 354–363.
Christensen, C. M., & Overdorf, M. (2000). Meeting the challenge of disruptive change. *Harvard Business Review, 78*(2), 66–76.
Christensen, C. M., Raynor, M. E., & McDonald, R. (2015). What is disruptive innovation? *Harvard Business Review, 93*(12), 3–11.
Christensen, C. M., Hall, T., Dillon, K., & Duncan, D. (2016). Know your customers' "jobs to be done." *Harvard Business Review., 94*(9), 54–62.
Davenport, T. H., Prusak, L., & Wilson, H. J. (2003). Who's bringing you hot ideas (and how are you responding)? *Harvard Business Review, 81*(2), 58–64.
Dhebar, A. (2016). Bringing new high-technology products to market: Six perils awaiting marketers. *Business Horizons, 59*(6), 713–722.
Duan, W., Gu, B., & Whinston, A. (2008). The dynamics of online word-of-mouth and product sales: An empirical investigation of the movie industry. *Journal of Retailing, 84*(2), 233–242.
Ganesh, J., Arnold, M. J., & Reynolds, K. E. (2000). Understanding the customer base of service providers: An examination of the difference between switchers and stayers. *Journal of Marketing, 64*(3), 65–87.
Gary, L. (2003). *Ambidextrous innovation*. Harvard Business School Publishing.
Giamanco, B., & Gregoire, K. (2012). Tweet me, friend me, make me buy. *Harvard Business Review, 90*(7–8), 88–93.
Govindarajan, V. (2012). A reverse innovation play-book. *Harvard Business Review, 90*(4), 120–124.
Hanna, R. C., Rohm, A., & Crittenden, V. L. (2011). We're all connected: The power of the social media ecosystem. *Business Horizons, 54*(3), 265–273.
Hansen, M. T., & Birkinshaw, J. (2007). Innovation value chain. *Harvard Business Review, 85*(6), 121–130.
Hildebrand, C., Haubl, G., Herrmann, A., & Landwehr, J. R. (2013). Conformity and the crowd. *Harvard Business Review, 91*(4), 23–24.
Holt, D. B. (2016). Branding in the age of social media. *Harvard Business Review, 94*(3), 40–50.
Iansiti, M., & Lakhani, K. R. (2014). Digital ubiquity: How connections, sensors, and data are revolutionizing business. *Harvard Business Review, 92*(11), 91–99.
John, L. K., Mochon, D., Emrich, O., & Schwartz, J. (2017). What's the value of a like? *Harvard Business Review, 95*(2), 108–115.
Jones, M. Y., Spence, M. T., & Vallester, C. (2008). Creating emotions via B to C websites. *Business Horizons, 51*(5), 419–428.
Kalyanam, K., & Zweben, M. (2005). Perfect message at the perfect moment. *Harvard Business Review, 83*(11), 112–120.

Kuratko, D. F., Hornsby, J. S., & Covin, J. G. (2014). Diagnosing a firm's internal environment for corporate entrepreneurship. *Business Horizons, 57*(1), 37–47.

Lim, C., & Fujimoto, T. (2019). Frugal innovation and design changes expanding the cost-performance frontier: A Schumpeterian approach. *Research Policy, 48*(4), 1016–1029.

Lindgaard, G. G., Dudek, F. C., & Brown, J. (2006). Attention web designers: You have 50 milliseconds to make a first impression! *Behaviour and Information Technology, 25*(2), 115–126.

Magids, S., Zorfas, A., & Leemon, D. (2015). The new science of customer emotions. *Harvard Business Review, 93*(11), 66–76.

Majchrzak, A., & Shepherd, D. A. (2021). Can digital innovations help reduce suffering? A crowd-based digital innovation framework of compassion venturing. *Information and Organization, 31*(1), 1–7.

Malhotra, A., Malhotra, C. K., & See, A. (2012). How to get your message re-twitted. *MIT Sloan Management Review, 53*(2), 61–66.

Mangold, W. G., & Faulds, D. J. (2009). Social media: The new hybrid element of the promotion mix. *Business Horizons, 52*(4), 357–365.

Mankins, M., & Garton, E. (2017, February 9). How spotify balances employee autonomy and accountability. *Harvard Business Review Web Article*.

McLaughlin, P., Bessant, J., & Smart, P. (2008). Developing an organization culture to facilitate radical innovation. *International Journal of Technology Management, 44*(3), 298–323.

Miranda, M., Konya, L., & Havira, I. (2005). Shopper's satisfaction levels are not only the key to store loyalty. *Marketing Intelligence and Planning, 23*(2), 220–232.

Nidumolu, R., Prahlad, C. K., & Rangaswamy, M. R. (2009). Why sustainability is now the key driver of innovation. *Harvard Business Review, 87*(9), 57–64.

O'Reilly, C. A., III., & Tushman, M. L. (2011). Organizational ambidexterity in action: How managers explore and exploit. *California Management Review, 53*(4), 5–22.

O'Reilly, C. A., III., & Tushman, M. L. (2013). Organizational ambidexterity: Past, present, and future. *Academy of Management Perspectives, 27*(4), 324–338.

Piskorski, N. J. (2011). Social strategies at work. *Harvard Business Review, 89*(11), 116–122.

Porter, M. E., & Heppelmann, J. (2014). How smart, connected products are transforming competition. *Harvard Business Review, 92*(11), 64–88.

Prandelli, E., Verona, G., & Raccagni, D. (2006). Diffusion of web-based product innovation. *California Management Review, 48*(4), 109–135.

Rajagopal. (2006). Innovation and business growth through corporate venturing in Latin America: Analysis of strategic fit. *Management Decision, 44*(5), 703–718.

Rajagopal. (2012). *Systems thinking and process dynamics for marketing systems: Technologies and applications for decision management*. IGI Global.

Rajagopal. (2019). *Contemporary marketing strategy: Analyzing consumer behavior to drive managerial decision making*. Palgrave Macmillan.

Rajagopal. (2020). *Transgenerational marketing: Evolution, expansion, and experience*. Palgrave Macmillan.

Rajagopal & Behl, R. (2017). *Start-up enterprises and contemporary innovation strategies in the global marketplace*. IGI Global.

Sarkees, M., & Hulland, J. S. (2008). Innovation and efficiency: It is possible to have it all. *Business Horizons, 52*(1), 45–55.

Shankar, V., & Malthouse, E. C. (2007). The growth of interactions and dialogs in interactive marketing. *Journal of Interactive Marketing, 21*(2), 2–4.

Taylor, D. G., Lewin, J. E., & Strutton, D. (2011). Friends, fans, and followers: Do ads work on social networks? *Journal of Advertising Research, 51*(1) 258–275.

Trusov, M., Bodapati, A. V., & Bucklin, R. E. (2010). Determining influential users in internet social networks. *Journal of Marketing Research, 47*(4), 643–658.

Valcour, M. (2014, April 28). The power of dignity in the workplace. *Harvard Business Review Web Article*.

Villanueva, J., & Ferrandiz, L. (2017). 3 steps to market-driven digital transformation: Stairway to digitalization. *ISES Insight, 32*, 15–22.

Whitla, P. (2009). Crowdsourcing and its application in marketing activities. *Contemporary Management Research, 5*(1), 15–28.

Wollan, R., Smith, N., and Zhou, C. (2011), *The social media management handbook: Everything you need to know to get social media working in your business*. Wiley.

Zhang, J., & Daugherty, T. (2009). Third-person effect and social networking: Implications for online marketing and word-of-mouth communication. *American Journal of Business, 24*(2), 53–63.

CHAPTER 7

Consumer Behavior and Cognitive Theories

Social power as a pivot to analyze the power structure consumers and consumers' involvement of firms in crowdsourcing. Accordingly, the managerial implications of 'consumer-firm' power balance are deliberated in the chapter. Crowdsourcing is a process that explores collective intelligence for resolving the complex behavioral issues by distributing tasks to a large group of people. The learning objectives of this chapter include understanding of how consumer cognitive (thinking) processes and limitations affect beliefs and social influences, and how other contextual factors influence consumer decision-making, choices, and behavior. This chapter focuses on learning from external factors on consumer behavior and relationships with other people that influence their decision-making processes. The behavioral analytics is discussed in this chapter, in the context of motivation and decision theories. Besides, this chapter discusses the role of consumer advocacy and psychodynamics (peer-to-peer opinion dissemination) as a tool for developing crowd-based business models.

Most companies are inculcating radical buying behavior among consumers by generating brand literacy through the interactions of consumer communities on social media. Facebook, Twitter, and Instagram have been the principal platforms of consumer networking for most of the customer-centric companies. Companies explore the consumer needs and preferences on the digital platforms and tend to meet consumers' rising expectations on the products and services they intend

Rajagopal, *Crowd-Based Business Models*,
https://doi.org/10.1007/978-3-030-77083-9_7

to buy. Simultaneously, to reaffirm their purchase intentions, consumers also stay critical to the multichannel experience of peers on their preferred brands. The customer experience is diffused by the user-generated contents on social media, which help them to review their perceptions, attitude, and behavior toward a brand in the marketplace. For example, Nordstrom customers can buy products not only in the physical and on the virtual stores, but also through a mobile app, on Instagram, or via text message. Consumers can pick, return, or exchange their online purchases at Nordstrom stores. Such convenience of digital marketing to access reviews and referrals, develop purchase intentions, and the possibility of decision reversals in case of change in the value perceptions has strengthened the consumer attitude and the behavior toward the brand.

Besides, innovation and social stimulation, consumer behavior is largely driven by the personal expectations and associate values. Therefore, customer-centric companies are investing in creating customer value through crowd-based motivation, customer relations, and offering products and services of sustainable utilitarian values. In addition, social health issues have taken a center stage to persuade consumers on well-being, diet, and organic consumption values, which have both crowd-based and individual appeals. Such dual focus of social and business development through the value creation, drives consumers to alter consumer behavior and ensure not only confidence in the brand and firm but also provide opportunity to firms for expanding the geo-demographic outreach. In such marketing approach brands play a critical role in shifting the consumer behavior to more profitable product portfolios. The social brands today have higher potential to both create and shift consumer behavior by stimulating consumers toward experimentation and value creation, aligning with the corporate goals and strategies, and judging the performance of products and services through collective intelligence and perceive values. In addition, partnering with social institutions and creating a crowd-movement to validate the corporate strategies on creating value among consumers and markets, also play a significant role in determining the consumer behavior today (Sidibe, 2020). This approach has allowed Unilever's sustainable living brands such as Dove, to help over 35 million young people around the world with self-esteem education since 2005 and Lifebuoy, which has reached over a billion consumers with its handwashing campaigns educating social preventive healthcare measures and created immense consumer value. Similarly, Ben & Jerry's food products, which are followed by the campaigns for social justice and climate change, and Unilever's social strategy of empowering rural women through the *Shakti program* (*Shakti* meaning Power in Hindi language) have created enormous customer value and sustainable behavior.

The acquired and shared culture among consumers drives awareness about the new trends, which in turn arouses new consumer preferences. For example, consumer preferences for 3-D games, virtual reality products, and trendy consumer electronics influence consumers in the emerging markets as *millennial effect*. The experience sharing over the digital platforms further influences the consumer behavior over a long time. Patterns of consumerism are changing in the society, as there are shifts in the consumer demography in the markets. The explosion of mass consumer segment, urbanization, and increase in the size of the population of aging consumers has contributed significantly to the shifts in consumer preferences and overall consumption behavior. Direct-to-customer marketing strategies, convenience shopping, and social media-driven marketing approaches of companies have increased social and cultural influence on developing the consumer behavior. However, disruption in technology and attraction toward local consumption also contribute in driving the consumer behavior dynamic across the geo-demographic segments. In addition, extended technology lifecycle builds positive consumer perceptions on higher value for money. Co-creation and co-designing approaches of customer-centric companies like IKEA has established business philosophy of connecting consumers and developing an emotion-based relationship with consumers as the key to leveraging loyalty and advocacy behavior. Co-creation and coevolution appear to be an effective process in building consumer behavior. Firms relying on the crowd-based business models and collective intelligence like IKEA, LEGO, and Starbucks have experienced that customer engagement with crowd-motivation serves as best strategies to inculcate consumer behavior. Such strategies on one hand leverage a company's core capabilities and help in acquiring customers on the other, by generative emotions and sense of belongingness for the brand. Understanding both self-references-based and induced consumer perceptions plays a significant role behind conscious (self-and crowd-referred) and unconscious (imaginary and unclear choices). Research-oriented firms invest in exploring such consumer behavior in their customers and watch behavioral transitions. Customer-centric companies build cumulative advantage by mining the emotional connection of brands with the customers as

LEGO explores over time that many people have high satisfaction with the dark colors of building blocks (Lafley et al., 2017).

7.1 Cognition and Perceptions

Visual attraction of products, emotions, self-congruence and perceived experience, knowledge and beliefs, and psychosocial insights about the products, drives the perceptions of consumers, which later helps in developing attitude and behavior in future. The consumer philosophy today is woven around the practice of *touch, feel, and pick* of products and services, wherein the perceptual process among consumers is observed in four stages beginning with sensitive feeling, attention, review, and cognitive affirmation. The consumer perception is backed also by ACCA factors comprising awareness, comprehension, conviction, and action. Consumers develop purchase decisions from perceived value and crowd-based motivation. However, conscious choice also helps in determining behavioral dynamics among consumers' psychology. The buying behavior is often jolted by the chaotic crowd comments, incomplete information, and ambiguous customer advocacy on social media. Customer Intuitions, crowd-based brainstorming, collective opinions, and selected preferences that are learnt in customer communities affect consumer behavior. However, intuitive judgments stay as powerful moderators and often override the collective decisions induced on social media. They are heavily influenced by the cognitive dynamics of individuals, a phenomenon is known as cognitive processing fluency, which conforms the *just feels right* notion of individuals at the given time (Lafley & Martin, 2017). In addition, brand commercials, in-store and online promotions, marketing events, referrals, and social media help in generating awareness among consumers to develop self-perceptions on the products and services. Consumers explore further information on the seeded perceptions to comprehend their knowledge and rationale in developing conviction toward the purchase decisions. Conviction is a state of cognition, which builds an inclination toward the products or services to buy. Consumer perceptions justified over the conviction may turn into action, as consumers finally buy the products or services (Rajagopal, 2011).

Consumer perceptions are often agile, and need to be endorsed by the peers, friends, and family to support decision-making and to put them into practice over a long term. Such cognitive process creates consumption attitude among consumers. Perceptions linked to emotions are commonly impulsive and temporary, which do not make a dent in cognitive process continuity, and help in decision-making. Consumers form perceptions on the viable solutions to the predetermined needs (recognized as problems) which match with their self-congruence, and could offer sustainable value (satisfaction). Consumers review their perceptions formed on products, services, brands, or business companies in reference to the public opinions and own observations. Accordingly, consumers justify their perceptions and develop purchase intention upon developing the right perceptions, consumers try to refine their needs, and find means and ends to acquire the product. Consumption of products establishes the perceived value among consumers and validates their buying decision. Perceptions initially formed by the consumers are often subject to change in view of the reviews, referrals, and self-reflections. Perceptual mapping is a useful exercise for customer-centric companies to understand various underlying cognitive dimensions that affect the decision-making process. Perceptual maps have been proved as a useful tool for marketers in understanding product design, product differentiation, product positioning, and product preferences among consumers. Commonly, the perceptual maps are constructed by asymmetric observations, perceived values, and self-reference criteria to determine the product optimization and value-led marketing strategies. Consumers exhibit many perceptual dimensions corresponding to a product or brand in the market (Chaturvedi & Carroll, 1998).

Perceptions are reconstituted accordingly by moving to new market ambiance, building brands with new attributes, and redefining the need. Accordingly, new perceptual criteria are set by the consumers to pursue their needs. Companies need to analyze the perceptual maps of consumers to measure the intensity of their persuasion by developing appropriate strategies for advertising and communication. In order to analyze the consumers' perceptions and judgment to support their decision-making process, consumer-centric companies offer array of consumer choice, product performance reviews over the social media (Jost, 2017). Self-enhancement by acquiring knowledge and shared experiences on products and services helps consumers in developing sustainable perceptions to make right purchase intentions and buying decisions. Social networking sites such as Facebook or Twitter serve as an interesting platform in self-enhancement process, which enables consumers to compare different goals and behaviors over a predetermined mindset. Social media is an attractive medium where consumers with a changing mindset interact among peers demonstrating their perceptual rationale, and validate their feelings and emotions. Their objective in engaging in social media is to learn about recent trends, new development of knowledge, or certain skillsets for further improvement in making buying decisions (Mathur et al., 2016).

Self-perception is associated with the self-congruence among consumers, form attitude among consumers toward a specific brand. Consumer attitude is developed based on the self-perception and the opinions they publicly express on particular issues encouraging social interactions. Direct-to-customer companies, such as Avon Cosmetics, Mary Kay, and Eureka Forbes (India), have benefited from marketing initiatives associating the company with a socially beneficial cause. Consumer attitude is a convergence of perceived expectancy and perceived value evolved through the cognitive process of consumer perception (Fishbien & Ajzen, 1975). The self-perception, propagation of views on the products and services over the social media, celebrity endorsements, and brand promotions support the consumer attitude, and drive emotional bonding. Crowd-based companies have developed *mass customization* tools using the collective intelligence resources that allow consumers to design their own products through social media, which encourages peoples' participation with social or business objectives and get input from peers before finalizing their product preferences. Such cognitive state of mind stimulates emotions, and consumers tend to get associated with the products and services by buying them repeatedly. The repeat buying phenomenon generates loyalty by upholding the emotions among consumers, which helps in inculcating the consumption behavior. Consumer with such learned behavior enjoy consumer lifetime value and turn social ambassadors of the brands by engaging in brand advocacy alongside the companies. Consumer perceptions are sensitive to their experiences, and help in building attitude if sustained for a reasonable period. Most consumer-centric companies ensure that consumers gain favorable and sustainable perception through brand campaigns, digital communications, social media forums, and product and service trials.

Broadly the consumer buying process involves pre-purchase, purchase, and post-purchase behaviors. The consumer decision-making units ranging from individuals to family in particular and community in general play significant role in inculcating buying behavior. Besides buyers, the behavior has effects on influencers (users), gatekeepers (informants and analysts), and approvers (decision-makers). The marketing campaigns for new products also influence consumer behavior and decision-making process in the context of the information inflow from social media, co-creation experience, and consumer engagement (Gourville & Norton, 2014). Consumers behave in the market in four different ways as proactive, reactive, interactive, and inactive. All four ways of expressing consumer behavior refer to their cultural background. Proactive consumers are experimental to new products, and are prone to accept the cultural changes induced by the market. The proactive consumers are largely induced by the markets through lifestyle interventions and cross-cultural fusion. Reactive consumers are critical to new products, strategies, and corporate initiatives and prefer the conventional culture that has grown over the period in the society. The reactive consumers are aggressive in sharing their experience, and are often critical about the products and services of the company. Interactive consumers express their views logically, and analyze the products and services of a company rationally and comparatively. Inactive consumers are passive and non-responsive. Consumers in the acquired culture are prone to behavioral changes, adapt to modern values, and are interactive in the market. These attributes of acquired culture drive multinational companies to develop dynamic marketing strategies, build their brand, and augment market share (Rajagopal, 2016).

Learning process among consumers is complex. They tend to seek comprehensive information on products and services and pool them, and face difficulty in filtering the information and analyzing to converge the available information and self-perceptions. Knowledge accumulation does not attribute to the consumer learning process. They need to develop articulation, codification, and subsequent routine development in making buying decisions where judgment and rules of thumb need to be clearly determined by the consumers. The consumers need to evolve their learning process through contextual enablers such as salespeople, fellow consumers, point-of-sales information sources, participants of social media, family, and peers, and self-reference determinants. Learning about new products, brand image, innovation and technology, and role of the company requires commitment among the consumers, as improper transfer of knowledge might cause biasness in developing perceptions and attitudes. Knowledge articulation and attributes of consumers to share multi-lateral of information across the social media help in creating the psychodynamics and opinion trends among consumers. Social platforms support in updating consumer knowledge and learning process on product innovation, and create positive influence on community learning process. Such knowledge transfer practice implies that firms can stimulate communication and interaction among people (Carmona-Lavado et al., 2010). Social media and peer reviews deliver knowledge directly on products and services, which helps in consumer learning process and enhances their decision-making skills. The participatory learning model as demonstrated by the community, family, and social media platforms not only helps consumers in acquiring information and knowledge on brands and markets, but also constitutes consumer behavior. Consumer knowledge leads them to explore new products and user opportunities, influence cognitive abilities, and draw motivations for experimenting new consumerism models (Neeley, 2005).

Diffusion of knowledge through social media and developing effective relationship are most popular ways to co-create consumer behavior. Some consumers not only want to acquire knowledge through crowd sources but also want to be *confident friends* with a brand while others might look for a *passionate fling* and would welcome a closer bond. Companies following a crowd-based business model search for kick-start signals from multiple sources to understand the consumer perceptions in the context of various relationship portfolios (Smedslund, 2011). Accordingly, firms co-create consumer perceptions and build a strategic mix of connections to gain competitive advantage, augment customer value, and inculcate strategic relationships with customers. In the growing perspective of dynamic market competition, it has been evidenced in many customer-centric companies like Hindustan Unilever Limited, Samsung, and PepsiCo, that relationship-driven consumer behavior is sustainable and more profitable than other market-oriented strategies as these companies tend to co-create and coevolve with consumers (Avery et al., 2014). Creating digital communities for social knowledge transfer also serve as public referrals and help companies in acquisition of new consumers and retention of existing consumers (Geisler, 2007). Learning communities are developed by the consumer-centric companies to transfer knowledge on social consumption causes like healthy foods, green consumption, organic farm products, and the like. Such learning communities are designed primarily to increase consumer attitude toward learning new consumption patterns and building convergence with social, ethnic, and personal values. Companies monitor consumer needs, perceptions, and expectations through the learning communities, and identify marketing strategies, which contributes to augment the consumer involvement in learning new consumption experiences and augmenting perceived satisfaction. Digital consumer learning communities do attain positive outcomes; however, consumer education programs need to be developed specifically to the requirements of geo-demographic segments (Andrade, 2007). The digital marketing strategies with hybrid self-experience stations attract more consumers to experience the products online, develop and share experience, and measure the perceived use value (satisfaction) of the products. Such web exposure for the product and services are accessible to a large number of consumers today, which drives them to develop perceptions and attitudes for the products and services of their choice (Jost, 2017).

7.2 Behavioral Analytics

Consumer behavior is getting multifaceted in the global marketplace due to the rapid increase in competition, innovation, and technology in products and services. Hence, architecting sustainable companies is not getting any easier. A longitudinal growth of brands across the companies has altered the perception, attitude, and behavior of consumer rapidly over time. Thus, companies are engaging consumers in building confidence on brands and the company by developing symbiotic relationships between consumers and market for sustainable growth. Companies build consumer perceptions on the product and services by disseminating continuous and sustainable communication through various cable channels to the Internet, product placement in movies, and even mobile-phone display screens. The first order of business is to take a hard look at the sustainable consumer segment that has the long-term profit potential for delivering right brands for segments, and to plan for required investment in building the customer-centric markets. While no good company ignores shifts that are clearly underway, they traditionally segment markets in reference to the size, income, age, and ethnicity of various target populations; estimates of their consumption and loyalty; and information about their locations, lifestyles, needs, and attitudes. Well-managed companies have moved from emphasizing customized items to offering globally standardized products that are advanced, functional, reliable, and low priced. They benefit from enormous economies of scale in production, distribution, marketing, and management. Such dynamism in the business and related activities portrays the functional concepts of globalization (Rajagopal, 2008).

Consumer behavior is a continuous process and is improved time and again with the experience. The trial and error constitute a part of the experimental consumer behavior, which is refined by sharing the experience and improving on the basis of collective intelligence. Consumers often make mistakes while making decisions due to ad hoc reasoning and influences. A stream of experimental evidence in recent years has evidenced that human elements are contribute significantly to the right or wrong decisions. However, at the same companies have also the role of managers in decision-making in consumer business and financial markets (Fox, 2015). Consumer preference and value placed on designer apparel is largely influenced by the social differentiation of products and self-esteem of the consumer. These attributes are likely to vary depending on the consumers' cultural orientation. The cultural dimensions of individualism, uncertainty avoidance, power distance, and masculinity, should be a useful framework to explain cross-cultural differences in customer acceptance of designer products. Consumer use destination brands for its symbolic value, reflecting the personality and status of the user. Destination brands are perceived as an ostentatious display of wealth. Thus, consumers are motivated by a desire to impress others with their ability to pay particularly high prices for prestigious products (Rajagopal, 2011). Consumption patterns are largely governed by social value of the product, which determines the purchasing intentions, consumer attitudes, or perceptions on brand or advertising slogan. Consumer experience with high socio-economic power perceptions creates distinct psychological motives toward new products that develop unique consumption patterns (Rucker & Galinsky, 2009).

Customer engagement in product design, packaging, and marketing is an integrated approach to create consumer behavior and implementing pro-consumer marketing strategies. Most companies have found that co-creation by persuading consumers in developing product expansion strategies (particular products, product line, or full product portfolio) has been an effective solution. However, some companies felt that engaging customers in internal strategies such as production and operations have caused pitfalls of such collaborative customer strategies. The strategic role of each customer becomes muddled when it is specialized or segmented. Many snack foods companies have discovered that a carefully focused and well-managed customer engagement helps in developing customer emotions and values on the product, which contributes to the consumer behavior (Quelch & Kenny, 1994). Diverse patterns of consumption create a consumption behavior that can be described as extemporaneous, expedient, and emergent behavior. The nature of the consumption process depends on a host environment, and the drivers influencing the consumption pattern. These drivers include culturally diverse decisions of the consumer, multicultural identities, social cues, contextual factors, and tendency of consumers toward experimentalism. Consumers living in frequently changing social and cultural environment across the geo-demographic segments become culturally plural, and turn experimentalists. Accordingly, the learning process among consumers stretches beyond boundaries, and becomes adjustable to the current state of socio-cultural diversities (Sankaran & Demongeot, 2011).

Consumption activities are driven by the lifestyle goals and sustain if they satisfy the basic needs and provide social and personal distinctions in using the product and services. Consumers are also often interested in higher satisfaction by consuming innovative and socially differentiated products to achieve self-realization, fairness, freedom, participation, social relations, and balance among the consumption ecosystem. Consumer value and lifestyle influences significantly the consumer behavior. Consequently, companies are leaning toward developing lifestyle brands to inculcate consumer behavior and have prolonged association. In the competitive marketplace every brand aims to grow as a *lifestyle brand*. Godiva chocolates have plans to reposition its brand as a lifestyle brand to develop a strategic impact on consumer behavior. The company aimed at repositioning Godiva as a lifestyle brand by leveraging its culinary experience to drive consumer values and product feel beyond common chocolates. The customer-centric businesses have realized that a premium and sustainable consumer lifestyle contributes meaningfully to indoctrinate consumer behavior and iconic values in the society. Customer engagement develops intuitive and intimate, lifestyle values through the preferred brand attributes of brand (Taylor, 2018). Such consumer aspirations may be served either by unique selling proposition, self-esteem, corporate image, or by new-generation products launched by the companies. For many consumers, consumption defines a significant part of their role in society, as sharing experiences about products among peers helps in creating and maintaining relationships. It may be a basis for self-respect, and a significant part of what gives life interest and meaning.

Consumerism has emerged historically across the changing market environment and has created mass markets, industrialization, and cultural attitudes that ensure that rising incomes are used to purchase an ever-growing output (Sharpe, 2008).

7.2.1 *Motivational Theories*

There are many motivational theories that still guide managers to attract consumers, retain them over the changing preferences, and develop loyalty. One of the most vulnerable cognitive dimensions among the consumers is *acquiescence effect*, which has several implications in the decision analytics of a consumer. This effect inculcates a sense of superiority and exhibitionism among consumers by evaluating self over others, as 'how a consumer will appear to others?' Another person can explain such cognitive dimension upon asking a question about how he or she looks. From the consumers' point of view, they consider such state of mind as superiority complex. Most consumer-oriented companies trigger such psychodynamics among the consumers by launching advertising campaigns that are informative as well as challenging. Nissan Automobile had brought to the market, 'shift the future' campaign in 2002, with an intention to draw the acquiescence effect among the mass consumers. Often acquiescence effect among consumers is turned as forced choice. Generally, companies present comparative benefits to the consumers to create such effect. For instance, Unilever had launched a commercial for its detergent cake in India with the verbal conversation 'Mine is whiter than yours' in 2006. This commercial has been successful in attracting consumers and creating stronger acquiescence effect among consumers. Acquiescence effect may also be explained as consumers *think every idea is a good idea*, and find it themselves liking, buying, and acting upon every option that is proposed. Some consumers have acquiescent personalities, while others acquiesce because they perceive others are better than they are. Creating acquiescence effect among consumers is the easy way out for companies, as it takes less effort than carefully weighing each option and ensures a quick strategy for driving motivation.

From the corporate perspectives acquiescence in business signifies to accept the consumer behavior at its face value even with reluctance. The retailing philosophy of Sam Walton, the founder of Wal-Mart and group of business, is based on acquiescence theory, which is reflected in the retailing mission of Wal-Mart stating 'Customer is always right' (if no, the point of view of customer is reluctantly accepted). Although most customer-centric firms are integrated vertically in the context of ownership and operational processes, such business models are often associated with high agility, operating costs, and driven by the collective intelligence. Therefore, for these firms, adapt to the most viable business model that involves establishing relationships, developing behavior, and collaborations with customers that allow them to complement their own operations and building sustainable value chain. Acquiescence, conceptually refer to as compliance management and focus operational relationships between consumers, manufacturers, operations and service providers, and retailers (Mwesiumo & Halpern, 2018). However, in the context of collective intelligence derived by the crowdsourcing- and crowdfunding-based business projects, acquiescence may be understood as the tendency to respond to attitudes with agreement (promise acquiescence) or disagreement (counter-acquiescence) regardless of their content. As customers and investors interact on the digital platforms, which provides a liber environment to express acquiescence. Most crowd-based business models categorically examine the nature and degree of acquiescence associated with the information to support strategic marketing decisions (Rammstedt et al., 2017). The salient attributes of motivational and decision theories are illustrated in Fig. 7.1.

The business practices today have integrated the social foundations of customers and business governance by empowering and engaging customers from ideation to profiteering stages of businesses. Such convergence of social and business domains is endorsed by various theoretical propositions as illustrated in Fig. 7.1. Collective intelligence helps consumers not only to gain awareness about the peer perceptions but also provides motivation to make decision at par with the community on consumption of innovative products. Nonetheless, specific needs of consumers are acquired and shaped by their experiences over time. Most of these needs can be categorized as achievement, affiliation, and power. A person's motivation and effectiveness in certain decisions on consumption are influenced by the above taxonomy. Cognitively a consumer describes his achievement over the need in terms of the degree of satisfaction gained in reference to his decision on buying. The decision on new products and services embedded with innovation and technology often becomes complex for the consumers, as it is difficult to measure the level of achievement or satisfaction emerging on their decision (McClelland, 1978). Consumers tend to experiment with relevant

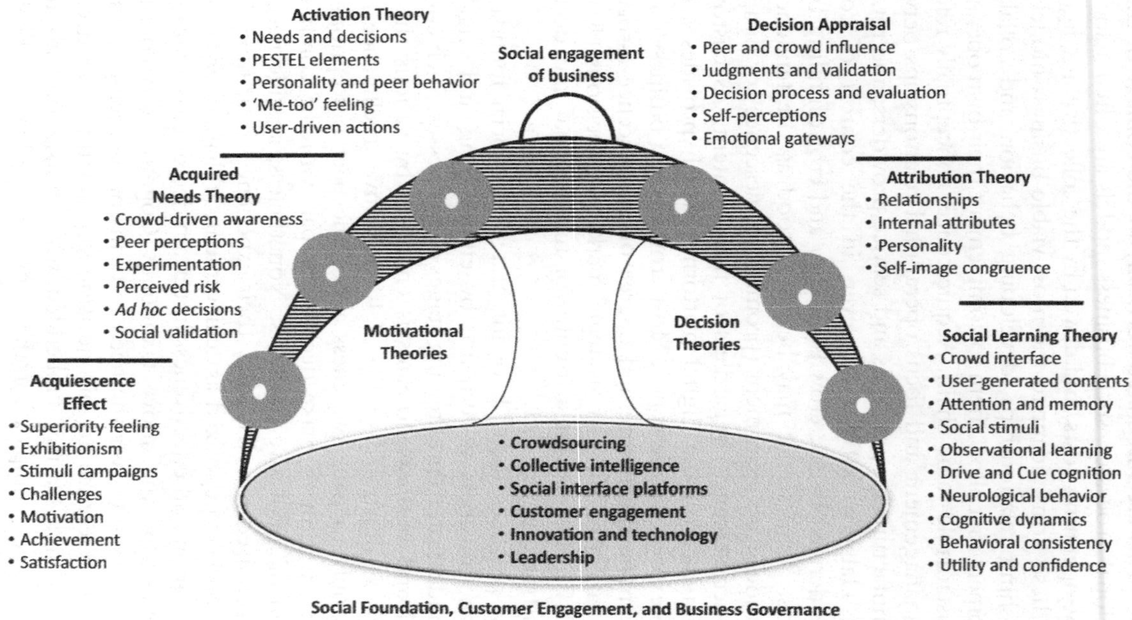

Fig. 7.1 Attributes of behavioral theories (*Source* Author)

brands and analyze perceived risk over the perceived value to measure desired satisfaction. During such cognitive process consumers gradually reach their decision whether to associate with the brand or otherwise. To support the cognitive evolution among consumers in achieving satisfaction, companies should improve their organizational policies in view of competitive marketplace, and develop motivational approaches accordingly. Consumers develop acquired needs as they are often influenced by the peer or crowd behavior and tend to make shifts in the buying decisions. The influx of information about the brands on social media and crowd-based digital platforms affect the cognitive perceptions and emotions of consumers. Most consumer searches on the digital environment result an ad hoc purchase decision. Such crowd influence is growing swiftly with the proliferation of information technology, electronic retailers, and virtual malls (Pookulangara & Koesler, 2011).

The *acquired needs theory* determining the consumer behavior to support the above rationale. Consumers who achieve satisfaction by using products and services for the identified needs, and justify their decision, further move to the stage of affiliation with the company and the brand. This stage is highly significant to the companies, as consumers get engaged in analyzing attributes of products and services, excel on their functions, evaluate perceived use value, measure anthropomorphic value, find conformity to the decision, and indulge in repeat buying. The need for affiliation among consumers is a conscious drive in view of the AATAR elements comprising awareness, attributes, trial, availability, and repeat buying. The success of trial of products among consumers congruent to their decision leads to repeat buying, which creates affiliation or belongingness of consumers to the brand (Rajagopal, 2018). Consumers tend to conform to the norms of social needs by widening their brand affiliation and product usage. Consumers feel empowered when their decisions are right. They seek and obtain leadership positions in social groups, professional associations, and with the sales people (Uduji & Ankeli, 2013). However, the consumers need to be motivated differently on crowd-based platforms for specific products and services portfolios as common arguments of values might not be encouraging to consumers universally.

The *activation theory* of consumer behavior explains that consumers often need a motivational push to activate their need and action toward implementing the decision. Motivations are driven by factors such as perceived values, social and peer behavior, individual personality, and exogenous factors including political, economic, social, technological, environmental, and legal perspectives that help in determining the consumer behavior. The motivational push factors relate to both the conscious and unconscious perceptions, which drive the cognitive dynamics toward making decisions on a given consumption or market situation. Accordingly, the motional arousal leads to achieving satisfaction, product experience, buying behavior, and evaluating the decisions made. In the process of motivational push, the effectiveness of customer relations and crowd-behavior support plays transformative role in constituting, reinforcing, or altering the consumer behavior (Prayag et al., 2013). Consumer-centric companies often launch advertising and communication campaigns to drive consumers by using several motivational tactics in reference to price, promotion, customer services, product and services delivery and guarantee, and technology benefits. The uniqueness of products and services, and scope of consumer stand-alone in the marketplace develops the *me too* feeling and generate arousal among consumer to experiment products, intention to purchase, and develop perceived value. Activation theory describes how cognitive arousal is necessary for effective functioning of people and achieving desired satisfaction. A person requires a certain level of activation psychologically, physiologically, and environmentally in order to get sufficiently motivated to achieve goals, take right decisions, follow logical action, and get perfect convergence with motivations, mind, and means. Consumers seek activation to justify needs, refine preferences, making right decision, developing perceived value, and get associated with the products or services. Companies tend to activate consumers through advertising and communication to educate consumers, derive experience through 'do-it-yourself' virtual and physical platforms, simulations, and experience sharing on digital media (Rajagopal, 2018).

Successful companies invest time and resources in understanding customers first, before developing products and developing cost-effective distribution systems. Companies do so by exploring customer problems, needs, and probable solutions by analyzing customer perceptions and user-generated contents on the digital platforms. The collective intelligence contributes significantly in understanding customers and developing appropriate customer engagements. Such corporate approach is able to constitute an insights engine comprising a set of people, psychodynamics, and processes. Companies are not only able to understand customers' attitude and behavior by activating the insight engine but also develop abilities to build user-driven actionable strategies. People contribute to the creative insights by sharing ideas and perceptions through brainstorming, expressing emotions, and engaging in storytelling with evidences rather than dry recitations of data. Unilever's Consumer Markets and Insights group may be cited as an epitome of a powerful insights engine, which has helped the company generate not only impressive revenue and sales growth but also to deliver high consumer value (van den Driest et al., 2016).

Consumer attitudes developed over the long-sustained perception, and actual behaviors, are commonly aligned unless the attitudes over time have shown cognitive disruption (abrupt shifts in attitude). Consumers have many opportunities to express attitude through behavior. However, sometimes attitude and behavior are both constrained to very specific circumstances. Consumer attitudes are based on personal experience and are endorsed by either the previous self-experience or peers. Attitude is strongly built around core beliefs of consumers on temporal, spatial, and personal experiences. Attitude–behavior consistency among consumers exists, when there is a strong relation between consumer perceptions, purchase intentions, actions, and perceived value. For example, a consumer with a positive green products and services buying attitude concerning about the environment, and recycling paper and bottles, shows high attitude–behavior sustainability and behavioral consistency. Companies need to develop strategies to encourage such attitude–behavior consistency among consumers, as it is important for co-creating behavior among potential consumers and guide their actions (Verma & Duggal, 2015).

7.2.2 *Decision Theories*

Most consumer-centric companies communicate brands through advertisements and peer interactivity in way that builds emotions among consumers and helps in developing perceptions over time. *Decision appraisal theory* argues that emotions play a significant role in developing right perceptions and judge decisions among consumers. Emotions are extracted from situational evaluations, appraisals of communication, and trial of products or services that raise specific observations among consumers. Essentially, appraisal of a situation causes an emotional, or affective response among consumers, which stands as a base for further judgments on adaptability of products or services, quality of the brand,

and building perceived value. Consumers also stay reflective, brainstorming, and analytical about their experience with the brands and products, and feel good or bad about them accordingly. Consumer judgments are affected by several biases including personal, social, corporate, and political leading to decision-making. The ability to combine self-perceptions with relevant knowledge pools and user experiences tend to form opinions and make decisions often with personal or crowd-based biases. Consumers often carry out self-appraisal to validate the judgments on buying decisions and determine rationale in their tactical decisions. The consumer communities share experiences on innovations, market promotions, social trends, and use values on products and services, which enables customer's choices with relevant data to inculcate consumption behavior over time. It has been observed in various market research studies that precision in understanding the consumer behavior enhances the scope of good judgment. Consumers share their observations on social network platforms helping others to make collective judgments through community-based learning, trust, experience, inclusivity, perceptual semantics, and strategic values (Likierman, 2020).

Emotions are valence[1] and specific affective reactions to the perception of situations, events, objects, or people. They influence thoughts, motivations, and behaviors, and can play an important role in family business strategy and decision-making. Specific discrete emotions influence judgments and decision-making processes (Bee & Neubaum, 2014). The appraisal theory of emotion proposes that emotions are extracted from appraisals of events leading to different opinions of peers and the society. As the popularity of e-commerce has risen to prominence in the twenty-first century, most consumers are able to appraise multiple brands online and emotionally perceive the brands, products, or services. Cognitive appraisals and emotions are the dominant determinants of online shopping behavior. Online consumers are more likely to disclose personal information when they have positive cognitive appraisals and liking toward the website in terms of safety and confidence (Li et al.,

[1] In psychology Valence is one of the most important scientific concepts that explains the experience of emotions. This term was introduced by Lewin (1951), which refers to the forces that attract individuals to desirable objects and repel them from undesirable ones. There is strong agreement that valence, expressed with terms such as positive–negative, good–bad, or pleasure–displeasure, captures something essential about affect related to human emotions.

2017). Cognitive appraisals on judgments are often a natural course of action, which makes persons to reconfirm their decisions and actions innumerable times beyond normal. The passion to take decision prevails with some consumers, who demonstrates also leadership and social controlling attitude. Such activities are personalized and embedded in self-concept, which is streamlined with the *Self-Determination Theory*. Individuals have tendency to integrate various cognitive elements around them into their judgments and strategic decisions (Moors et al., 2013).

Companies need to work beyond communicating successful advertisements and brand communications, and understand the integrated communication action paradigm toward convergence of awareness, comprehension, conviction, and action (ACCA). To generate emotions among consumers, it is essential to create awareness through substantial comprehension. These factors would be able to build emotions among consumers and drive intention toward associating with the brand (conviction). This stage is sensitive for both consumers and companies, because most consumers review their decision on brand association and purchase intentions, and tend to seek opinion of other consumers. Reviewing opinion of other consumers might override the self-reference of a consumer and defer the action. Customer acquisition and retention are largely based on the perceptions, corporate strategies, and social recognition of the brand. Companies make continuous efforts to acquire new customers by educating them on the brand performance and promotions, while the existing customer is retained by experience sharing across the spatial and temporal metrics. Consumer involvement in social networks and company's external relations helps in developing sustainable customer value. The customer value is an important parameter for the companies to play defensive role in the marketplace to acquire and retain customers. Building up customer value, involving them in the various products and services from designing to delivery, and serviceability helps the company to gain competitive advantage (Rajagopal, 2011).

Attribution theory deals with how a social perceiver analyzes public information to arrive at causal explanations for making decisions. This theory examines the relationship between the nature of information gathered and the way it has been combined to form a causal judgment (Fiske & Taylor, 1991). This theory discusses how and why people explain events as they do. However, attributions, comprehend consumer behavior to adopt a brand, product, or service and analyze their experience with it. Internal attribution refers to the process of cause and effect to the consumer needs, personality, and perceived use value. A consumer analyzes the brand behavior and experience of other consumers in the marketplace, and generally relies on internal attributions, such as personality traits, to judge his decision. The external characteristics of consumer attribution widely focus on the social and market effects than the internal attributes and self-congruence. The attribution elements that affect consumer cognition include choice, intentions, social desirability, hedonistic relevance, and congruence to personality. These elements affect short-run perceptions among consumers and help in developing intentions of brand association. However, to develop long-run brand associations, and build attitude and behavior of consumers toward the brand, the factors concerning consensus, distinctiveness, and consistency of behavior also influence the decision process of consumers (Kelley, 1967).

In the age of advanced information, technology, and access to the digital space, consumers interact and learn from the experience of each other, and evaluate public opinions before taking any decision. The *social learning theory* argues that people learn from one another through observation, imitation, and modeling. The theory has often been called a bridge between behaviorist and cognitive learning theories because it encompasses attention, memory, and motivation as strong drivers of learning (Bandura, 1977a). More than the digital space, television plays a significant role in learning among young consumers. In society, many influential models, such as family and friends, television, peers, and teachers at schools, colleges, and universities, surround consumers. Often consumers seek endorsement from peers, family, or social representatives, during the decision process. Observational learning occurs through observing the behavior of others. It is a form of social learning, which embeds in individual and group behavior. Observational learning could occur when cognitive processes are active in a person. These mental factors intervene (mediate) in the learning process to determine if a new response for decision process is needed (Bandura, 1977b). Cognitive drive is a psychological state of mind that controls the needs, decision process, and emotional touch points. The stages of need recognition, information analytics, emotions and arousal, and achieving satisfaction, largely form the path of cognitive drive among consumers. In psychology, the *drive theory* is based on the principle that physiological changes in a person take place when certain needs are not satisfied, and it create a state of stress. When a need is satisfied, the drive is reduced and the organism returns to a state of homeostasis and relaxation. However, considering the positive perspective of the drive theory, it is argued that cognitive drive has facets of both positivity and negativity in consumers, while measuring the extent of satisfaction to their needs. Neuromarketing studies reveal that the encoding specificity principle states 'the greater the similarity between the encoding event and the retrieval event, the greater the likelihood of recalling the original memory.' The consumer neuroscience explores the functions of brain to predict and manipulate consumer behavior and decision-making. Some ground-breaking studies in the past have demonstrated that it has potential to create value for marketers. However, it has been taken up more as an art to manipulate consumers than learning the cognitive and perceptual role of neuroscience in building attitude and behavior of consumers. Neuromarketing tools are superficially used to correlate the physiological and neural signals to gain insight into consumers' motivations, preferences, and decisions. Scientifically and medically, it contains methods of brain scanning, which measures neural activity, and physiological tracking, eye movement, and other physiological proxies associated with the cognitive dynamics. Nonetheless, some customer-centric firms tend to collaborate with the specialist consulting firms to use neuromarketing as a marketing tool. Consequently, the concept of neuromarketing is being oversold by the firms and with unrealistic expectations (Harrell, 2019).

Cue theory from the cognitive perspectives of consumers can be interpreted also in reference to consistency, utility, and confidence. Cues, such as the smell of cookies baking, smell of perfume/cologne, sound of ice falling into a whiskey tumbler, sight of a bowl of ice cream, and sight of a pack of cigarettes, if demonstrated or shown in a visual advertisement at periodical intervals, not only reinforce brand image but also help consumers in retrieving information easily to the top-of-the-mind. Optimal distinctiveness is a social psychological theory explaining within-group and outside-group differences. It asserts that individuals desire to attain an optimal balance of inclusion and distinctiveness, within and between social groups and situations. The behavior of everyone needs to belong to a group, and at the same time everyone needs to be unique, is the core argument of optimal distinctiveness theory. According to *Optimal Distinctiveness Theory*, individuals strive to maintain a balance between the need to be assimilated by the peers and family, and the need for autonomy and differentiation. Optimal distinctiveness is a social psychological theory toward understanding internal and external differences within a group of people or consumers. Consumers often form their groups of interest to share experiences and information about consumption practices. Hence, the distinctiveness theory explains the consumer behavior very closely. This concept asserts that individuals desire to attain an optimal balance of inclusion and distinctiveness within and between social groups and situations (Brewer, 1991).

Social institutions play a significant role in nurturing the cultural heritage, which is reflected in the individual behavior. Such institutions include family, education, and political structures. The media affects the ways in which people relate to one another, organize their activities to live in harmony with one another, teach acceptable behavior to succeeding generations, and govern themselves. The status of gender in society, the family, social classes, group behavior, age groups, and how societies define decency and civility, are interpreted differently in every culture. Social institutions are a system of regulatory norms and rules of governing actions in pursuit of immediate ends in terms of their conformity with the ultimate common value system of a community. They constitute underlying norms and values making up the common value system of a society. Institutions are intimately related to and derived from the value attitudes common to members of a community. This establishes institutions as primarily moral phenomena, which leads to enforce individual decisions on all human needs including economic and business-related issues. The primary means for enforcement of norms is moral authority whereby an individual obeys the norm because that individual believes that the norm is good for its own sake. The relationship between the business and religion truly poses a self-challenge. Mary Kay Inc., an international direct marketing cosmetics company operates on the *Go-Give philosophy* (Weston, 1999).

7.3 Consumption Philosophies

Crowd-based cognition often alters the innate consumption behavior and induce quick shifts in the perceptions, attitude, and behavior of consumers. The crowd focus is categorical in the context of premier, mass, and bottom of the pyramid consumer segments. The categorical crowd of upstream consumers debates the value of products and services from the hedonic perspectives in reference to price-quality and self-esteem correlations while the collective intelligence of mass consumers highlights concerns on value for money from the utilitarian standpoint. Commonly, consumption behavior is built around two prime consumption philosophies—utilitarianism and hedonism. Utilitarian consumption emphasizes gaining the consumer surplus and long-term association with the products or services, whereas hedonic consumption behavior grows over the emotive and multisensory cognition supported by the societal values and shopping experience (Hirschman & Holbrook, 1982). The lifestyle-oriented consumption behavior is widely driven by social consciousness, personality factors, and market-driven stimulants, which widely appeal to the consumers of upstream segments. Consumers tend to maximize happiness following the social trend, crowd behavior, and emotions. They are widely driven by the collective intelligence and social behavior, which motivates consumers to lean toward hedonic consumption (Tsai & Hsee, 2008).

Conspicuous consumption exhibits the tendency of buying and displaying high-value products to indicate wealth, social status, and live aligned with the social trends. According to evolutionary psychology (Griskevicius & Kenrick, 2013), conspicuous consumption may represent a means of competition in mate attraction. Consumers with low income tend to buy conspicuous goods on credit as it signals high status to compensate for their feelings of economic powerlessness and the relatively inferior social value and lifestyle (Rucker & Galinsky, 2008). Emotional attachments lead to stronger consumer self-image congruence on brands. Consequently, people with emotions blended with inferiority and alienated feelings suffer from deprived social values and become dissatisfied with the quality of life. Consumers indulging in the consumption of high-value brands create unique positions and identities of consumers in the society. In conspicuous consumption, behavior shows strong evidence toward self-image congruence that explains and predicts different aspects of consumer behavior. The consumer homophily often drives consumers to compartmentalize their social values and lifestyles because of either superiority or inferiority cognitive attributes. Such state of mind drives inferiority-driven consumers to adapt to conspicuous consumption behavior (Ghiglino & Goyal, 2010). Higher perceived social value is associated with more positive feelings toward value and lifestyle satisfaction, as well as relates to less depression, anxiety, and stress social value and status are also associated with increased self-efficacy and self-esteem, which leads to more positive self-perceptions and positive feelings.

Social image and self-image congruence are two of the major factors that affect conspicuous consumption behavior. Accordingly, consumer achieves the sense of hedonic fulfillment on consumption of high value-high technology products as their attributes match with the consumer's desired self-image. Consumers develop strong emotional attachment with conspicuous products as they add value to their lifestyle and societal identity (Foroudi et al., 2014). Hedonic value, therefore, reflects the emotional worth of consumers in experiencing self-image congruence and societal lifestyle. Such cognitive perceptions lead to conspicuous consumption behavior. Conspicuous behavior is developed with cognitive focus on societal value and attention to hedonic elements. Such consumption experience is elicited from emotive and multisensory elements that focus on affective consumer behavior (Jiang & Benbasat, 2007). The *theory of conspicuous consumption* explains the behavior of high economic class people in the society of displaying excess wealth to promote their social status. Conspicuous behavior exhibits the tendency of buying high-value goods to display wealth on products and goods that have either emotional or utilitarian values. Veblen and Banta (2009), explained conspicuous consumption behavior as a tendency of wasting excess wealth. The innovation diffusion theory primarily focuses on users as buyers, who buy innovative products considering cost, perceived use value, and societal value. However, this theory downplays the role of firms, policymakers, and referrals within the geo-demographic segments to create upmarket value of a product (Geels & Johnson, 2018). The social cognitive theory can also be explained in the context of continuous social learning emphasizing the importance of motivation and social variables in human behavior. This theory explains an individual's belief and reinforcement of self-image to improve social value and lifestyle (Schunk & DiBenedetto, 2020).

The peer-to-peer and crowd information sharing platforms connect across bi- or multi-directional channels comprising firms, service providers, referrals, and users through online dissemination of ideas, experiences, and trends. Such collective information integrated intangible features like space, time, and knowledge along with the tangible resources and assets to customers. The crowd information sharing platforms including social media channels, blogs, and corporate media not only disseminate the peer discussions, dialogues, and disruptions across various categories of customers but also create value by educating them on key decision indicators such as prices, accessibility, promotions, competitive leverage, shopping flexibilities, ease of use, technology, and developments. Most consumer debates on products and services on crowd platforms are led by a user-focused mission with transparency, privacy protection, and interactive communications, which influence the tactical (short term), ad hoc (temporary), and strategic (long-term) consumption behavior (Dolnicar, 2019). Contrary to hedonic consumption behavior, utilitarian motivations are related to functional, economic, rational, practical, or extrinsic benefits, which make the consumer experience and decision on buying products or services with the utilitarian values agreeable and pleasant. In direct and crowd-referred buying consumers are motivated toward buying in the context of following information:

- Availability of products and services,
- Information on competitive pricing,
- Navigation for desired products, and
- Deliberation on utilitarian values and brand strategy.

The main interest of consumers to look into the crowd-based information is a set of reliable and relevant information that advocates easy navigation for a wide assortment of products and categories on various online shopping channels. Such pro-product and pro-shopping channel information on social media channels trigger planned or impulse buying. Alternatively, the collective intelligence helps consumers in knowledge building and exploring the availability of useful information to make conscious purchasing decisions (Moe, 2003).

Personal influences, which include cognitions, beliefs, perceptions, and emotions, are widely derived from peers and the society. Personal influences include processes that help to instigate and sustain motivational outcomes. The social cognitive theory explains that goals of consumers are driven by the social motivational outcomes. A goal is a mental representation usually driven by self-image, which is based on personal values. Consumers tend to establish their self-image congruence with the societal values. Therefore, consumers lean toward conspicuous behavior to reinforce cognitive satisfaction by staying at par with the societal values and lifestyle. Social values and lifestyle are psychographic variables that distinguish patterns of personal beliefs, cognitive ergonomics, and living standards in the context of prevailing societal values (Green et al., 2006).

References

Andrade, M. S. (2007). Learning communities: Examining positive outcomes. *Journal of College Student Retention: Research, Theory & Practice, 9*(1), 1–20.

Avery, J., Fournier, S., & Wittenbraker, J. (2014). Unlock the mysteries of your customer relationships. *Harvard Business Review, 92*(7), 72–81.

Bandura, A. (1977a). *Social learning theory*. Prentice-Hall.

Bandura, A. (1977b). Self-efficacy: Toward a unifying theory of behavior change. *Psychological Review, 84*(2), 191–215.

Bee, C., & Neubaum, D. O. (2014). The role of cognitive appraisal and emotions of family members in the family business system. *Journal of Family Business Strategy, 5*(3), 323–333.

Brewer, M. (1991). The social self: On being the same and being different at the same time. *Personality and Social Psychology Bulletin, 17*(5), 475–482.

Carmona-Lavado, A., Cuevas-Rodríguez, G., & Cabello-Medina, C. (2010). Social and organizational capital: Building the context for innovation. *Industrial Marketing Management, 39*(4), 681–690.

Chaturvedi, A., & Carroll, J. D. (1998). A perceptual mapping procedure for analysis of proximity data to determine common and unique product-market structures. *European Journal of Operational Research, 111*(2), 268–284.

Dolnicar, S. (2019). A review of research into paid online peer-to-peer accommodation: Launching the Annals of Tourism Research curated collection on peer-to-peer accommodation. *Annals of Tourism Research, 75*, 248–264.

Fishbien, M., & Ajzen, I. (1975). *Belief, attitude, intention, and behavior: An introduction to theory and research*. Addison-Wesley.

Fiske, S. T., & Taylor, S. E. (1991). *Social cognition* (2nd ed.). McGraw-Hill.

Foroudi, P., Melewar, T. C., & Gupta, S. (2014). Linking corporate logo, corporate image, and reputation: An examination of consumer perceptions in the financial setting. *Journal of Business Research, 67*(11), 269–2281.

Fox, J. (2015). From "economic man" to behavioral economics. *Harvard Business Review, 93*(5), 78–85.

Geels, F. W., & Johnson, V. (2018). Towards a modular and temporal understanding of system diffusion: Adoption models and socio-technical theories applied to Austrian biomass district-heating (1979–2013). *Energy Research and Social Science, 38*(1), 138–153.

Geisler, E. (2007). The metrics of knowledge: Mechanisms for preserving the value of managerial knowledge. *Business Horizons, 50*(6), 467–477.

Ghiglino, C., & Goyal, S. (2010). Keeping up with the neighbors: Social interaction in a market economy. *Journal of European Economic Association, 8*(1), 90–119.

Gourville, J. T., & Norton, M. I. (2014). *Marketing reading: Consumer behavior and the buying process*. Harvard Business School Press.

Green, G. T., Gordell, H. K., & Betz, G. J. (2006). Construction and validation of the national survey on recreation and the environment's lifestyles scale. *Journal of Leisure Research, 38*(4), 513–535.

Griskevicius, V., & Kenrick, D. T. (2013). Fundamental motives: How evolutionary needs influence consumer behavior. *Journal of Consumer Psychology, 23*(3), 372–386.

Harrell, E. (2019). *Neuromarketing: What you need to know*. Harvard Business School Press.

Hirschman, E. C., & Holbrook, M. B. (1982). Hedonic consumption: Emerging concepts, methods and propositions. *Journal of Marketing, 46*(1), 92–101.

Jiang, Z., & Benbasat, I. (2007). Research note- investigating the influence of the functional mechanisms of online product presentations. *Information Systems Research, 18*, 454–470.

Jost, J. T. (2017). The marketplace of ideology: "Elective affinities" in political psychology and their implications for consumer behavior. *Journal of Consumer Psychology, 27*(4), 502–520.

Kelley, H. H. (1967). Attribution theory in social psychology. In D. Levine (Ed.), *Nebraska symposium on motivation* (Vol. 15, pp. 192–238). University of Nebraska Press.

Lafley, A. G., & Martin, R. (2017). *Customer loyalty is overrated*. Harvard Business School Press.

Lafley, A. G., Martin, R., McGrath, R. G., Cook, S., Knudstorp, J. V., & Champion, D. (2017). Cumulative advantage. *Harvard Business Review, 95*(1).

Lewin, K. (1951). *Field theory in social science: Selected theoretical papers*. Greenwood Press.

Li, H., Luo, X., Zhang, J., & Xu, H. (2017). Resolving the privacy paradox: Toward a cognitive appraisal and emotion approach to online privacy behaviors. *Information & Management, 54*(8), 1012–1022.

Likierman, A. (2020). *The elements of good judgment*. Harvard Business School Press.

Mathur, P., Chun, H. H., & Maheswaran, D. (2016). Consumer mindsets and self-enhancement: Signaling versus learning. *Journal of Consumer Psychology, 26*(1), 142–152.

McClelland, D. C. (1978). Managing motivation to expand human freedom. *American Psychologist, 33*(3), 201–210.

Moe, W. W. (2003). Buying, searching, or browsing: Differentiating between online shoppers using in-store navigational clickstream. *Journal of Consumer Psychology, 13*(1–2), 29–39.

Moors, A., Ellsworth, P. C., Scherer, K. R., & Frijda, N. H. (2013). Appraisal theories of emotion: State of the art and future development. *Emotion Review, 5*(2), 119–124.

Mwesiumo, D., & Halpern, N. (2018). Acquiescence and conflict in exchanges between inbound tour operators and their overseas outbound partners: A case study on Tanzania. *Tourism Management, 69*, 345–355.

Neeley, S. (2005). Influences on consumer socialization. *Young Consumers, 6*(2), 63–69.

Pookulangara, S., & Koesler, K. (2011). Cultural influence on consumers' usage of social networks and its impact on online purchase intentions. *Journal of Retailing and Consumer Services, 18*(4), 348–354.

Prayag, G., Hosany, S., & Odeh, K. (2013). The role of tourists' emotional experiences and satisfaction in understanding behavioral intentions. *Journal of Destination Marketing and Management, 2*(2), 118–127.

Quelch, J. A., & Kenny, D. (1994). Extend profits, not product lines. *Harvard Business Review, 73*(5), 153–160.

Rajagopal. (2008). Measuring brand performance through metrics application. *Measuring Business Excellence, 12*(1), 29–38.

Rajagopal. (2011). Impact of radio advertisements on buying behaviour of urban commuters. *International Journal of Retail and Distribution Management, 39*(7), 480–503.

Rajagopal. (2016). *Sustainable growth in global markets: Strategic choices and managerial implications*. Palgrave Macmillan.

Rajagopal. (2018). *Consumer Behavior Theories: Convergence of Divergent Perspectives with Applications to Marketing and Management*. New York: Business Expert Press.

Rammstedt, B., Danner, D., & Bosnjak, M. (2017). Acquiescence response styles: A multilevel model explaining individual-level and country-level differences. *Personality and Individual Differences, 107*, 190–194.

Rucker, D. D., & Galinsky, A. D. (2008). Desire to acquire: Powerlessness and compensatory consumption. *Journal of Consumer Research, 35*(3), 257–267.

Rucker, D. D., & Galinsky, A. D. (2009). Conspicuous consumption versus utilitarian ideals: How different levels of power shape consumer behavior. *Journal of Experimental Social Psychology, 45*(3), 549–555.

Sankaran, K., & Demangeot, C. (2011). On becoming a culturally plural consumer. *Journal of Consumer Marketing, 28*(7), 540–549.

Sharpe, M. E. (2008). *Microeconomics in context*. Routledge.

Smedslund, J. (2011). Meaning of words and the use of axiomatics in psychological theory. *Journal of Theoretical & Philosophical Psychology, 31*(2), 126–135.

Schunk, D. H., & DiBenedetto, M. K. (2020). Motivation and social cognitive theory. *Contemporary Educational Psychology, 60*, 101832. https://doi.org/10.1016/j.cedpsych.2019.101832

Sidibe, M. (2020). *Marketing meets mission*. Harvard Business School Press.

Tsai, C., & Hsee, C. (2008). Hedonomics in consumer behaviour. *Rotman Management Magazine*, Spring, 45–49.

Taylor, B. (2018). *Lifestyle brands are building hotels now*. Harvard Business School Press.
Uduji, J. I., & Ankeli, M. O. (2013). Needs for achievement, affiliation, and power: The possible sales manager's actions for exceptional sales force performance. *Research Journal of Finance and Accounting, 4*(9), 96–103.
van den Driest, F., Sthanunathan, S., & Weed, K. (2016). Building an insights engine. *Harvard Business Review, 94*(9), 64–74.
Verma, H. V., & Duggal, E. (2015). Environmental concerns, behavior consistency of emerging market: Youth and marketing. *Emerging Economy Studies, 1*(2), 171–187.
Veblen, T., & Banta, M. (2009). *The theory of the leisure class*. Oxford University Press.
Weston, H. (1999). *Mary Kay cosmetics-sales force incentives*. Harvard Business School Press.

CHAPTER 8

Crowd-Based Service Design

The collective intelligence not only offers ideation, but also helps firms in decision-making. The crowd-based business models also share control rights between stakeholders and management. This chapter discusses the crowd-based business models in service industries, collective governance, and shareholder rights. The concept and modalities of reverse service pyramid are argued in this chapter as 'putting the customers first.' In addition, the concept of thinking triangle comprising design thinking, systems thinking, and value thinking has been discussed in this chapter in the context of coevolution of services firms with crowd value chain. The discussions on designing services-based crowd platforms, reverse service pyramid, social domain of services, and systems thinking and value management in crowd-based services are central to this chapter. This chapter argues that services firms using collective intelligence develop value-driven services business model and provide cost-effective utilitarian services with embedded aesthetic and emotional values.

Collective approach in services designing has been successful in social services sectors including public health, education, housing, transportation, and ecological conservation. Crowd cognition in developing community services has contributed significantly in building public–private partnership. In general, the collective services are those that are provided by the government, self-help community groups, and large

Rajagopal, *Crowd-Based Business Models*,
https://doi.org/10.1007/978-3-030-77083-9_8

non-governmental organizations. Nonprofit institutions engaged in delivering community services are socially governed and largely crowdfunded, which broadly include social enterprises engaged in offering green energy to households, water conservation services, social health (out-patients services), and farm and non-farm activities designing at the grassroots. Such collective services are also partially supported by the local governments through capital and human resources. Designing Internet-based social heath application together with crowdsourcing and social networks is able to generate a digital *living and learning* system, which has contributed through BioGames application in diagnosing malaria parasite in human blood. This application on mobile phones helped laypersons to diagnose red blood cells infected with malaria parasite. The rapid diagnostics for malaria through this gamification tool have improved the management of malaria diagnosis in low- and middle-income countries, where the process of diagnosis is expensive, unreliable due to climatic disorders (temperature variations) and inadequately equipped laboratories. BioGames was made available on Android and online. Gamers were given a tutorial, then in the game had a syringe to *kill* infected cells and *collect* healthy ones. Similarly, another example of crowdsourcing in social health management is in managing public health emergencies through digital tools. Frontline SMS, also called Frontline SMS Medic, enables users to request needs via SMS. It has been used in Malawi, Burundi, Bangladesh, and Honduras. Ushahidi is an open source crowdsourcing application that collects individual reports via web, SMS, and email. It can classify, translate, and geotag results. Ushahidi software was initially created in response to election violence in Kenya, but it has been used most popularly deployed to manage health and social emergencies following the aftermath of the Haitian earthquake in 2010 (Wazny, 2018).

8.1 Designing on Crowd Platforms

Crowdsourcing in large organizations have been practiced to develop service designs and has become central to the companies like Netflix, Amazon, and travel and tourism companies, which develop new services and improve those existing through customer engagement and open-innovation processes. Travel and tourism companies learn from customers and stakeholders about developing new tourism ventures and develop new service designs. Consequently, collective intelligence has emerged as a principal source to understand customers and improve service efficiency. This shift in services design process is considered more as requirement for designing customer-centric services, implementing servitization process, and creating value among customer than involving crowd potential merely as aesthetics to acquire new customers. Designing services collectively employs design-thinking *en masse* throughout the organization and within its ecosystem. The crowd-based approach in services management and marketing helps in resolving value embedded complexities of many services and processes. People attempt to pave path cater to their needs by exploring right solutions through interactions within and outside the community (Eisenmann et al., 2006). The interactions are often supported by information technology platforms and other audio-visual interface systems to create intuitive and pleasurable feeling among the crowd participations. Crowd-based design thinking is a simplified way to learn consumer perceptions, experiences, and emotions by humanizing the services designing and implementation process. Understanding the cognitive dimensions of users, crowd-based services motivate the creation of physical models, such as diagrams and sketches, to explore problems, identify ways to resolve them, and develop prototypes for experimentation (including community avenues, do-it-yourself, or experiencing through augmented reality platforms. The crowd interface also explores the chances of failure of new services and suggests the tolerance limit with the break-even point and social acceptance level. However, in creating crowd-based design-centers it is difficult to quantify the returns on investment accurately as crowd may not focus on all mediating and intervening elements of business ecosystem that affect the profitability of ventures or services programs (Kolko, 2015).

Most social services are redefined in the crowd-based business landscape as they meet with several realities that emerge out of perceptions, experience, and expectations of the service users. The crowd-based services revisions, redesigns, and reengagement of customers reveal core competitive thinking as compared to in-company appraisals of services. The social network involves customers, referrals, and stakeholders of distinct groups of users in a network. Crowd brainstorming helps bidirectionally the markets and firms as they not only benefit users of services but also enlighten the decision-makers of companies. Crowdsources and crowdfunded social health programs, which are run by the community centers or self-help groups connect ambidextrously with the patients and pharmaceutical industry comprising pharmaceutical companies, pharmacies, medical doctors, and laboratories. Such organization link patients to a web of health care providers and vice versa and connect with collectively designed operating systems, which interlinks computer users and application developers for periodical evaluations of the functionality of platforms and to carry out need improvements. Two-sided networks differ from traditional value chains as in the traditional system, value is evolved from cost–benefit (profit) ratio while in the crowd-based business modeling value is considered in the context of customer relationship, satisfaction, and loyalty, which ensures sustainability in business. Putting the service users first in the crowd-based business models reduces the service costs on one hand and improves the sustainable network effects on the other.

Civic crowdfunding is a crowdfunding practice, which is applied to social development projects. Such projects are difficult to quantify about the share of resources as they hold both tangible (capital and human resources, and infrastructure) and intangible (voluntary services offered by people) share in implementing service projects. However, as they represent a significant opportunity for the society, such organizations are governed by the self-help groups and non-governmental organizations. Such social institutions leverage funds for public interest projects, more broadly for projects aiming to improve social well-being. Crowdfunding for local social goods has been implemented to carry out various small-scale and community projects within the region, such as designing public parks, raising public facilities, and community centers by revamping distressed areas. Most civic crowdfunding is *place-based* as against general crowdfunding, which relies on web technologies and online communities. Crowdfunding on social services like health, infrastructure, and transportation relies mainly on offline communities in suburban and rural areas and contributes to concrete local impact. Such service design approaches are stimulated through personal relations, community meetings, public–private partnerships, and corporate initiatives. In these cases, the crowdfunding platform plays the role of intermediary and catalyst for people who have a common stake in the crowdfunded project (Charbit & Desmoulins, 2017).

With the advancement and outreach of information technology to millions of social network users in developing nations has an influx of applications and tools that help people to connect on various crowd platform to manifest their ideas and experiences. The popular crowd interaction tools range from Facebook to YouTube to Instagram that endorses new paradigms of social and commercial innovations, which have emerged as co-creation and coevolution. Services co-creation in suburban and rural geographies has emerged as a new approach of hearing people on finding innovative solutions for chronic, casual, or predetermined social problems. It is the process by which services are developed jointly by companies through the user-generated contents. While the co-creation of services is in process, customers and stakeholders, tend to create value by opening up in the niche, regional, national, and global markets. Startup, small and medium enterprises largely rely on the co-creating process for designing new services and cultivate a co-creative engagement platform based on brainstorming, discussions on ecosystem elements, innovations dialogue, accessibility of innovated and improved services, risk assessment, and transparency in the disseminating the user-generated contents (Ramaswamy, 2009).

Crowdsourcing is an open-innovation approach to solve problems, create new products, and improve consumer experiences. Upstream and mainstream consumer brands adapt to grow as crowd brand for achieving quick success in the competitive markets. Crowdsourcing provides as strategic pool of collective intelligence by engaging consumers as a part of a brainstorming exercise and action. It delivers interesting and dynamic marketing opportunities for services brands like Netflix, Amazon Prime, and Disney Channel, through effective consumer engagement (Bal et al., 2017). Crowdsourcing has emerged as powerful tool to promote services brands by empowering services brand communities within the social and ethnic ecosystem. Brand communities segmented from a larger crowd enables customer-centric firms to make decisions that influence image of services brands and product offerings in a controlled and planned way. Such move in managing crowd-motivated services brands reveal powerfully positive effects, as the campaign of Ryan Air, a low-cost airline of Ireland was endorsed by the crowd as an economic value-based service in Europe. Crowdsourcing offers mutual benefit for firms and consumers as users receive benefits of value for money, social comfort, and comparative self-esteem among peers. The crowdsourcing firm benefits from the collective intelligence to build future collaboration with people and gain confidence on its services brands. McDonald's Twitter hashtag campaign in 2012, #McDStories, designed to impart information about the restaurant chain's suppliers and to allow customers to share their own McDonald's stories publicly (Estellés-Arolas & González-Ladron-de-Guevara, 2012).

Crowd behavior is often unpredictable. Though crowds serve as social change agents, the information generated on crowd platforms can be perceived as either positive or negative. The unification of crowd communication, emotions, and ideation is a major challenge to the firms that rely on crowdsourcing and try to understand the crowd's cognitive inclination and meaning of structured or random deliberations. The group activities such as participating in contests, creating a visuals and videos collectively (social photo journalism), organizing debates, or triggering social revolutions would complement the positive crowd manifestations. As crowdsourcing has gained critical importance in business, the power, intelligence, influence, and impact of the crowd has been seen as a positive force for companies. Ultimately, crowdsourcing is an approach to harness the collective intelligence, create end user value, and motive people for a common good. Ideally, the collective intelligence has emerged as a stronger social backup than that of a few individuals within an organization or community (Xu et al., 2015).

Crowdsourcing has attained global focus as many social issues such as sustainability, public health, organic cultivation, and regional development congregated as civic and corporate social responsibility. Integrating people with business to achieve profit with purpose and social values has encouraged service-led growth through practical techniques. The collective intelligence has encouraged low-cost service innovation integrating the following elements of *services ecosystem*:

4As:Awareness (collective intelligence), attributes (need-based design), affordability (cost-effective services), and adaptability (social and economic stimuli to consume services)

4Cs:Cost to customer (tangible and intangible costs), convenience (availability and perceived ease of use), communication (transparency and clarity in user-generated contents), and conflict resolution (customer relationship management)

4Vs:Value (customer and social values), validity (collective decision), venue (social marketing of services), and vogue (value and lifestyle)

4Es:Exportability (crowd-based innovation), expansion (improvements in services and processes), experience (sharing with community), and emotions (sense of belongingness with crowd-based services design)

4Is:Interest (public interest), information (crowd-based, recurring, and strategic), image (social and personal congruence), and implementation (people-led growth).

4Ms:Marketing of services (strategic and tactical focus), mobility (geo-demographic fit), management (crowd and social governance), and maintenance (public–private partnership)

Services are intangible and dynamic, which need periodic user intervention to improve in real time using affordable technology and design driven by the crowd. Most product innovations unlike services focus on partial dynamic attributes like pricing and promotion, which have impact on commercialization innovated products. The product designs are relatively static with predetermined physical properties. Services are largely driven by the experience and emotion. Therefore, perceived values for services are vulnerable unlike products and need frequent interventions of users to improve the services attributes in collaboration with the service providers. Services blueprinting is a process for designing new and improving services based on changing customer preferences and is securely grounded in the customer's experience, which allows value-based dynamic service processes (Bitner et al, 2008).

8.2 Reverse Services Pyramid

Crowd-based interactive platforms support the designing of customer-centric and social services. Collective approach in designing of sectoral services such as education, health, housing, and sustainability are not only a valuable source of human capital but also provide an interface for community learning and awareness. The social services are successfully managed using the collective intelligence, which encompasses contemporary ideas, solution to existing problems, and value creation perspectives. In this process customers, stakeholders, and collaborators (social and corporate) share their experience to design new services or improve existing services and tend to build social cohesion (Barthel et al., 2014). Crowd interactions develop coherent learning platforms to deal with new ideas for existing problems. The collective information in designing social services focuses on special issues and sets goals, approaches, accountability, and explores possible pitfalls. The crowd-based services projects aim at exploring social or business ecosystems and develop service approaches based on the customer-generated contents. Therefore, a collective intelligence system embeds multiple ideas from customers and stakeholders, which are built on community-based technologies (Shams, 2016).

Crowd, comprising customers, referrals, technocrats, and stakeholders constitute the bottom of pyramid while the top management as decision-making unit in an organization stays atop the pyramid. In the crowd-based business models this pyramid stand reversed empowering the bottom line, which contributes to the customer-centric products and services designs, operation strategies, and competitive performance through stakeholder governance. Crowd-based service companies observe reverse accountability, which empower stakeholders to monitor, evaluate, and raise performance-related clarifications to the administration and top management of the company. Crowdsourcing has a significant positive impact on products and services design quality in the initial phase while the user expertise positively moderates the role of crowdsourcing on the design quality, development of services, and delivery management. In addition, crowd-connectivity and expert networking play an inverted effect on crowdsourcing-product design quality relationship (Jiao et al., 2021). Crowdsourcing strengthens services innovation and its performance in a given social context. Service innovation through crowd stimulated ideation process is a major challenge faced by an organization to streamline crowd-based ideas from the perspective of their economic viability and technological feasibility. Most customer services companies rely on crowd and customer engagement designing, implementing, and solving services issues. Companies broadcasts open calls to engage individuals with suitable knowledge and expertise outside the organizational boundaries in developing customer-centric services. Commonly the crowdsourcing projects are frequently applied to develop new service insights, identify solutions for existing services, find new technology applications, get 3-D designs, build customer-centric virtual service automation prototypes, and even develop low-cost software solutions (Füller et al., 2014).

In services marketing firms, loyalty is influenced by the existing knowledge of consumers and is found to be positively and significantly related to the quality of information, right to information, and organizational competencies. Consumer education was found to be positively associated with consumer knowledge or expertise on the products or services. The consumer education significantly affects consumer loyalty and service quality delivered by the firms (Bell & Eisingerich, 2007). It has been observed that a service firm with consumer-orientation approach increases relationship quality, while a low-profile selling approach decreases relationship quality. The relationship quality significantly affects the possibilities of future retention of consumers. Firms should emphasize on training their employees on consumer orientation, which would add additional value to a firm's service offering and influence acquisition and retention of the consumers (Huang, 2008). An empirical research, conducted for differentiating the various types of knowledge, evidences that the relative effects of the self-assessed and objective knowledge depend on the type of the information source. The new strategies were supported by the Internet of Things (IoT) concepts to develop and manage the cost-time-risk triangulation in business. Accordingly, a consistent business-operating model with transparency, new governance, and improved processes emerged across regions and industries. Consequently, the digital business-to-business marketing approaches helped companies control the growth in costs and time spreads and brought new discipline into managing the impact of risk in marketing products to business clients. As a result, returns on investment in industrial marketing has improved significantly in the late twentieth century.

The concept of sharing economy has emerged as foundation for the people-led social and economic development and has been encouraged to strengthen the developing economies. The sharing economy is treated as an umbrella growth concept to motivate collective innovation, community consumption, crowdsourcing, crowdfunding, and social entrepreneurship. It explores new opportunities and encompasses customer-centric competencies to develop products and services to cater to customer needs and share for usage rather than own or buy them. The digital publishing industry is one of the contemporary examples of shared business as promoted by the Kindle books of Amazon. The practice of crowdsourcing in service design has become popular over the years. Suburban and rural economies in developing countries have also been leveraged by the crowdsourced ideas, people's participation, and public–private partnerships in implementing local transportation, sharing production infrastructure, and using the essential community services. The peer-to-peer logistics in urban areas commonly known as car-pools to facilitate community mobility is a good example of shared services which in rural areas in India community productions centers for handloom weavers is revolutionary experiment in the cooperative sector.

The social network platforms are used by the consumers to compare prices among competitors. These platforms have also opened freeways to exhibit products online and share their opinion or experience on the products and services. Consequently, marketers have lost control over how and where their products are presented to potential customers. Some of the more sophisticated online retailers have used this trend to their advantage, employing recommendation algorithms, user reviews, and unique customer-generated content to build trust and increase a consumer's propensity to purchase. A variety of online players including Amazon.com, Netflix, and Internet radio site Pandora are recognized for having state-of-the-art recommendation systems that effectively match customers with the products, movies, and music they love.

The reverse pyramid of crowd-based services design is gaining strength over time with the growing advancement in information technology, communication devices, and user outreach to interactive crowd platforms. The widespread usage of mobile phones and other communication devices has enabled crowdsourcing and peer interactions easy and enjoyable, which has volunteered people to participate in the crowd discussions and share their views and experiences. Consequently, increasing number of customers are using their mobile devices to find information not only about the products and services brands, their performance, and associated corporate image. Using the social networks customer-centric firms empower customers with mobile offers, mobile information, and mobile customer service and motivate them to participate in the crowd brainstorming, dialogues, and design contributions (social, economic, engineering, and management-related themes). Mobile web users, who serve as connoisseurs and spend their time in content channels to explore information and conduct data-text mining across blogs and corporate websites. However, the following strategies would help firms in managing a successful crowd interactions:

- A careful selection of people in various crowd segments,
- Briefing them with crowdsourcing objectives,
- Explaining corporate strategy path and expected contributions from the crowd cognition, and
- Encouraging technology-driven services blueprint through crowd conversations

It is observed that such people's empowerment would inculcate a positive perception among the participants to state positive views about the services, brands, and the company in the independent blogs (Bernoff & Schadler, 2010).

Some studies discuss that though service quality has attracted considerable attention within the services marketing literature, high profile consumer education has not been considered as a valuable strategy. It is argued that consumer education is a powerful quality strategy in a variety of service contexts, and that it is already being used by an increasing number of service organizations. Firms delivering services influence the degree of quality of services in references to the education of consumers, skills, and cognitive abilities toward reviewing the efficiency of services. Thus, services marketing firms try to build co-shopping and co-reviewing with customers of different levels of education (Sabrina, 2005). It has been observed that consumers with high level of education often develop negative perceptions on services marketing firms. These consumers resist the services firm's deceptive practices (perceived deception) on consumer's relational variables (satisfaction and loyalty intentions to the online retailer). Also, the level of education in consumers plays moderating role in determining consumer attitude toward the Internet (Sergio, 2010). Co-creation is used today as a democratic business approach not only to develop new service designs but also applied in services recoveries as an effective tool. Co-creating a service recovery has been proved worth over the conventional service recovery systems and evaluations. Customers involved in co-creating a service recovery strategies exhibit confidence as they could explore the reasons for services failure and contribute most favorable solutions to revive the services. Co-creating a service recovery reveals better results for low equity brands than for high equity brands. A co-created service recovery demonstrates the knowledge and skills of customer to join systematically the disrupted operations blocks between the customer and service provider within services value. Previous researches illustrate that there is a positive effect of a co-created service recovery on customer satisfaction and repurchase intentions, as the co-creation process generates effective customer engagement, which creates also emotions and sense of belongingness among customers. Consequently, co-creating services recovery process generates high-perceived value and stimulates quick acceptance of revived services among peers (Hazee et al., 2017).

Over time, the distribution and logistics functions in large companies have transformed from dealer-based perspectives to channel-driven logistics. This management approach has seeded value-based channel management (VBCM) model through a holistic vision on managing distribution and logistics operations with several customer-centric parameters. The VBCM model has been a beginning toward integrating the cost and risk factors with 5Ts comprising time, target, territory, task, and thrust on services efficiencies. Implementing dynamic capabilities into practice is a major challenge not only for small and medium organizations but also for many multi-domestic companies operating in emerging markets. Therefore, the power of organizational design, showing how managers can harness new organizational forms to build a capacity for sensing, shaping, and seizing competitive opportunities, is a strategic operations decision. Fast-moving business scenarios lean toward decentralized organization design and self-organizing processes that quickly convert individual capabilities into actionable collective intellect. However, self-organizing processes require managers to design and execute them. The new organizational design principles include multi-functional teams to build dynamic capabilities for sustained innovation in dynamic environments (Feline & Powell, 2016).

Crowd-based ideation process is easier and can be streamlined during the process; however, driving these ideas marketable is a challenging task as group discussions on crowd platforms often collapse due to evidence-based discussions and outcomes. Co-creating marketing strategy needs enormous experience among customers and stakeholders in the context of new product responses in the competitive markets and their predicted lifecycle. Nonetheless, the innovation paradigm has significantly shifted in the twenty-first century from centralized to decentralized strategies and from manufacturer-centric to democratized designing of products and services. The trends of services marketing have also moved from closed organizational strategies to open-market concepts and the organizational monopoly of internal discovery has been overridden by the external engagements significantly. Consequently, open innovation, which is based on crowdsourcing serves as a means to exploit both internal and external resources, ideas, and channels to commercialize the services using customer-generated inputs and create business value (Wang et al., 2021).

Commercializing new ideas and turning them into innovative products are one of the many challenges among small and medium enterprises. Commercializing crowdsourced ideas and realizing profits from them are different for every company. Small firms may excel at finding good ideas but have a weak design to market—and operation systems for commercializing them in the competitive marketplace. However, complex organizational design and unclear decision-making process in ideation, resources management, manufacturing process, and marketing make the commercialization of innovative products less market competitive. Companies using the innovative approaches and tools without pilot testing and without understanding their technology-specific innovation systems damage the market performance of such products and services. In managing any innovative products in the market, the innovation value chain needs to be carefully developed and implemented for consumers, market players, and stakeholders of the company. The value chain comprises the main phases of innovation including idea generation, conversion, and diffusion. Besides determining the appropriate innovation management strategies, firms need to evaluate the consistency among the ideas and their anticipated perceived values among consumers. Therefore, selecting ideas and investing on them, and converting and marketing ideas are complex.

Open innovations are designed and developed by the crowd and are commercialized by social and public organizations, and private firms. Therefore, both individual companies and public economies face the growing challenge to engage crowd and social entrepreneurs in innovating in-service concepts and design them based on the user-generated contents. The open-innovation processes rely more on external knowledge and ideas than the in-company resources and human capital. Yet crowd stimulation for open innovation has not fully evolved over the traditional research and development process of developing new services. Open innovation works somewhat differently in-service businesses as customer is continuously engaged in sharing revealing his emotions and sharing experience to guide the service designing process. For example, Amazon.com has not only created open service innovation by bringing the outside-in information customer reviews to benefit third parties selling products and services via Amazon's site (Chesbrough, 2011).

Using the value for money framework, managers can evaluate an end user view of their innovation efforts before launching them in markets. Firms can engage employees, customers, suppliers, and other third parties as active participants in the innovation process, expanding the range of ideas and gathering real-time feedback on their potential take-up. For example, Nokia operates an online lab that allows users around the world to download beta applications and provide feedback to its product development teams. This strategy provides an early opportunity to identify potential problems and alerts customer differences across geographic markets. Social media websites provide a public forum that gives individual consumers opportunity to present their observations, as well as access to product information that facilitates their purchase decisions. User-generated online reviews on products and services have proliferated among the peer consumers through social media that drives a great impact on marketing (Trusov et al., 2010). The word-of-mouth which percolates down the neighborhood not only increases guiding messages for the consumers, companies, and marketers toward converging better value chains but also alters the processing of consumer information in building customer-centric marketing strategies. In particular, peer communication through social media has emerged as a new form of consumer socialization which is driving the consumer decision-making and helping companies to develop value-added marketing strategies (Casteleyn et al., 2009).

The electronic word-of-mouth has significantly replaced the conventional customer interfaces and contributed to the collective intelligence, which has opened collective services opportunities as an emerging domain. The crowd-based services models in education, health, transportation and logistics, and sustainability sectors have offered significant competitive leverage to firms engaged in social businesses. The user-driven business models in services have presented new opportunities to the physically challenging and low-resources entrepreneurs operating in downstream niches, while simultaneously the collective intelligence also enhances the scope of collaborative services between entrepreneurs and corporate houses. The crowd inputs determine the collective values of the firm and help in building sustainable customer through the crowd capital concept (CCC). The CCC analyzes the tactics and practices of community services to overcome the marketing challenges by putting the customers' preferences, perceptions, and personality first and manage such services business models effectively (Täuscher, 2017). Firms need to involve consumers in co-creation and co-designing of products and services to establish a customer-centric business strategy. Co-design activities are performed at dedicated interfaces and they allow for the joint development of products and solutions between individual customers and manufacturers (Berger et al., 2005). Knowledge sharing through face-to-face communication is positively related to both product and financial performance, while technological knowledge sharing has a positive impact on product performance under conditions of high technological dynamism. Supplier involvement in the buying process is related to product and services performance, while use of knowledge-management tools is related to financial performance (Lakshman & Parente, 2008).

Most companies have developed a parallel communication channel around the social media along with their business propositions. Hence, the emerging firms feel that there should be a social marketing strategist who needs to play the role in stimulating discussion in the media, filtering communications, picking new ideas, and analyzing opportunities for co-creation of strategies with the consumers. The role of social media strategist should be to develop customer-centric approaches for the company and integrate social experiences into products and services. The role of social media strategists should be to figure out how the current relationships of customers exist and determine the ways to bring out those relationships into the experiences of every product and service of the company. The role of strategist should also ensure to build new social experiences as well as embrace existing experiences with the company, and make the customers stay on the network platforms with their friends and family.

8.3 Social Domain of Services

The services domain has shifted from transactional to relationship philosophy over time and customer engagement in designing and implementation of services has been observed as an effective strategy. Such shift has underpinned the importance of long-term, value-driven customer interactions and relationships, and involving community in managing social and customer services. The services domain today is central to cognitive, emotional, and experiential resources of customers and founded on the behavioral interactions in designing and implementing services. The customer-centric orientation in services has stimulated wider interactions of customers on the crowd platforms including social media channels. The collective intelligence offers insight into the dynamics of consumer behavior, perceptions on services branding and marketing by contributing not only ideas to design services but also reinforces customer commitment in imparting services as a successful business venture. The customer-centric philosophy has narrowed the proximity of companies to the social ecosystem and gained significant importance in the twenty-first century (Kumar et al., 2019). Social engagement aligns with individual, community, civic, and institutional benefits including leverages from business and economy. While social scholarship focuses on the individual and community attributes as a state of engagement, the social perspective of engagement endorses collective impact on co-created businesses through a socially determined process. The design-to-society philosophy is, therefore, aligned with the social engagement theory and social presence maxim, which refers to the degree of presence perceived by the community participants in generating and disseminating communication. Social presence theory argues that social media (physical and digital interactions) should align with psychological perception of involvement (presence), and transmit visual and verbal cues. Social presence broadly includes the activities of sharing ideas and experiences, communicating social postures, social brand expressions, social needs, upholding customer voice, and monitoring checks and balances on business to society value transfers (Calefato & Lanubile, 2010).

Customer participation and engagement on crowd platforms lead to developing applied psychosocial outcomes including brand trust, attachment, and loyalty, which help services delivering firms to develop competitive strategies and enhance sales, market share, and profitability (Islam et al., 2018). Crowdsourcing has also emerged an approach for innovation in services. This approach has proved helpful in improving logistics services. The fast-growing practice of e-commerce involved heavy load on delivery services as the demand for product deliveries has been increased manifold in suburban and rural geo-demographic grids. Consequently, company like Amazon has moved to public to seek ideas for improving logistics and inventory services and over time customer engagement in the services improvement process has contributed significantly to speeding up the last-mile logistics in remote areas. The crowd-driven evolution of services and the growing concept of sharing economy along with the advancement of communication and mobile device technologies have accelerated new opportunities to improve various customer-centric services. One of those innovative opportunities is designing a crowd-sourced delivery system (Devari et al., 2017).

Effective social networking on digital and face-to-face interactions enables companies to design network marketing. Engaging customers in marketing process drives psychodynamics and enhances the scope of peer-review-led brand building. Direct marketing and retailing companies largely view sales networks in terms of direct contacts, and often depend upon the social networks. However, the companies intensively involved with customers like financial services, may not necessarily have an effective network because networks often pay off their value through indirect contacts. Moreover, a thumb rule in customer-centric companies is to adopt relevant social networks and let them grow with the support of the company so that it can embark on such platforms to gain competitive advantage in the marketplace. Hence, the density of the connections in a network is important. However, thin networks are also better for generating unique information (Rajagopal, 2021). Understanding social needs is an essential challenge for the companies to create social value by delivering right solutions. In order to dive deep into the social needs, communication is critical to explore the social cognition, and construct strategic or tactical solutions. Therefore, social participation through active engagement is the underlying requirement for most customer-centric companies. Marketing today is evolving inside the participatory conversations with customers and stakeholders. Precise, positive, promotional, and personality-building marketing communications with distinct and identifiable brand or corporate focus provide a streamlined path for the social conversation on business modeling. However, chaotic market-oriented communications with multi-target audiences spread across customers, competitors, observers, and employees affect the strategy implementation and decision systems across the market players within the industry (Muniz & Schau, 2011).

Most efforts to promote corporate social network collaboration are chaotic and built on the implicit philosophy that the higher the connectivity, the better the performance of an organization. It is challenging for executives to learn how to promote connectivity only where it benefits an organization or individual, and how to decrease unnecessary connections. The customized response network excels at reducing the redundancy in communication and filters out the ambiguous problems involved in innovative thinking on business strategy-specific conversations with the customers. Strategy consulting firms and new product development groups tend to work on this format. Managers need to develop a strategic view of the collaboration with social network participants within the policy of the company, which supports the types of social networks that best fit their goals (Cross et al., 2005).

Many services organizations initiate crowdsourcing process to develop community services with an objective of design new sustainable practices to improve social and economic performance. Social innovations are complex as they have to pass through several checks and balances especially on behavioral perspectives. Consequently, the innovation, managers reply to community participation as often they have opaque insight into the real problem, needs, and expected solutions. Community services make greater impact today as their internal effectiveness affects the business performance both tactically and strategically. Crowdsourcing and collective intelligence offer designs, community blueprints, interventions, and competitive approaches to design and implement services. The company carry out the information analytics and measure them through metrics in terms of network connectivity, participation, congruity, and predicted business outcomes to improve such services initiatives. The social network analysis might move services project from an ad hoc team lying as an informal group to a value-producing network through crowd engagement. Such crowd-based services approach broadly focuses on the following attributes (*e.g.*, Cross et al., 2006):

- Driving influx of information on the desired problem and needs,
- Improving information flow and knowledge reuse,
- Encourage customer engagement with emotions and commitments,
- Developing the sense of belongingness during the participation,
- Developing an ability to sense and respond to key problems or opportunities,
- Stimulating frugal, planned, and basic innovation at the initial round of crowdsourcing,
- Delivering value creation,
- Promoting health and unbiased community interactions, and
- Engaging employees through community efforts.

Design-to-society approaches offer a vigilant marketing system to gain competitive leverage in the market by integrating the social business process. Many marketers actively solicit user-generated content (UGC) on various food (diet, alcohol, and organic products) and fashion (apparel and accessories) products for occasional and short-term use in advertising campaign. Accordingly, the UGC is successfully integrated into broad objectives of firms to harmoniously co-produce the brand content, which is recommended for the innovation and service-dominant logic (Vargo & Lusch, 2004). Design-to-society approach to the targeted community provides a significant benefit to the customers and stakeholders over the conventional for-profit marketing methods. However, in some cases, such as in sustainability projects, the social investment involves high cost in terms of either money or intangible measure (difficulty, for instance, in quitting smoking); it becomes harder for the company to connect the payback to the existing revenue streams. Social marketers face their greatest challenge in converging the intangible social benefits with business growth and performance with the purpose (Rangan el al., 1996). Social network analysis is valuable in facilitating collaboration among various strategic groups in the company such as leadership networks, strategic business units, new product development teams, communities of practice, joint ventures, and mergers. By making informal networks visible, social network analysis helps managers systematically assess and support strategically important collaboration (Cross et al, 2002).

A good social strategy for a company requires an analysis of all internal marketing and sales assets. In this way, the company can gather up all customer/client-facing online content, including policy papers, published reports, presentations, messaging, online videos, and mobile applications. In order to get close involvement with the social media, a company needs to list all relevant contents appearing on blogs, any on-site communities, Facebook, and Twitter, to inculcate an active discussion. To be an effective and hassle-free involvement with the social networks, a company should assess what has been communicated (content types, length, and messaging per target), and how, and how often, it has been communicated with the network users. In order to work with social media platforms, business-driving keywords need to be identified and set onto the search engines by the company.

Crowdsourcing and social media together significantly contribute to the workplace dynamics in companies by empowering participants to make liberal expressions and confront biases in the workplace. Nonetheless, most people stay abreast with the information and cognitive inputs from their near circles of peers as their audience. The crowd information has snowballing effect, which multiplies rapidly in a reverse pyramidal shape until the rate of its absorption in the society and target audience is maximum. Crowd information influences businesses also through the selected workplace teams who analyze the information to leverage existing strategies for the products and services and drive a collective social impact (Brands & Rattan, 2020). The social media strategists figure out the existing relationships of customers with companies and determine the ways to bring out those relationships into the experiences of every product and service of the company. The social strategist ensures to build new social experiences and embracing customer experiences with the company and makes the customers stay on the network platforms with their friends and family. Social networks also help firms go sustainable by building loyalty and trust corporate policies. Successful sustainable enterprises in developing countries often involve informal networks that include businesses, nonprofit organizations, and local communities. These networks prompt the firms to go for investments in the financial, social, human, and ecological capital areas. Successful sustainable networks require business enterprises to sponsor for ensuring the network's financial sustainability and serve as the anchor of the company. Multinational corporations sometimes support social networks to anchor with specific operational objectives (Wheeler et al, 2005).

Most firms are biased with the size of the social network assuming that the larger the size of network the larger the efficiency. Many research studies indicate that the size of network does not affect the quality of information. In pooling collective intelligence, the focused brainstorming, peer or social validation, and its applicability influences the business strategies than the size of network which steers the ideas, concepts, and processes. A right social network irrespective of the number of participants can contribute to the firms successfully. However, the key contacts with their personal networks (active or passive) also determine the power of social networks. Business organizations can capitalize on employees' social networks, as they are more focused and possess adequate knowledge in dealing with the issues. A combination of active and committed staff members and highest-performing executives in a compact workplace network might contribute to high-quality relationships with people despite diverse thinking varying spheres of market experience with the brands. Small networks can be effective that are typically range in size with membership of 12–18 people. Such network units help managers learn, make decisions with less bias, and grow in the workplace with common community understanding. The small networks can be effective with the following attributes (*e.g.*, Cross & Thomas, 2011):

- Knowledge and experience of network members,
- Clarity in understanding of issues and precision in thinking,
- Ability to play with cognitive semantics to interlink ideation process,
- Quality of information and drafting ideas,
- Admitting formally and informally powerful people to the network,
- Periodically eliminating the redundancy in thought processes,
- Unbiased mentoring members and adherence to the core of ethics,
- Carefully examining the social, political, or external supports,

- Welcome diverse developmental feedback,
- Develop sense of purpose or worth in participation, and
- Promote work–life balance.

Consequently, new ideas in business and innovative concerns are increasingly shared in a niche market or social networks, which often open the corporate boundaries for creating customer value and pro-customer business modeling. Informal networks, though small in size, provide both strategic opportunity and potential threat, while they can increase creativity within a firm. Informal social networks like person-oriented or brand-led blogs are growing manifold. Companies or business associations need to recognize relevant informal social networks to collect quality information. Validation of information communication networks has emerged as major challenge as the communication embedded therein might damage the brand image or corporate reputation. Managing unrecognized social networks is sensitive for many firms as they help firms in the diffusion of creative knowledge to other firms through personnel and knowledge transfer on one hand, but are susceptible to information infidelity on the other. Firms that operate within small worlds, such as information technology-based services firms, fell into such damage caused by the social networks.

Co-creation is an upcoming phenomenon in business ecosystem, which involves society and business in sharing and adapting experiences of people, respectively. It is a bidirectional dynamic of exchanging ideas, experiences, innovation concepts, developing prototypes, and commercializing generic thought into the business avenues. Experience co-creation is an art, which is portrayed by the business communities with the support of personal and digital interfaces to know the insights of all players in market operations including customers. Co-creating business models with the underlying customer and stakeholder experiences have emerged as a new paradigm of strategy innovation. Customer-centric companies like Nestlé, Conagra, Amazon, Unilever, and Tata India are able to explore the public domain holistically today to innovate products and services with compelling value propositions through co-creating strategy with effective employee engagement (e.g., Ramaswamy & Gouillart, 2008). Successful co-creation of innovations has major challenge of commercialization, which has driven the co-created products and services to evolve ambidextrously with society and corporations.

Employee engagement and customer involvement are the pillars of coevolution process, besides resource pooling, distribution, and managing marketing-mix (product, price, place, promotion, and psychodynamics) functions. Social business design is largely based on the psychosocial drivers that affect co-creation of innovations and strategies, and the commercialization process. Customer and stakeholder participation in co-creating innovation and marketing strategies co-creation is effective in exploring the solutions to social problems and determining the needs. Participation in a social purpose is interactive and emotional as compared to the involvement of customers and stakeholders in an absolute commercial project. The social, cultural, and ethnic foundations nurture belief, trust, and loyalty perceptions during the collective efforts in innovation and developing marketing strategies.

Improving innovations on the experience of lead users is a controlled form of crowdsourcing and information pooling. Most customer-centric companies such as Amazon, Nike, Adidas, LEGO, Gourmet foods are practicing the lead user approach not only to carry out incremental innovations but also to develop new ideas. This approach is congruent with the open services innovation, the concept of co-creation using the customer guidance as a best practice for companies. There are a number of companies that have benefited from embracing the idea of co-creating with customers. Webasto Group, in Germany, is a diversified products and services family-owned company, which believes in fair customer cooperation for sustained growth and focused on product innovation by incorporating a lead user method. The company invests in continuous learning from its customer on innovating the roof sensor module, which is a roof system for autonomous vehicles with attractively integrated sensors and related thermo and cleaning systems. The company has also encouraged customer-centric innovation in lighting effects, which create a pleasant and personalized ambiance inside the passenger compartment. The lighting elements are integrated into the guide rails of the roof system or roof element, whereby the panels remain transparent. In addition, the solar roof developed by the company has been listed by an ecological innovation in the European Union. The company has created an elaborate open-innovation process in order to not only create innovative products, but also to differentiate itself as an innovative company (Chesbrough & Stern, 2012).

Companies carrying out the co-creation process gain societal insights from the knowledge, attitude, and practices (conventional of intermediate) toward finding the social solutions. Most social entrepreneurs join co-creation projects and set mutual benefit goals with the business corporations. In addition, the companies benefit from co-creation process in socializing their existing and upcoming brands by developing referrals and brand gatekeepers in the societal niche, which helps in enhancing the customer outreach. Societal engagement of business corporations opens avenues to enter the downstream markets alongside the mass and premium market segments, driving them to conquer the universe of market (comprising premium, upper mass, regular mass, lower mass, and bottom of the pyramid market segment). In an interactive social and business environment, coevolution of businesses with the societal values provides competitive leverage to the companies and helps in achieving corporal social identity. The intrinsic factors within the social ecosystem that stimulate the co-creation process of social entrepreneurs, customers, and stakeholders include social responsibility-led self-esteem, voluntary behavior, social leadership, and active involvement in social media. The extrinsic factors of business ecosystem that attract co-creation and coevolution process with social stakeholders comprise social governance, public policies, public–private partnership, and the leverage of empowering social stakeholders toward promoting the social businesses (Rajagopal, 2021).

8.4 Systems Thinking in Services

Systems consist of people, structures, technologies, and processes that work together to make organizations viable. Systems thinking, a part of operations and management research, essentially looks at the whole as a basis for understanding, designing, and managing its components. Systems thinking is applied in organizational management for decades in the field of operations but it has also been conceptualized in the functional areas of marketing. Systems thinking offers a powerful new perspective, a synchronized flow of thoughts, and a set of tools that can be used to address the most complex problems in everyday business operations. Systems thinking may be considered as a way of understanding reality that emphasizes the relationships among various components in a process, rather than the independent constituents of the process. Based on the attitude of employees toward change proneness, the systems thinking in innovation works effectively with proactive strategies of the company.

Accordingly, the company is able to harness creative potential while maintaining accountability instead of reacting to employees for resisting to change. Most organizations clarify the roles of each employee in the innovation process while enhancing organizational flexibility, aligning internal processes to facilitate change, and builds the innovation leadership pipeline in association with the customers and stakeholders (Judge, 2011).

Based on a field of study known as system dynamics, systems thinking has a practical value that rests on a solid theoretical foundation. In marketing operations, systems thinking can be described as a tool in tracing and linking various activities in a particular function. To be competitive, companies must develop innovative new businesses on competitive market platforms. Firms may face several operational barriers and seldom mesh smoothly with well-established systems, processes, and cultures. Nonetheless, success requires a balance of conventional and new marketing strategies to keep the competitive forces in equilibrium (Garvin & Levesque, 2006). Emerging companies face various challenges when they pursue new businesses and the usual problematic responses to those challenges. The systems thinking is usually driven by many smaller systems, or subsystems. For example, an organization is made up of many administrative and management functions, products, services, groups, and individuals. If one part of the system is changed, the nature of the overall system is often changed as well by definition. Systems theory has brought a new perspective for managers to interpret the patterns and events in their organizations. Organizational system consists of people (crowd), structures (policies), technologies (infrastructure), and processes (manufacturing and marketing) that work together to make organizations viable. Of these system's elements, crowdsourcing has emerged as one of the strong approaches for customer-centric co-creation and coevolution of innovation projects. Systems thinking therefore, has emerged today as a part of collective research, which essentially looks at the whole as a basis for understanding, designing, and managing its components (Norton, 2010).

Interactive design offers a constant critical assessment, and continuous learning and understanding of mental models. This dimension of systems thinking is based on intuitive thinking that stimulates creativity and provides an organization with a conceptual foundation to create a unique competitive advantage. The success of systems thinking approach needs a transformational leadership at both business organizations to help in redesigning organization, creating value chain, developing global standards, investing in business process improvement, and strengthening the backward and forward business linkages. The business growth exhibits building synergy between the society and business firms. The concept of synergy refers to the achievement of integrating the social values with business goals for developing competitiveness, trust among consumers, and ensuring growth. The concept drives the firms to make an additional effort over the sum of the conventional decisions focused on market leadership and profit-oriented business goals. Systems thinking stimulates cooperation between several elements and allows for greater overall effects integrating the social and business values (Carayannis & Campbell, 2009). The coevolution of small and big companies enhances investment on innovation, technology, and research and development. Such mergers or acquisitions help companies strengthen their marketing strategies by developing customer-centric branding and promotion strategies. The convergence of technology, entrepreneurship education, and public policies on entrepreneurship development programs promote hybridization, business performance, and corporate citizenship behavior ambidextrously between small and large enterprises.

It is observed that knowledge management fully mediates the impact of organizational culture on organizational effectiveness, and partially mediates the impact of organizational structure and strategy on organizational effectiveness. There are a possible mediating role of knowledge management in managing relationship between the systems thinking attributes comprising organizational goals, employee engagement, stakeholder values, work culture, decision-making process, and organizational effectiveness (Zheng et al., 2010). The systems thinking is usually driven by many smaller systems or subsystems. For example, an organization is made up of many administrative and management functions, products, services, groups, and individuals. If one part of the system is changed, the nature of the overall system is often changed as well by definition. Systems theory has brought a new perspective for managers to interpret the patterns and events in their organizations.

8.5 Value Management in Services

Experience sharing over the digital platforms further influences the customer behavior over a long time. Patterns of consumerism are changing in the society, as there are shifts in the customer demography in the markets. The explosion of mass customer segments, urbanization, and increase in the size of the population of aging customers have contributed significantly to the shifts in customer preferences and overall consumption behavior. Direct-to-customer marketing strategies, convenience shopping, and social media-driven marketing approaches of companies have increased social and cultural influence on developing the customer behavior. However, disruption in technology and attraction toward local consumption also contribute in driving the customer behavior dynamic across the geo-demographic segments. Extended technology lifecycle builds positive customer perceptions on higher value for money. Co-creation and co-designing approaches of customer-centric companies like IKEA has established business philosophy of connecting customers and developing an emotion-based relationship with customers as the key to leveraging loyalty and advocacy behavior.

The perception of customers toward shopping is commonly influenced by the social psychodynamics, need, enthusiasm for experimentation, benefit seeking, and obsessive behavioral attributes. Thus, customer perceptions influence customer behavior with their ecosystem, which often creates *me too* feeling, and induce the pro-perception buying decisions. In addition, perceived benefits in terms of price, associated promotions, and perceived use value of products significantly influence purchase intention. Perceived customers' effectiveness, occupation, and income level also have a significant effect on confirming the positive customer perception toward willingness to pay for the product of high-perceived value (Zhao et al., 2018).

Customers behave in the market in different ways comprising proactive, reactive, interactive, and inactive behaviors. All four ways of expressing customer behavior refer to their cultural background. Proactive customers are experimental to new products and are prone to accept the cultural changes induced by the market. The proactive customers are largely induced by the markets through lifestyle interventions and cross-cultural fusion. Reactive customers are critical to new products, strategies, and corporate initiatives and prefer the conventional culture that has grown over the period in the society. The reactive customers are aggressive in sharing their experience and are often critical about the products and services of the company. Interactive customers express their views logically and analyze the products and services of a company rationally and comparatively. Inactive customers are passive and non-responsive. Customers in the acquired culture are prone to behavioral changes, adapt to modern values, and are interactive in the market. These attributes of acquired culture drive multinational companies to develop dynamic marketing strategies, build their brand, and augment market share (Rajagopal, 2016). Customers experience brands emotionally, not through individual communications, i.e., advertising, packaging, online presence, or promotions, but in their totality. There exists in every country a *culture screen*, which generates cognitive and affective influences, and shapes the interpersonal and personal determinants to form the customer behavior.

References

Bal, A. S., Weidner, K., Hanna, R., & Mills, A. J. (2017). Crowdsourcing and brand control. *Business Horizons*, 60(2), 219–228.

Barthel, S., Parker, J., Folke, C., & Colding, J. (2014). Urban gardens: Pockets of social-ecological memory. In K. Tidball & M. Krasny (Eds.), *Greening in the Red Zone* (pp. 145–158). Springer.

Bell, S. J., & Eisingerich, A. B. (2007). The paradox of consumer education: Consumer expertise and loyalty in the financial services industry. *European Journal of Marketing, 41*(5), 466–486.

Berger, C., Möslein, K., Piller, F., & Reichwald, R. (2005). Co-designing modes of cooperation at the customer interface: Learning from exploratory research. *European Management Review, 2*(1), 70–87.

Bernoff, J., & Schadler, T. (2010). *Applications: How to boost your company's image using social technologies*. Harvard Business School Press.

Bitner, M. J., Ostrom, A. L., & Morgan, F. N. (2008). Service Blueprinting: A practical technique for service innovation. *California Management Review, 50*(3), 66–94.

Brands, R., & Rattan, A. (2020). *Use your social network as a tool for social justice*. Harvard Business School Press.

Calefato, F., & Lanubile, F. (2010). Communication media selection for remote interaction of Ad Hoc Groups. *Advances in Computers*, Elsevier, *78*, 271–313.

Carayannis, E. G., & Campbell, D. F. (2009). Mode 3' and 'Quadruple Helix': Toward a 21st century fractal innovation ecosystem. *International Journal of Technology and Management, 46*(3–4), 201–234.

Casteleyn, J., Mottart, A., & Rutten, K. (2009). How to Use Facebook in your market research. *International Journal of Market Research, 51*(4), 439–447.

Charbit, C., & Desmoulins, G. (2017). Civic crowdfunding: A collective option for local public goods? *OECD Regional Development Working Papers*, No. 2017/02, Paris: OECD Publishing. https://doi.org/10.1787/b3f7a1c5-en.

Chesbrough, H. W. (2011). Bringing open innovation to services. *MIT Sloan Management Review, 52*(2), 85–90.

Chesbrough, H. W., & Stern, A. (2012). *Webasto: Co-creating innovation with lead users*. Harvard Business School Press.

Cross, R., Borgatti, S. P., & Parkar, A. (2002). Making invisible work visible: Using social network analysis to support strategic collaboration. *California Management Review, 44*(2), 25–46.

Cross, R., Liedtka, J. M., & Weiss, L. (2005). Practical guide to social networks. *Harvard Business Review, 83*(3), 124–132.

Cross, R., Laseter, T., Parker, A., & Velasquez, G. (2006). Using social network analysis to improve communities of practice. *California Management Review, 49*(1), 32–61.

Cross, R., & Thomas, R. (2011). A smarter way to network. *Harvard Business Review, 89*(7–8), 149–153.

Devari, A., Nikolaev, A. G., & He, Q. (2017). Crowdsourcing the last mile delivery of online orders by exploiting the social networks of retail store customers. *Transportation Research Part e: Logistics and Transportation Review, 105*, 105–122.

Eisenmann, T. R., Parker, G., & Alstyne, M. W. V. (2006). Strategies for two-sided markets. *Harvard Business Review, 84*(10), 92–102.

Estellés-Arolas, E., & González-Ladron-de-Guevara, F. (2012). Towards an integrated crowdsourcing definition. *Journal of Information Science, 38*(2), 189–200.

Felin, T., & Powell, T. C. (2016). Designing organizations for dynamic capabilities. *California Management Review, 58*(4), 78–96.

Füller, J., Hutter, K., Hautz, J., & Matzler, K. (2014). User roles and contributions in innovation-contest communities. *Journal of Management Information Systems, 31*(1), 273–308.

Garvin, D. A., & Levesque, L. C. (2006). Meeting challenges of the corporate entrepreneurship. *Harvard Business Review, 84*(10), 102–110.

Hazée, S., Vaerenbergh, Y. V., & Armirotto, V. (2017). Co-creating service recovery after service failure: The role of brand equity. *Journal of Business Research, 74*(1), 101–109.

Huang, M. H. (2008). The influence of selling behaviors on consumer relationships in financial services. *International Journal of Service Industry Management, 19*(4), 458–473.

Islam, J., Rahman, Z., & Hollebeek, L. (2018). Consumer engagement in online brand communities: A solicitation of congruity theory. *Internet Research, 28*(1), 23–45.

Jiao, Y., Wu, Y., & Lu, S. (2021). The role of crowdsourcing in product design: The moderating effect of user expertise and network connectivity. *Technology in Society*, **64**, Article 101496. https://doi.org/10.1016/j.techsoc.2020.101496.

Judge, W. Q. (2011). *Organizational capacity for change dimension 5: Systems thinking*. Business Expert Press.

Kolko, J. (2015). Design thinking comes of age. *Harvard Business Review, 93*(9), 66–71.

Kumar, V., Rajan, B., Gupta, S., & Pozza, I. D. (2019). Customer engagement in service. *Journal of Academy of Marketing Science, 47*(1), 138–160.

Lakshman, C., & Parente, R. C. (2008). Supplier-focused knowledge management in the automobile industry and its implications for product performance. *Journal of Management Studies, 45*(2), 317–342.

Matteis, R. J. (1979). The new back office focuses on customer service. *Harvard Business Review, 57*(2), 146–159.

Muñiz, A. M., & Schau, H. J. (2011). How to inspire value-laden collaborative customer-generated content. *Business Horizons, 54*(3), 209–217.

Norton, B. (2010). Language and identity. In N. Hornberger & S. McKay (Eds.), *Sociolinguistics and language education* (pp. 349–369). Bristol: Multilingual Matters.

Rajagopal. (2016). *Sustainable growth in Global markets: Strategic choices and managerial implications*. Palgrave Macmillan.

Rajagopal. (2021). *The business design cube: Converging markets, society, and customer values to grow competitive in business*. Business Expert Press.

Ramaswamy, V., & Gouillart, F. J. (2008). *Co-creating strategy with experience co-creation*. Harvard Business School Press.

Ramaswamy, V. (2009). Are you ready for the co-creation movement? *IESE Insights*, Third Quarter, *2*, 29–35.

Rangan, V. K., Karim, S., & Sandberg, S. K. (1996). Do better at doing good. *Harvard Business Review, 74*(3), 42–54.

Sabrina, N. (2005). Influence on consumer socialization. *Young Consumers: Insight and Ideas for Responsible Marketers, 6*(2), 63–69.

Sergio, R. (2010). Relational consequences of perceived deception in online shopping: The moderating roles of type of product, consumer's attitude toward the internet and consumer's demographics. *Journal of Business Ethics, 95*(3), 373–391.

Shams, S. M. R. (2016). Capacity building for sustained competitive advantage: A conceptual framework. *Marketing Intelligence & Planning, 34*(5), 671–691.

Täuscher, K. (2017). Leveraging collective intelligence: How to design and manage crowd-based business models. *Business Horizons, 60*(2), 237–245.

Trusove, M., Bodapati, A. V., & Bucklin, R. F. (2010). Determining influential users in Internet Social Network. *Journal of Marketing Research, 47*(4), 643–658.

Vargo, S. L., & Lusch, R. F. (2004). Evolving to a new dominant logic for marketing. *Journal of Marketing, 68*(1), 1–17.

Wang, Y. C., Phillips, F., & Yang, C. (2021). Bridging innovation and commercialization to create value: An open innovation study. *Journal of Business Research, 123*, 255–266.

Wazny, K. (2018). Applications of crowdsourcing in health: An overview. *Journal of Global Health, 8*(1). https://doi.org/10.7189/jogh.08.010502

Wheeler, D., McKague, K., Thomson, J., Davies, R., Medalye, J., & Prada, M. (2005). Creating sustainable local enterprise networks. *Sloan Management Review, 47*(1), 33–40.

Xu, Y., Ribeiro-Soriano, D. E., & Gonazalez-Garcia, J. (2015). Crowdsourcing, innovation, and firm performance. *Management Decision, 53*(6), 1158–1169.

Zhao, R., Geng, Y., Liu, Y., Tao, X., & Xue, B. (2018). Customers' perception, purchase intention, and willingness to pay for carbon-labeled products: A case study of Chengdu in China. *Journal of Cleaner Production, 171*(1), 1664–1671.

Zheng, W., Yang, B., & McLean, G. N. (2010). Linking organizational culture, structure, strategy, and organizational effectiveness: Mediating role of knowledge management. *Journal of Business Research, 63*(7), 763–771.

PART III

Times Ahead

CHAPTER 9

Future Perspectives

The future business paradigm is going to change from competition to cooperation. Factors supporting collaboration are observed as trust, common goals for cooperation, and existence of cooperation mechanisms, while barriers are related to three factors such as lack of trust, risk–benefit evaluation, and lack of common goals for cooperation. Therefore, the challenges ahead include triangulation of people, business, and governance. This chapter argues that crowdsourcing has no exclusivity to meet this challenge by overriding the market competition. The co-creation of customer value is critical in helping firms achieve a competitive advantage through crowd-based business models and social marketing strategies that influence not only customer satisfaction and loyalty. In view of the above perspectives, this chapter discusses optimistically the ways to harness collective intelligence and develop crowd entrepreneurship as an alternative to conventional business modeling. This chapter also discusses the pros and cons of interactive planning process and the importance of collective innovations as a process for companies to ensure consistent growth in business amidst increasing market competition.

9.1 Harnessing Collective Intelligence

Most companies with transformational leadership are making efforts to integrate people and the concept of profit with purpose. This drive has

Rajagopal, *Crowd-Based Business Models*,
https://doi.org/10.1007/978-3-030-77083-9_9

encouraged empowering people (broadly constituting customers, potential crowdfunding investors, and social services experts in exploring new innovation opportunities. A latitudinal survey with international business organizations has observed that empowering people in brainstorming social innovation ideas to self-organize by promoting emotional connection with leaders, communities, and employees has emerged as a new trend not only to create value but also to improve the business performance of firms with a predetermined social purpose. The crowdsourcing therefore can be identified as an open approach to new ideas and experimentation with commitment to implement the crowd-based business models and use prolifically the collective intelligence resources. The crowd contributions to the triple bottom line of a business organization comprising need-based innovation, value creation, and profit with purpose enhance the corporate competencies and reputation within the social and business ecosystems. Though it is a challenging task to streamline crowd behavior with corporate behavior and practices, the business leaders would require learning to manage effectively the cost, time, and risk propositions to leverage from the crowd-dynamics. Crowd-based business models are difficult to predict and might cause small failures in short term but the strategic output of the crowd engagement in developing social business might be beneficial as against the conventional business plans (Giles, 2016). The crowdsourcing leverages human knowledge, expertise, and enthusiasm for customer-centric and value-based innovation. Crowd contributions can be harnessed for optimizing performance considering the following principles:

- Corporate openness in analyzing the for and against discussions of the crowd on a given theme,
- Preparing an unbiased and knowledge-intensive crowd segment for contributing to innovations,
- Inculcating a social viewpoint of discussion as against personal opinions,
- Encouraging classified discussions than reiteration of opinions,
- Inculcating the sense of commons (focusing on 'We') than highlighting personal credits (imaging self or focusing on 'I'),
- Streamlining crowd deliberations based on 3V paradigm,

- Contribution should be subjected to ***verification*** (some firms organize consumer jury to validate the innovation concept and prototype)
- Crowd ideas need to ***validate*** instantly by encouraging evidence-based discussions
- Focusing on creating social and business ***values*** and sharing with participants while designing need-based innovations

- Reinforcing the notion of reverse innovation (local innovations with conventional wisdom) and reverse accountability (people and stakeholders) in the crowd-based discussions„
- Ensuring transparency in crowdsourcing policies, communication documentation, and data transfer,
- Establishing clarity in expected outcome,
- Encouraging self-organization among the participants in a team,
- Briefing on the principles of continuous learning and systems thinking,
- Mapping perceptual semantics (participatory cognitive appraisal), and
- Encouraging transformational leadership in managing the crowd-segmented teams for innovation.

While harnessing the crowd, a consistent challenge is to optimize the returns on time invested and develop something significant. Therefore, crowd-based co-creation strongly relies on the best human abilities despite the technological aides. Collective intelligence is a human element and builds balance between minds and machines, between products and platforms (digital), and between the core (team) and the crowd (McAfee, 2018). Besides business perspectives, co-creating innovation is also culturally driven. The interactions among the members of crowd-based teams are found effective with homogeneity in cultural values. Linking crowdsourcing with the culture perspectives delivers higher promise to achieve the desired results. Therefore, choosing crowd segments to build teams can be based on a culture map, by plotting various common and differential attributes. Broadly such cultural attributes can be as classified below:

- Language, communication, and clarity of expressions,
- Collective evaluation pattern,

- Ability to be proactive to persuasion and guidance,
- Leadership abilities and working skills in teams,
- Documenting discussions systematically and in a synchronized manner,
- Abilities to make right decision based on contents analysis,
- Adhering to mutual trust, listing agreements, and filtering disagreements to reinforce right decisions, and
- Managing time, task, and target to reach consensus.

Consequently, culture significantly influences the workplace dynamics in an organization and also in the market ecosystem. However, in managing crowd deliberation it is not wise to misjudge the cognitive dynamics to meet the challenge and abruptly shift the rules of engagement of crowdsourcing on preconceived assumptions. Most participants may not feel comfortable with prejudiced work-styles of crowdsourcing managers or discussion leaders. The contrary of imposing control standards, it would be helpful to build the brainstorming crowd sessions with positive parameters and team-friendly approaches. The differences of opinion that people of varied backgrounds bring to a work group can be great assets (Meyer, 2014).

Visualizing and measuring market attractiveness in the context of new incumbents, rise of substitutes, and the extent of bargaining power of customers and supplier is a complex process for the firms emerging with the crowd-based business model. Crowdsourcing and social media interactions help firms in overcoming the conventional business models and succeed with the value-based business strategies. Most customer-centric companies like Apple, Mary Kay Cosmetics, Samsung have grown initially with the crowd and learn about the regional presence of competitors, consumer preferences, and supplier options to develop appropriate manufacturing and marketing strategy. These firms have opened their social media channels, controlled blogs, and e-commerce platforms, which were widely driven by the collective intelligence. In the twenty-first century, the platform (digital)-based businesses are growing popularly along with the active crowd participation that bring together innovators, manufacturers, service providers, marketers, and customers within close proximity. However, among many, few companies like Uber, Alibaba, and Airbnb required a different approach to strategy. The network effects with dynamic external interactions increase the value to customers and crowd participants (Van Alstyne et al., 2016). It is time for companies to get close with the customers and evaluate emerging digital threats and opportunities and create new business options with crowd-based business models to stay connected with the digital ecosystems as a future perspective. Despite the pressures from platform-based companies including Uber, Airbnb, and Amazon, opportunities for companies are continuously increasing with the digitization. Such situation leverages strong customer relationships and increase cross-selling. The combination of creating value chains within the business ecosystems and effective using collective intelligence has significantly contributed to the business performance. Over time the crowd-based business models have companies in improving the organizational capabilities and relationships with customers, crowd-based innovators, modular manufacturers, suppliers, multichannel distribution system managers, and with other contributing factors within the social and business ecosystems (Weill & Woerner, 2015).

However, collective intelligence has an embedded challenge of trustworthiness due to lack of evidential support to the presented information. This cognitive factor often succumbs to the groups failure and raises doubts on the wisdom of crowds. Some research studies have observed that erroneous information, deviations in discussions, and intentional silence or indifference of participants interrupt information flow and affect the quality of contents. In addition, polarization of participants during discussions and the inculcating the notion of *everybody knows* or *no one knows* caused biasness in crowd brainstorming to generate collective information. Consequently, the contributions from the crowd are subjective as the discussions in crowd often grow as a 'mind of its own,' which may raise a pertinent question on its congruity with the organizational goals (Sunstein & Hastie, 2014; Wilson et al., 2017). Organizational cultures that value relationships are build through consensus and developed as collaborative strategy for implementation. A recent study suggests that women are more likely to serve the groups systematically with the sense of belongingness and favor work–life balance commitments than involving into the time-intensive commitments. Therefore, the managers engaged with the crowdsourcing and crowd-based information analytics should view the quality of information in the context of profile of customers, their work–culture, and the level of cognitive stress, to overrule information biases. Building a team culture that recognizes and responds to the work–life balance, stress, and experience in crowd collaboration requires clear profiling of participants, contracting, and transparency to ensure the quality of information (Cullinan, 2018).

9.2 Crowd Entrepreneurship

Crowd entrepreneurship is a process of collective renewal and development of new customer and social innovation projects and improving an existing business by understanding stakeholder value perceptions and potential competitive postures in the market. The performance of this process drives social creativity and the individual initiatives, which enhances the organizational productivity and helps in creating favorable conditions for harnessing entrepreneurial potential. The development of crowd-based innovation models and collective intelligence offers new innovation insights and enables corporate entrepreneurship in the long run to continue with the products and services emerging out of the crowd platforms. Developing a congruence with crowd cognition and building strong employee engagement by reaching out extensively the collective intelligence, corporate entrepreneurship process can be successfully fostered and implemented in customer-centric business organizations. A combination of crowdsourcing and corporate venturing practices leads to crowd-based business modeling and motivates crowd-venturing process within an organization. Such business process captures both individual and organization-related factors to manage customer-centric products and services in competitive marketplace. Such entrepreneurship processes within organizations are evolving toward more distributed and participative forms. In the context of the concepts of corporate entrepreneurship, collective intelligence, and crowdfunding, crowd-venturing can be defined as a structured and systematic process aimed to leverage the distributed intelligence and creativity inside the organization (the crowd). The crowd-ventures tend to initiate and develop effective entrepreneurial innovations and supports social and collective processes, and businesses (ventures). Broadly, the performance of crowd-venturing is related to the ability of the crowd (random or classified) to nurture employee contributions with the goal of developing new business ideas to develop crowd-based entrepreneurial ventures (Elia & Margherita, 2018).

The recent boom in the social media users and technologically supported crowd platforms in exploring advanced innovations such as social robots in managing domestic information or providing community services in hospitals, airports, and other public places. Such automated devices manage to disseminate programmed information and process quick responses. Some of the robots[1] that are engaged in social services are as discussed below:

- Kismet—a robot head that understands and exhibits emotion when interacting with humans,
- Tico—a robot developed to improve children's motivation in the classroom,
- Bandit—a social robot designed to teach social behavior to autistic children, and
- Jibo—a consumer-oriented social robot, which understands speech and facial expressions and seeks to form relationships with the family that adopts it.

Increasing number of customer-oriented services are being innovated and commercialized based on the collective intelligence. Some common ideas such as greeting people, delivering pre-programmed information, serving food, and even completing simple cooking jobs tasks are contributed by the crowdsourcing platforms. Social sharing today has become easy, rapid, and significant through the electronic word-of-mouth and mobile word-of-mouth through the social network platforms (Vilnai-Yavetz & Levina, 2018; Davenport & Kirby, 2015).

Several new ventures have crowdsourced ideas to sense the need for innovation and explored opportunities in various social sectors like education. These firms developed business models to capitalize on crowd contributions and deliver value-based services enhancing specific expertise. *Skillshare*, a technology venture founded in 2011 has developed a digital platform that supports innovative education as a highly desired social service by facilitating online learning on a broad variety of topics. The embedded novelty in this platform is, it uses a crowd of independent experts to teach classes related to their expertise and interests instead of employed teachers in a conventional school system. *Skillshare* variety of relevant crowd-created content, which is also used by the other to train their employees. As a reward for their contributions, Skillshare pays a royalty to its crowd members depending on the number of students they can attract to their live classes (Kietzmann, 2017). The success of such crowd entrepreneurship has encouraged companies to conceptualize

[1] For details see https://searchenterpriseai.techtarget.com/definition/social-robot.

and implement crowd-based business model (CBBMs) to increase their outreach to customers and proximity to society to create value. These business models can be highly effective and need to be implemented by conducting a comprehensive analysis of the collective information and its potential value to the firm. For implementing CBBM in a business organization effectively an optimal size of crowd including the participants inside the firm (employees and stakeholders) and outside the firm (customers, entrepreneurs, and innovators). However, the optimal size of the crowd is a relative measure, which involves various micro- and macro-factors of the company. The micro factors are the key performance indicators of the firm emerging out of the internal ecosystem while the macro-factors include the profile of crowd members, level of experience and skills, knowledge of basic business, and leadership. The optimal size of the crowd size leads to effective decision-making, value creation to customers, and delivering strategic outputs. Consequently, the crowd-based business model has both positive and negative attributes, which affect the overall performance of the firm. It is necessary for the crowd-sourcing firms to consider the following perspectives meticulously, while planning for crowd interface (Täuscher, 2017):

- Setting strategic objectives for crowd-based innovation,
- Building effective crowd teams with discussion agenda,
- Corporate investment in crowdsourcing,
- Cost implications of crowd creation,
- Value creation inside the crowd teams and in the company,
- Measuring risks from the crowd, and
- Direct and indirect network effects.

The collective intelligence resources of crowd explore new business opportunities. In fact, crowdsourcing has reinforced customer values and encouraged social interface with business. Therefore, CBBM drives competitive advantage though it poses new challenges to crowd-based enterprises and executives. As the Internet of Things (IoT) begins to dominate the technology landscape, the next generation of crowdsourcing may emerge as a game changer in crowd entrepreneurship and explore new entrepreneurial opportunities. As crowdsourcing systems diversify, the inflow of categorical information can be acquired from data sensors, artificial intelligence (AI), bots, and other devices in the changing facets of information technology by 2030. As a result of advancements in artificial intelligence, the variety of product and service opportunities are expected to inflate as entrepreneurs become more aware of technologies. Converging crowd-based business model with advanced crowdsourcing driven by the AI data mining tools, the crowd entrepreneurship would be able to transform into the sensor-based entrepreneurs with the planning, developing, and mapping actions to launch new products and services within the AI ecosystem (Brown, 2017).

9.2.1 Interactive Planning Process

Planning process suggested by Ackoff is an outgrowth of his broader vision on systems thinking in an organization. The emphasis on interactive planning has become an applied perspective in organizational planning, which was embedded in the planning theory (Ackoff, 1999). The Interactive Planning (IP) methodology has been developed as a conceptual tool to guide systematic and systemic (overall) development of organizations. Such approach is idealistic and often considered as a guiding paradigm. IP offers a comprehensive layout for demonstrating a systematic, step-by-step, process of organizational development with focus on the design of an ideal organization (Haftor, 2011). Growing organizations use interactive planning models that are intertwined and interdependent, and tend to evolve as learning organization involving stakeholders, customers, managers, and functional leaders. The interactive and reactive planning processes are able to predict collective outcomes within the organizational ecosystem. However, managers looking to navigate these difficulties need to adopt new approaches. Often reactive managers are typically dissatisfied with the way interactive decisions appear. They are quite satisfied with the way things were dealing with problems in a way to return to that state. They have nostalgic longing for conventional wisdom (Sargut and McGrath, 2011). Ackoff's interactive planning process relies on averages, which are often less important than outliers. Therefore, large organizations use models that simulate the behavior of stakeholders within the organizational system. During the interactive planning process risk mitigation is crucial in planning. Ackoff (2001) explained that planning consists of the design of a desirable present and the selection or invention of ways of approximating it as closely as possible. It creates its future by continuously closing the gap between where it is at any moment of time and where it would most like to be. It included parts of interactive planning as formulating the mess, ends-planning, means-planning, resource planning, design of implementation, and design of control. The advantages and disadvantages of interactive planning paradigm are exhibited in Table 9.1.

Table 9.1 Advantages and Disadvantages of Interactive Planning Process

Indicators	*Advantages*	*Disadvantages*
Formulating the Mess	Interactions between the stakeholders and managers lead to consensus building	Differences in opinion develop non-congruence with the predetermined organizational objectives
Ends Planning	Determining collective measure on quality aspects of planning Time and risk management can be predetermined	Multilayering of ideas causees fragility in organizational planning Over powering the scope of the organizational planning jeopardizing the time framework and enhancing risk factors
Means Planning	Interactivity on means of planning help in resource mapping and developing action plans	Scope creep in planning process enhancing the cost-time-risk factors. According to Pepper (2007), the fulfillment of people's needs, together with the understanding of people's level of knowledge, can be achieved through the service strategy of socialization and trainings (Pepper, 2007)

(continued)

Table 9.1 (continued)

Indicators	*Advantages*	*Disadvantages*
Resource Planning	Sharing ideas on resources planning would help in systems thinking	Ideological and operational differences might jeopardize the planning process
Implementation design	Interactive modules can help implementing organizational plans with stages and review gates and maintain appropriate checks and balances	Design vulnerability might demotivate employees, stakeholders, and leaders in effective implementation of plans
Design of control	Interactive planning will help in developing effective design of control integrating the perspectives of employees, stakeholders, and leaders	Heterogeneity of ideas might cause gaps in establishing control standards toward monitoring and evaluation of organizational plans

Source Author

Interactive planning is directed at predicting organizational growth, which is based on the belief that an organization's future depends at least as much on what it does between now and then, as on what is done to it (Ackoff, 2001). Meanwhile, interactivity dissolves problem by altering characteristics of one entity owned, or altering surroundings to eliminate problems entirely. It can be done by upholding desired design of the future and discover a way to realize it. Therefore, interactive planning methodology derives from interactivity concept and is a participatory method administering a set of problems, correlated when believed that if a step is not taken, then desired future will possibly not happen, and that if the step taken it is the right one, and desired future can possibly be realized. (Rachma-Fitriati, 2014).

9.3 Collective Innovations

Innovation of new products is a complex process that needs to be carried out meticulously in the firms integrating the business and consumer use values in the marketplace. Firms engaged in innovating products should map consumers' needs, attributes of close substitutes, competitive threats, required product services, and estimated cost of marketing of the product in different markets. However, the rate of failure of innovative services is higher as compared to the consumer products. These products largely include credit cards, insurance schemes, hire purchase schemes, investment plans, and the like. The major factors that obstruct the process of innovative products development include:

- Limited creativity and paucity of customer-centric innovative ideas on products and services
- Fragmented markets and consumer segments
- Disruptive social networks for the diffusion of innovations
- Social and economic limitations of consumers
- Government policies and legal conditions
- Cost-effectiveness of the process of new product development
- Competitive marketing-mix strategies to promote the innovative products and services,
- Resource crisis at various levels in the process of innovative product development and inappropriate strategic decision toward launching innovative products in the market
- Innovation life cycle and sustainability of innovative products.

Most companies consider the process of innovative product development as colossal due to the cumbersome stage gate process of manufacturing, organizational and market-led intricacies in analyzing key indicators to launch and manage the products in the competitive marketplace. However, the process of developing an innovative product can be made easier by rationally dividing the chronology of process into two parts—an early stage, which focuses on evaluating prospects and eliminating bad bets, and a late stage that optimizes the market potential.

The pivotal role of creativity in organizations has been widely recognized by the academic community. Creativity is associated with that part of the innovation process which is labeled as idea generation (Coyne et al, 2007). Ideation process for new product development can be stimulated through metaphors, pictures, and experiences. It is rooted in the philosophy of rationalism and empiricism, implying 'the truth is out there' approaches. It is observed that defining cognitive idea generation is based on personal experiences and beliefs driven by individual and social information. However, these forms of cognitive-based idea generation process are individualistic and not amenable to team contexts (Bhatt, 2000). There is typically an indirect connection between investment in research, innovation, and commercial benefit. Research is more likely to help generating ideas through the available information and public resources. More significantly, as discoveries are likely to be in the form of laws of nature, abstract ideas, and physical phenomena, they are likely to be converged with the end user values and market potential from the perspective of business firms (Abernathy & Utterback, 1978). New-product ideas or innovation concepts should be documented on the following lines:

- Use consumer language.
- Keep idea simple, focused, and organized.
- Keep clarity from the consumers point of view.
- Do not overpromise or oversell.
- Focus on major consumer benefits.
- Differentiate the brand from the competition.
- Keep all concepts that will be tested in the same format.
- Use experienced professionals to prepare the concepts.
- Address to right target audience.
- Understand the level of errors in information acquisition.
- Include diagnostic questions.

Ideas generated and acquired from internal and external resources need to be carefully screened in the interest of consumer satisfaction as well as company's profit. In this process the company should avoid the *Drop* and *Go* errors. The former attempts to dismiss the good idea while the latter attempts to allow the poor ideas to move into the process of commercialization. Hence the purpose of screening the idea needs to be understood carefully. It is advised that the company should develop an idea-rating matrix on the basis of the emerging ideas and their usefulness. Product ideas have to be turned into concept and product concept can be turned later into the brand concept. The concept testing calls for testing of these competing concepts with an appropriate group of target consumers. The concepts can be presented physically or symbolically. The consumers' response may be summarized and the strength of the concept may be judged. The need gap and product gap levels may be checked and modified thereafter. The concept testing and product development methodology applies to any product or service. The business analysis includes estimating the sales as it would be of one-time purchase, frequently purchasing product or at regular interval purchase product (Rajagopal & Rajagopal, 2011). The estimates should also be made in relation to the tendency of first purchase, replacement purchase, or repeat sales.

Apple (Consumer electronic and technology), Merck (Pharmaceutical), IKEA (crowd ideation-based interior designing), and Wikipedia (crowd-based nonprofit information enterprise) are some companies that are engaged in turning to crowds for exploring the customer need-based solutions. These enterprises have accepted the probable risks in doing business with crowd comprising a vast group of strangers distributed around the world, and seeking a one-stop customer solutions through new or incremental innovations. In refining the crowdsourcing process to achieve desired quality outputs, people can be motivated by contests, collaborations, and rewarding complementary decisions. Contests may draw crowd attention for highly challenging issues, design revisions, and contributing to creative business projects (Boudreau & Lakhani, 2013).

As a greater number of crowd participants began to contribute in the crowdsourcing process, cross-pollination of ideas and innovation concepts makes higher impact in co-creation of an innovation blueprint. Co-creating blueprints, infrastructure layouts, and building cognitive cosmos in the innovation project charter lead to develop customer-centric and social business models. Most companies in the competitive marketplace shift ideas to gain competitive leverage and tend to seed, synergize, and serve the market target. The most important lesson for entrepreneurs and leaders to learn in the innovation process is how to think about innovation and nurture it in the interest of the firm and market (Hargadon & Sutton, 2001). The creation of the processes required for efficient manufacture and market delivery of a commercial product based upon the prototype characterizes innovation in the commercial stage. Innovative emphasis shifts from product function to process development and refinement. Process-focused innovations during this stage are likely to be radical rather than incremental. Besides Fintech projects, entrepreneurs today leverage investor networks to attract donations or equity-based crowdfunding through designing campaigns on social media channels. Though many resources to improve venture success have emerged by the end of twentieth century, the organizational challenges have also grown manifold in managing crowd-generated funds. These challenges represent an obstruction to crowd openness toward developing new ventures (Di Pierto et al., 2018).

Innovation-led products become sustainable in the mature stage as they gain desired market share and position them strategically in the market competition with long-term goals. In this stage both the consumer value and brand equity for the innovation-led products and services enhance. However, as the technology grows and consumer preferences for the products change over time, the products turn obsolete in the decline stage depleting their market share and increasing the substitution risk. Firms thus should be engaged in continuous improvement or innovation process to develop next generation products at the edge of the mature stage and avoid falling into the decline stage. Products, which fall into the decline stage, are difficult to revive as the dynamic market forces weaken the product significance and turn them idle in the marketplace. Often investing on the products trapped in the decline stage does not yield expected returns and turn as sunk cost that cannot be recovered.

Product innovation and marketing cycle are also affected by the innovation diffusion cycle spread across the same stages as of product innovation cycle. In the introduction cycle, often the diffusion of information is low as firms do not put adequate resources in generating awareness on the innovation. Firms invite lead users in this stage to test the innovated product and influence early adopters on the usage of product. Lead users form a small group but act as powerful referral and brand carriers. Firms spend adequate resources in the growth stage to diffuse product innovation attributes through direct communication on one-on-one basis to drive intensive effect on the innovation-led products among early adopters. Consumers in this group are strong followers of lead users and stand as effective opinion leaders for influencing the early majority of consumers. Most companies deploy enormous resources in advertising, communication, and social media involvement during the late growth and maturity stage to drive customers who are less affluent, less educated, but ready to experiment the innovative products. The early majority consumer segment constitutes relatively larger segment than the previous consumer segments but is confined to niche. However, the following stage is of late majority, which is a very large segment and often represent about half of the total number of consumers in a given market area. This consumer segment exhibits high adaptability with the innovative products and derives satisfactory value for money that makes the late majority consumers as frequent buyers. Consumers in this segment are price sensitive and post the threat of defection when more attractive substitute products penetrate in the market. However, a small number of (about 20 percent) consumers in each market segment are hard to drive for buying any innovative product as they are indecisive and difficult to convince. Such segment of consumers is found in all stages of growth of innovative products but is apparently huge in number during the decline stage of the product lifecycle.

Consumer perceptions play a key role in the life cycle of a brand. The role varies according to the stage in the life cycle, market situation, and competitive scenario. A company to invest on appealing communication strategies for creating awareness and may need to influence the decision of consumers toward buying the brands they have not tested before. Systematically explored concepts in the field of customer value and market-driven approach toward new products would be beneficial for a company to derive long-term profit optimization strategy over the period. On a tactical level, managers need to consider the optimum spread of customers on a matrix of product attractiveness and market coverage. This needs careful attention and application of managerial judgment and experience to measure the customer value-driven performance of the retail stores considering the innovative sales approaches for organic products, store layouts, product displays supported with comprehensive point-of-sales information, brand information, and other loyalty parameters of the consumers. Customer value in terms of satisfaction, use value, retailing practices, price, quality, and media appreciation is one of the indicators for building brand value for the nonconventional products and unfamiliar brands of a firm. Customer value concepts may be applied by the firms to evaluate the product performance of an innovative product in the given market and determine the approach for gaining competitive advantage over the traditional products. In order to gain the returns in the long run on the aggregate customer value, firms may need to methodically estimate the profitability associated thereof in terms of product attractiveness, volume of buying and market share while introducing the new products in a competitive market environment. The study proposes a framework for future research in measuring the customer value in specific reference to the nonconventional products (Rajagopal, 2014).

References

Abernathy, W. J., & Utterback, J. M. (1978). Patterns of Innovation in Industry. *Technology Review, 80*(7), 40–47.

Ackoff, R. L. (1999). *Re-Creating the Corporation: A Design of Organizations for the 21st Century*. Oxford University Press.

Ackoff, R. (2001). *A brief guide to interactive planning and idealized design*. May 31. Interact Consulting, Lancaster.

Bhatt, G. (2000). Organising knowledge in the knowledge development cycle. *Journal of Knowledge Management, 4*(1), 15–26.

Boudreau, K., & Lakhani, K. R. (2013). Using the crowd as an innovation partner. *Harvard Business Review.*

Brown, T. E. (2017). Sensor-based entrepreneurship: A framework for developing new products and services. *Business Horizons, 60*(6), 819–830.

Coyne, K. P., Clifford, P. G., & Dye, R. (2007). Breakthrough thinking from inside the box. *Harvard Business Review, 85*(12), 70–83.

Cullinan, R. (2018). *In Collaborative Work Cultures, Women Carry More of the Weight*. Harvard Business School Press.

Davenport, T. H., & Kirby, J. (2015). Beyond Automation. *Harvard Business Review, 93*(6), 59–65.

Di Pietro, F., Prencipe, A., & Majchrzak, A. (2018). Crowd equity investors: An underutilized asset for open innovation in startups. *California Management Review, 60*(2), 43–70.

Elia, G., & Margherita, A. (2018). Assessing the maturity of crowdventuring for corporate entrepreneurship. *Business Horizons, 61*(2), 271–283.

Giles, S. (2016). *The Most Important Leadership Competencies, According to Leaders Around the World*. Harvard Business School Press.

Haftor, D. M. (2011). An evaluation of R.L. Ackoff's interactive planning: A case-based approach. *Systemic Practice and Action Research, 24* (4), 355–377.

Hargadon, A., & Sutton, R. I. (2001). Building innovation factory. *Harvard Business Review, 78*(3), 121–130.

Kietzmann, J. H. (2017). Crowdsourcing: A revised definition and an introduction to new research. *Business Horizons, 60*(2), 151–153.

McAfee, A. (2018). Harnessing the Crowd in the Age of the Machine: The New Business Playbook. *IESE Insights, 37*(3), 1–6.

Meyer, E. (2014). Navigating the Cultural Minefield. *Harvard Business Review, 92*(5), 119–123.

Pepper, J. (2007). *What Really Matters: Service, Leadership, People and Values*. Yale Univesity.

Rachma-Fitriati, A. (2014). Applying Interactive Planning on Leadership in the Organization: The Case of Transforming Public Transport Services in Banjarmasin. *Procedia - Social and Behavioral Sciences, 115*(3), 283–295.

Rajagopal. (2014). *Architecting enterprise: Managing innovation, technology, and global competitiveness*. Palgrave Macmillan.
Rajagopal and Rajagopal, A. . (2011). *Product strategy and six sigma: Challenges, convergence, and competence*. Nova Science Publisher.
Sargut, G., & McGrath, R. G. (2011). Learning to Live with Complexity. *Harvard Business Review, 89*(9), 68–76.
Sunstein, C. R., & Hastie, R. (2014). Making Dumb Groups Smarter. *Harvard Business Review, 92*(12), 90–98.
Täuscher, K. (2017). Leveraging collective intelligence: How to design and manage crowd-based business models. *Business Horizons, 60*(2), 237–245.
Van Alstyne, M. W., Parker, G., & Choudary, S. P. (2016). Pipelines, Platforms, and the New Rules of Strategy. *Harvard Business Review, 94*(4), 54–62.
Vilnai-Yavetz, I., & Levina, O. (2018). Motivating social sharing of e-business content: Intrinsic motivation, extrinsic motivation, or crowding-out effect? *Computers in Human Behavior, 79*(1), 181–191.
Weill, P., & Woerner, S. (2015). Thriving in an Increasingly Digital Ecosystem. *MIT Sloan Management Review, 56*(4), 27–34.
Wilson, M., Robson, K., & Botha, E. (2017). Crowdsourcing in a time of empowered stakeholders: Lessons from crowdsourcing campaigns. *Business Horizons, 60*(2), 247–253.

Index

Rajagopal, *Crowd-Based Business Models*,
https://doi.org/10.1007/978-3-030-77083-9

The manufacturer's authorised representative in the EU is Springer Nature Customer Service Centre GmbH, Europaplatz 3, 69115 Heidelberg, Germany. If you have any concerns regarding our products, please contact ProductSafety@springernature.com

Printed and bound by CPI Group (UK) Ltd, Croydon, CR0 4YY
28/09/2026
02224083-0005